Folklore and Literature

Folklore and Literature
Rival Siblings

Bruce A. Rosenberg

The University of
Tennessee Press / KNOXVILLE

Library of Congress Cataloging in Publication Data

Rosenberg, Bruce A.
  Folklore and literature : rival siblings /
Bruce A. Rosenberg.— 1st ed.
      p.   cm.
  Includes bibliographical references and index.
  ISBN 0-87049-681-6 (cloth : alk. paper)
    1. Literature, Medieval—History and criticism.   2. Literature
and folklore.   3. Folk literature—History and criticism.
4. Oral tradition.   I. Title.
PN681.R67   1991
809'.02 — dc20   *90-40630   CIP*

For Ann Harleman:
novelist, translator, scholar
(linguist and philologist),
poet, visual artist, critic,
inspiration

Contents

Acknowledgments

THIS BOOK WAS WRITTEN DURING the past decade or more, and some of the ideas behind it are more than twenty-five years old, dating to my first interest in the interrelations of folklore and literature. During that time I have incurred debt to many individuals and institutions, and their assistance has made this final project possible. Here I want to thank a few of them.

The John Simon Guggenheim Memorial Foundation enabled me to take a crucial year away from classroom and administrative duties and to begin writing during 1981–82. Several summers, supported by fellowships — spent at the Henry E. Huntington Library — enabled my work to continue. And the Rockefeller Foundation at Bellagio, Italy, provided a great many facilities to enable me to continue writing, though I was only the spouse of the grantee.

Publication of this book has been aided by a grant from the Faculty Development Fund of Brown University.

Portions of several chapters have appeared elsewhere during the past two decades, and the author gratefully acknowledges their granting permission to reprint them: Oxford University Press (from *The Art of the American Folk Preacher*), the University of Illinois Press (from *Can These Bones Live?*), the Trickster Press (from *Folklore on Two Continents*), the University of Wisconsin Press *Historical Studies and Literary Criticism*), the *Centennial Review of the Arts and Sciences*, *Journal of the Folklore Institute*, *Western Folklore*, *Folklore Forum*, *Oral Tradition*, and *Neuphiloloquische Mitteilungen*.

Several individuals have been of enormous assistance, for which this mention is certainly pale compensation. W. Edson Richmond has, as always, been helpful and supportive of the entire range of my comments on folklore and literature, and few scholars in the world know as much about this intersection as he does. Daniel Barnes was a constructive reader of this manuscript, and has helped me immeasurably with it. He was the ideal critic — always positive, his goal was the making of a better book. His generosity is hardly to be adequately equaled — or thanked. And Ann Harleman (Stewart) has been the center of this book for more than a decade. Among the least of her contributions to it has been my understanding of linguistics — her specialty. Among the most substantial has been her unwavering love.

Introduction

MY PURPOSE IN WRITING THESE PAGES is to address the theoretical intersection of the study of folklore and of literature, an interdisciplinary interstice seldom discussed today and not, to my knowledge, written about. One, but only one, of the reasons for this lack of scholarly interest has been the broadening of the conceptual framework of folklore scholarship. At the beginning of the twentieth century, folklore studies were concerned mainly with the ballad and the folktale, a situation brought about because some of the most influential folklorists—they were professors of literature—dominated the field. Today, many folklorists study what had formerly been the domains of anthropology, archeology, and linguistics, particularly material culture and the process of transmission of lore: folk narrative as communicative event. Narrative lore is only one of many aspects of scrutiny by contemporary folklorists; but because of its obvious relationship to literature, folk narrative is the aspect of folklore on which this book focuses. *Literature and Folk Narrative* might well have been its title.

In these pages I discuss in detail—with examples as needed—the important ways in which the disciplines of oral narrative and literary history and criticism interact. This book is necessarily a survey, largely of extant scholarship. The materials included—the ideas, the proposals, the conjectures, the theories, etc.—are here because they are relevant to the subjects of verbal folklore and literature, and not always because they are new and original thoughts of mine.

Much of the literature examined is from the Middle Ages, for biographical reasons (I was trained as a medievalist), but more significantly for practical ones: so much of medieval narrative derives from or is analogous to oral tales, and so is an obvious body of work from which to draw examples. I have, however, tried when possible to limit my forays into medieval literature to such "classics" as *Beowulf*, Chaucer, and *The Song of Roland* in the hope that most of my readers will be familiar with them. Many readers may well be more familiar with these medieval narratives than with the contemporary stories of Elizabeth Jane Howard or the novels of Willa Cather.

The intersection of folklore (in its limited perspective) and literature is here marked by several areas indicating the most important aspects of the contribution of one to the knowledge of the other, aspects in which literary criticism and analysis have benefited from theories and methodologies originally developed for folkloric study. Clusters of two or more chapters of this book mark each such area.

(1) Two chapters introduce the subject and define the nature of the symbiotic interests and conflicts between the students, readers, and scholars of literature and folk narrative, and then outline the nature of orality and of the oral tradition.

(2) The next three chapters describe the ways in which folklorists have analyzed folk narratives as well as the methods by which ancient and medieval folktales have been reconstructed in recent times, and evaluate the usefulness of such reconstructions to literary critics and historians.

(3) Then three chapters define and discuss what is probably the most important theoretical contribution of folklore to literary criticism. The structuralist system of Vladimir Propp, who was by no means the originator of this analytical approach to narrative, became the one best known to Western literary critics. Propp's specimens were folktales.

(4) The Milman Parry–Albert Lord theories of oral performances, and their literary interpolations, merit three chapters in the section of essays on oral performance and its literary applications.

(5) Folk custom, belief, and ritual — as they occur in literature — are described in two chapters. Suggestions are made about the enhancement of our aesthetic understanding when we understand these folkloric aspects.

(6) The final four chapters are devoted to the persistence of folk narrative in contemporary literature and life, ranging from the uses of folktales and ballads by narratologists, to contemporary/traditional legends now current, to urban legends in literature, to an analysis of lineality and simultaneity in literature and folktales.

Among the main aspirations of this book are: to set forth the assumptions, the methodologies, and the goals of each of these approaches; to describe to the professionals and students of each discipline the assumptions of their colleagues, as well as to show what they are doing and thinking when they analyze and evaluate narrative folklore according to the procedures of their own discipline. Necessarily, I think, many of my elucidations are of folklore theories which are here presented to those who may not be greatly familiar with them: literary historians and critics.

But this book is not merely a summary of previous studies and ideas, though such a volume might well prove useful; rather, I have ventured several new interpretations and discoveries that alter our understanding of the ratio among the components of narrative; it is my hope that the boundaries and frontiers of both folklore and literature will be thereby expanded. One of my most urgent aspirations for this book is that it be educative; it must not stand or fall on particular interpretations or analyses, as would a work pretending to be entirely original and inventive. Rather, to fulfill this instructional purpose, the procedures and goals of each discipline—particularly of folklore—are described throughout, sometimes in detail, however obvious these may appear to readers who already know such methodologies. Specific demonstrations are used to present the more important theories: structuralism, the oral-formulaic theory, the historic-geographic assumptions and methods, etc. Historians of folklore theory will here be traveling over familiar territory; that is a risk I have accepted.

The generic and historical range of the illustrative materials used, particularly the literature, is intentionally wider than the works of one nation or language: largely American and English, and occasionally European, beginning with the Bible and *Beowulf*, but encompassing Elizabeth Jane Howard and Frederick Forsyth. Asian literature is omitted solely owing to my ignorance of it. Shakespeare and Chaucer are given prominence, though some contemporary narratives are also included. This is not meant to imply any inferiority of contemporary narrative; learned narratives composed prior to 1600 are simply the richest in their use of folk materials, plots, and thematic subjects. The specimens examined here are analyzed by those methods appropriate to their genre and their individuality. Almost always my examples were chosen because I felt they well illustrated particular points.

Thus, *Beowulf* figures heavily in a discussion of the relationship of text narratives to analogous folktales. Elizabeth Jane Howard's short story "Mr. Wrong" is dissected in the chapter on contemporary urban legends. My remarks on folklore in contemporary literary theory consider the narratologist's perceptions of the folktale and the ballad as "minimal narratives." The heavily oral formulaic sermons of American folk preachers are examined in a chapter on oral-formulaic perspectives, as is that favorite subject of oral-formulaic analysis, *Beowulf*.

Several of Roland Barthes's concepts and terms appear in the book.

All derive their meaning from his system, which can't be easily or briefly defined. Nevertheless, it may be helpful for the reader to have a few of the terms defined here. "Nuclei" are essential narrative units the deletion of which will change the narrative's structure; "catalyzers" are narrative units or events that cause other events to happen; "integrational elements" contribute to the meaning of a narrative by being grouped hierarchically; "distributional elements" gain meaning when they are classified horizontally.

Folktale types and motifs are cited by the numbering systems of Antii Aarne and Stith Thompson in their standard works listed in the bibliography.

For the past twenty-five years or so, nearly all of my published writing has addressed the broad area of the intersection of folk narrative and literature. Thus, I was tempted to make this book a collection of those writings; however, in the interest of thematic balance, with the realization of how much substantial work has been done by others, I have rewritten most of the chapters for the sake of the present volume. A few chapters have appeared elsewhere in substantially the same form as they do here, but most of my own work, "borrowed" for use here, has been recast and rephrased to suit the present requirements of this book. My intention throughout has been to make this volume an authoritative statement on the subject; it is one that has occupied most of my professional life, and I want to say something important about it.

PART ONE

Interactions

THE FIRST TWO CHAPTERS OPEN the discussion of the interrelationship of folklore and literature. This monologue is especially important today—in the 1990s—when folklore is thought to be unrelated to literature. I want to recall to the reader the striking proximity of verbal lore and folk narrative to literature. And, following the lead of recent folkloric scholarship, I will argue further that many literary circles—literary communities, if you will—have several characteristics in common with folkloric ones. By close scrutiny of such living communities, we can make intelligent estimations of literary communities now deceased and presumed to be unapproachable.

Such essays as comprise this opening section might not have been necessary a few decades ago when folklore research in the United States was heavily under the influence of professors of literature. They studied narrative folklore with obvious literary connections—primarily the ballad and the folktale—in order to complement the study of the history of literature. Francis Child, the great compiler of English and Scottish ballads; George Kittredge; Archer Taylor; and Francis Utley were all English professors. Even Stith Thompson, the "father of American folklore," taught in the English Department at Indiana University.

But, around two decades ago, the American Folklore Society declared its independence from the Modern Language Association, led by several prominent Young Turks whose training was heavily anthropological. The direction of folkloric studies in America turned sharply away from literature and nearly all text-based products to studies of the folkloric, mainly oral, process. A narrative's tradition became less important than the communicative event of its transmission. And, of course, a myriad of other subjects, in no way related to oral narrative, came under the folklorist's purview.

So, in academic literary circles folklore is often thought of as research on rural, usually uneducated (and certainly unsophisticated) peoples, or it is watered-down anthropology-come-lately; in neither case is it thought to be contiguous with literary studies. Hence, the following chapters serve to supply the connective tissue between these two organisms, suggesting the many ways in which the subjects are quite similar and the similar ways in which they are studied. Future study for the scholars of each discipline, employing the goals and thus the methodology of the other, is implied.

Folklore and Literature:
Rival Siblings

THE STUDENTS AND SCHOLARS OF FOLKLORE and literature had long enjoyed mutual interests, to the benefit of each. The American Folklore Society antedates the Modern Language Association by only a very few years; and from the first, folklorists were more often than not teachers of literature. Many folklorists outside academies were antiquarians; but within colleges and universities, the interest of professors of literature in folklore was centered on the belief that the study of simpler, popular, unsophisticated forms could enhance an understanding of richer, literate genres. A similar idea has recently been expressed by William Labov, who felt that "it will not be possible to make very much progress in the analysis and understanding of these complex narratives [myths, folktales, legends, histories, epics, etc.] until the simplest and most fundamental narrative structures are analyzed in direct connection with their originating functions" (Labov and Waletzky 1967, p. 12).

Those early literary folklorists also believed that a study of folklore, particularly of the ballad and the folktale, would lead to a comprehensive knowledge of the early stages of all poetry. They recognized that, before lyric and narrative were committed to writing, an oral tradition flourished. Understand the early ballads, so this rationale went, and we will understand the genesis and development of the literary genres derived from them. This feeling was barely disturbed by the eventually established facts that very few ballads in our possession today are medieval in origin and that most of those with "medieval" subjects derived from known literary works, especially the romances (Richmond 1954). To educated tastes, the ballads were crude and primitive, as were the folktales, but it was from them that the sophisticated scholar had to learn in order to understand the origins of "worthwhile" literature.

Not only in those early days — during the last century and the turn of this one — were the popular ballads, as W. Edson Richmond put it

(1954, p. 173), "held to be too crude for the appreciation of a man of any literary taste." Francis Lee Utley often recalled his offer to play some records of Leadbelly, whose songs had (he felt) an important relationship with medieval narratives, to an audience of medievalists at an MLA meeting, and being coldly and unequivocally told, "No." Most of the Middle English popular romances are classified "popular" mainly because they are inferior — by the standards of literary critics (more about this later) — to the French romances from which so many of them are derived. If they were popular, they were not likely to be excellent.

Several folktales share many episodic constituents with the romances and epics of medieval England and Europe. Probably many of these folktales preceded those romances and epics chronologically, and some literary treasures of our European heritage derive from these simple narratives. Yet literary critics often question the folktale's priority, usually because of the datable romances and epics and the fact that no folktales, per se, were collected until the nineteenth century. There are other reasons for maintaining the chronological primacy of literature, but the demonstrable age of manuscripts seems to have been the most persuasive.

Ballads and folktales have been both revered and disdained by professors of literature for the same reasons. On the one hand, folk literature, folk art, and the oral tradition have been indelibly associated in the romantic and nationalistic context of the past century with a certain class of people and with certain notions about them. These products of the unlettered arose, spontaneously, from the soil of the nation and the soul of the people (Finnegan 1977, pp. 34–40). The widest range of folk art was considered non-art, but in a positive sense: it was unconscious (therefore free of artifice), sincere (and so not corrupted), and unself-conscious (and therefore genuine). Folklore was thought to be close to nature, and such ideas appealed to many nineteenth-century nationalist critics, and to many of ours. The Grimms' folktale collections were enormously popular in Nazi Germany. But being "primitive," "untutored," and "spontaneous" implies judgments of social class; and the other side of that coin may be contempt for "das Volk."

Roger Sherman Loomis, that most distinguished of American scholars of Arthurian literature from the 1930s through the 1960s, has stated the real reason why the idea of the folktale origin of literature was a priori unacceptable. Loomis's beliefs had nothing to do with literature, since only "plowmen, goose-girls, blacksmiths, mid-wives, yokels" (1959, p. 2) composed and transmitted folklore, while the literature that he studied was the product of sophisticated artists of genius. The "plowmen, goose-girls, . . . and yokels" is a favorite line of folklorists as an instance of the cultural snobbery of literary scholars. Loomis was guilty: elsewhere he characterized the purveyors of folklore as "swineherds, clodhoppers, fishermen" (1958a, p. 63), and in another essay they were "peddlers," "rustics," and "bogtrotters" (cited in Cormier 1972, p. 116). No relationship was demonstrated between "civilization" and poetic cultivation. Loomis's disdain of certain occupations is unhelpfully ad hominem. It is hardly descriptive of those who bear folklore, one of whose subjects has become the late Professor Loomis himself. Similarly, in 1975 one of my students at the Pennsylvania State University collected a number of often-told anecdotes about Harvard's illustrious George Lyman Kittredge transmitted entirely by academics, none of whom are "goose-girls" or "yokels."

If there is a social distinction made between the creators of folklore and of literature, another kind of differentiation is made on the basis of the materials of folklore. "Folktales," "fairy tales," fables," "myths," "legends," and "old wives' tales" are the genres folklorists study seriously—as they do monsters, giants, ogres, dragons, and trolls. Yet all of the former category are, in the marketplace vernacular, synonyms for "mistake," "falsehoods," "unreal fantasies," "vulgar errors," even for "lies."

Vladimir Nabokov, one of those writers who has merited the literary scholar's acclaim, has written about "a subtle balance of parts which attests to deliberate artistic endeavor [in *The Song of Igor's Campaign*] and excludes the possibility of that gradual accretion of lumpy parts which is so typical of folklore. It is the lucid work of one man, not the random thrum of a people" (1960, p. 6).

Literary scholars—as opposed to literary critics—much prefer to deal with datable, documentable data; this is especially true of research in medieval literature. The folklorist often does not have this luxury. When possible, the date and name and location, etc., are collected along with the item. But when the researcher explores the Middle Ages, such documentation is not possible. Most folklorists take oral transmission for granted, and assume that consequently change necessarily takes place (see Utley 1961, pp. 193–206). This change is tantamount for the literary scholar, to error and degeneration. A long time ago—in 1916—John Robert Moore wrote of his research that "I have yet to find a clear case where a ballad can be shown to have improved as a result of oral transmission. . . . As far as the narrative element is concerned, tradition works nothing but corruption in the ballad" (p. 387).

So there once was a golden age?

Though Kittredge was not especially deprecatory about the changes

inherent in oral transmission, he did establish the connection of change
with degeneration and chaos:

> The product as it comes from the author is handed over to the folk for oral
> transmission, and thus passes out of his control. If it is accepted by those
> for whom it is intended, it ceases to be the property of the author; it be-
> comes the possession of the folk, and a new process begins, that of oral tradi-
> tion. . . . As it passes from singer to singer it is changing unceasingly. Old
> stanzas are dropped and new ones are added; rhymes are altered; the names
> of the characters are varied; portions of other ballads work their way in;
> the catastrophe may be transformed completely. (Sargent and Kittredge, p. xvii)

More than nearly all of his contemporaries, Kittredge realized that
change per se was not degenerative; yet when he pointed out in the introduction to his edition of the *English and Scottish Popular Ballads*
that there are several texts, not one (p. xvii), his observation was anath-
ema to his literary-scholars audience, for whom a "distortion complex"
was tantamount to chaos (see Richmond 1954, p. 178).

If a narrative appears in print, some literary scholars seem to imply,
it is necessarily better than the same story related orally. Typical is Paul
Olson's comment that in the conclusion of *The Merchant's Tale* "the
great peartree scene . . . by any standards, must be one of the great comic
scenes in literature" (1961, p. 212). Similarly, Harvard's great editor of
The Canterbury Tales, Fred N. Robinson, once wrote that *The Pardoner's Tale* "has sometimes been called the best short-story in existence. . . . Certainly the tale was never better told than by Chaucer"
(1957, pp. 10–11). These scholars have been caught off guard, defending too vigorously the reputation of Chaucer, who does not need this
kind of unsupportable hyperbole; his critics' effusiveness will not stand
up under even slight scrutiny. "The Treasure Finders Who Murder One
Another" (Aarne-Thompson type 763), the basis of *The Treasure of
Sierra Madre* and of the Alex Guiness movie *The Lady Killers*, and
"The Enchanted Pear Tree" (type 1423), has been told thousands of
times, orally, only a microscopic portion of which has ever been recorded, and none by either Olson or Robinson. Based on such a limited
sampling, then, one should not say that *The Merchant's Tale* is the
"best short-story in existence" and that *The Pardoner's Tale* "was never
better told than by Chaucer."

Popular culture—and not necessarily popular literature—is also commonly denounced, though infrequently with Roger Sherman Loomis's
flair. As recently as 1981 two professors at Dartmouth College blamed

the low level of undergraduate writing on "the continuing presence of popular culture." Cited in Dartmouth's student newspaper, with no editorializing comment, they were further quoted as asserting that, in a world becoming increasingly visual because of the popularity of television, a way of life develops that tends to hinder the improvement of writing as well as thinking (*The Dartmouth*, November 1, 1981, p. 1).

Because a number of the riddles in the Anglo-Saxon Exeter Book are obscene, Professor Tupper assumed that the riddles' characters must have been of the lower class (1910, p. 203). A few had been interpreted by scholars as embedding philosophical content; but this seemingly contrary evidence — or is it contrary? — was disregarded. However, an analysis of several of the riddles' terms for men and women — and a comparison with their usage in other Old English poems — show that when the riddles refer to classifiable human characters, their social station is usually high (Stewart 1983, pp. 39–52). Kittredge used to reflect upon that golden age when folk ballads were first sung, "when there were no formal divisions of literate and illiterate; when the intellectual interests of all were substantially identical, from the king to the peasant" (Sargent and Kittredge, p. xii).

If there is a predilection toward associating certain genres — literary and oral — with specific social classes, there is a difficulty in accepting the currency of several legends known to have been popular in the Middle Ages. Shirley Marchalonis has identified three of them appearing in medieval manuscripts and in oral tradition in 1976. And in the late 1960s and 1970s stories persisted that John F. Kennedy was still alive on Skorpios, not in his grave in Arlington National Cemetery as the public supposed. He was never really killed in Dallas, but was spirited away by his wife and friend Onassis to the Greek magnate's island in the Mediterranean. Such stories that Kennedy is still alive on an island over the sea are no more improbable than the older beliefs (and accompanying narratives) that King Arthur was alive and well on the isle of Avalon; both men are awaiting the moment of their country's greatest need to return and to lead their people once again to glory. The medieval legend deserves our attention because it is often used as a vehicle in admirable literature; but its modern counterpart should not be disregarded out of hand: it is in outline an analogous inspiration.

But *analogous* is not *equal*; the literary critic prefers one form, one style, to others, regardless of analogous inspirations or analogous sequences of distributional elements. The folklorist — and those whose interests are oriented toward the social sciences — may admire the schooled artist, but will focus, professionally, on other qualities and other aspects of a performance. Both may admire Jan Peerce's rendition of Yiddish folk songs; the folklorist, qua social scientist, does not concede that this singer's artistic merit defines the boundaries of his or her interest.

Artistic merit is important to both audiences, to the literary critic (the musical critic in this hypothetical example) primarily, because in criticism the talent of the individual artist is foregrounded, it is cherished and revered. In folklore studies individual artists (singers, raconteurs, artisans, etc.) are also studied sometimes and partly for distinctive abilities, but largely for their relation to a tradition. The tradition of the schooled artist is also explored — its history (literary history) and the writer's milieu — and while these ancillary interests often become (limited) ends in themselves, ultimately they should detail the aesthetic genius of the artist. The difference in underlying assumptions is one of emphasis, not of kind; there is a "sociology of literary taste," just as some folklorists have carefully examined and evaluated the aesthetics — the ethnopoetics — of their informants. Folklorist Petr Rybnikov (1831–85) wrote of one of his informants that "a good narrator strings the words like pearls. One can feel the rhythm, even in whole verses. So it is with tales which he knows well and retells often" (in Jason 1977, p. 475).

Folklore studies seldom highlight artistic merit per se (though ethnopoetics is at the moment a hot topic); in the communicative folk event, researchers foreground the social dynamics (medium) more than they do the "text" of the performance. For over a century that text, the performance's product, ws the most important item in the transaction, because folklorists were, in the main, professors of literature. Contemporary American folklorists — those who have earned their degrees during the past thirty years — have adopted the anthropologists' interest in process and transmission. And process, including the communicative event, broadens into the socio-linguistics and the psychology of the performance, the cultural impact of the milieu; in such an intellectual environment, the product necessarily loses dominence. Concern with tradition — the tradition of textual transmission that concerned Child and Kittredge and a century of like-minded literary folklorists — is also necessarily diminished. The product as well as the environment are now seen to be in flux, and people's recollection of tradition is seen ever more strongly to be variable.

The similarities between oral narratives and those prepared in writing are greater than is commonly supposed. Both types of narrative are works of art; the early Russian formalists showed that the folktale is an individual creation, not a mindlessly reproduced variant of a tradition. Folk narratives are composed anew at each rendering, according to those deep structural rules of composition inherent to the genre. This understanding was one of the starting points of Russian formalist analysis of folktales (Jason 1977). The genres of literary fictions are similar in kind and are more flexible, more varied, less conservative. The folk artist usually feels that he/she is perpetuating a tradition, whereas the literary artist (of the past few centuries) may exalt his/her personality and the individuality of the work.

Both oral and written narratives necessarily unfold sequentially, linearly. Since this has been discussed in some detail in my "Simultaneity and Linearity in Narrative" (1979), it need only be alluded to here, though with the important revision that we do not read with absolute sequentiality, one word at a time. Rather, the eye takes in blocks at one gulp (as it were); speed-reading is based on the principle of many large gulps digested rapidly. But that does express a sense of simultaneity, that more than one event is taking place, more than one narrative strand is unfolding simultaneously with others — as in life.

Writing is necessarily sequential, and so the author is inherently unable to reveal his/her narrative except sequentially. Attempts to overcome this limitation — as in some of B. S. Johnson's novels, one of which prints two columns on a page, each one relating a different series of events, or his collections of discrete chapters which can be shuffled and absorbed at the reader's discretion and inclination — have not been successful. For one thing, each of Johnson's columns has to be read sequentially, so the final effect is that of switching back and forth between two simultaneous narrative strings, just as has been done in conventional writing for centuries.

The folktale raconteur has the advantage in trafficking in traditional, known narratives. During the recitation his/her audience will know what is going to happen and can actively "fill in" (internally, in their own imaginations) what is going on simultaneously.

If Father Ong is right (1981, pp. 128 ff., among many such places), sound, the medium of the oral narrator, situates the listener "in the middle of actuality and of simultaneity," an advantage not shared by the writer, who "situates man in front of things and in sequentiality." Sound is three-dimensional; it seems to emerge from the heart of things, to resonate from interiors. Of course this is a different kind of simultaneity.

Ong does not advert to the simultaneity of two discrete narrative strings and the possibility of their concurrent presentation, but of the enveloping quality of sound.

Nevertheless, this "other" simultaneity, that inherent in sound (and not in print), affords another important distinction between written and orally performed poetry. The written or printed word is necessarily of the surface, of the exterior space; it can never convey simultaneity, of either kind. The inscribed word cannot resonate as does the spoken. Sound manifests the speaker at a "maximum; hearing puts us in contact with the personal grounds of actuality . . . in a specially intense way" (Ong 1981, p. 174). It is only when the spoken word is treated as a transcribed typograph that it too can be said to be radically sequential; but that is to transform its presentational mode. Folklore is what gets left out of the event when it is transcribed. "At a given instant I hear not merely what is in front of me or behind me or at either side, but all these things simultaneously, and what is above and below as well" (Ong 1981, p. 129).

Both oral and written genres deal with human life, not always in radically different modes. The folktale hero, like his literary counterpart, is active (on a quest) or passive — things happen to him. As quester he seeks retribution, or a bride, or a prize of great worth. He may be successful (in the tales Propp studied he always was), or he may be persecuted; during the course of his story, he must overcome obstacles or pass tests. Other folktales are parodies of the genre itself. The hero is an insignificant tailor, and his feat is to swat a number of flies at one blow. The formidable and terrible enemy turns out to be stupid. And though the villain may be strong, his stupidity enables the hero's cleverness to win the day. Folk and learned literatures also share many "themes." The Swiss folklorist Max Lüthi explored this idea in a 1976 essay on "Parallel Themes" in folk and in art narratives. One of his examples is the theme — the idea — the philosophical kernel, that "man is always the cause of his own fall" ("Der Mensch fällt nur durch sich"). It appears in the twelfth-century Nestor Chronicle, in which Tzar Oleg is told, prophetically, that the horse he rides will be the cause of his death. Lüthi traces this theme in Shakespeare, Marston, Ben Jonson, Webster, and in several writers on the continent. Schiller incorporates the idea, as do Kleist and Gryphius. It is to be found in *Oedipus Rex*. But it is also a popular idea running through many folktales. Lüthi notes the witch who is burned to death in her own oven, the ogre who kills his own children in place of the intended victims because their hats have been exchanged, and other villains who pronounce their own sentences. Snow White (and others) do not heed sound advice they are given, and bring about disasters. Fairy-tale heroine-victims often urge their fathers to remarry, thus bringing the wicked stepmother into the household.

The popular Baroque theme of reality versus appearance is also present in the folktale: the swineherd is, in reality, a prince; the "scald-head" has golden locks; the *Dummling* is the best (and often the cleverest) of three brothers; the ragged Cinderella is the fairest of all; the limping or three-legged horse is the fastest. Lüthi concludes that the fairy tale "must not be accounted for as the result of a primitive technique of narration only, but as the expression of something essential. That is the reason why great writers like to adopt this form of narrative" (Lüthi, p. 9).

In 1908 the Danish folklorist and medievalist Axel Olrik first published what has since become one of the seminal essays on the form of folk narrative, "The Epic Laws of Folk Narrative" (in Dundes 1965, pp. 129–41). Based on his observations of oral forms, Olrik organized more than a dozen descriptive "Laws" (principles really, since "Laws" implies a fixity that is not always present). A brief review of them is to the point of this chapter, for in Olrik's formulations we will see with some precision the similarities between folk and written narrative.

Of all of Olrik's principles, the one that will strike the reader as being undoubtedly characteristic of oral performances of narrative (rather than written renderings) is the "Law of Two to a Scene." Olrik had observed this phenomenon so often that its violation—the appearance of more than two characters in an orally presented narrative—would constitute a "violation of tradition" (pp. 134–35). Three characters may congregate at one time; but only two may speak. The bird speaks to Siegfried only after Regin has gone to sleep. Nearly all conversation is dyadic, though Olrik wrote in times before communication theory, and so must be forgiven a certain lack of precision in his formulation of this "Law." Nevertheless, it seems almost always to hold true probably because (to extend Olrik's observation) neither speaker nor listener could keep a three-way (or four-way) conversation straight in their minds. When such events are written out, the reader has the leisure to sort out who is saying what to whom.

Olrik claimed that the "greatest law of folk tradition is *concentration on a leading character.*" This is true of nearly all oral narrative, often of the folktale, which is usually relatively brief and structurally uncomplicated in its European forms; a number of longer narratives—the Yugoslavian heroic songs, for instance—are more complicated. In any event, nearly all written narrative focuses on a leading character, and exceptions are rare, perhaps *War and Peace*. Olrik thought that *Hamlet* was concentrated "in spite of his [Hamlet's] verbosity" (Dundes 1965, p. 139). Olrik has in mind the tradition of this story as well as Shakespeare's version. The same cannot be said of *King Lear*, with its intricate subplotting. In its folktale form, "Love Like Salt," it was much more so. But a number of folktales are combinations of several constituent tales, and must strain to maintain their concentration on a leading character. Nevertheless, as with many of the other "Laws," Olrik's observations are to be taken as observations not of lawful certitude but of general tendencies. Still, they are valuable for all that.

The "Law" of folktale single-strandedness elaborates Olrik's observation that folk narrative is always "mono-linear" (Dundes 1965, p. 137). No study shows this more clearly than Eugene Vinaver's *The Rise of Romance* (1971 with its learned comparison of orally derived epic (the *Chanson de Roland),* written romances of the twelfth and thirteenth centuries, and the style of *interlacement* which developed at that time. However, some conflated oral narratives also interweave the threads of the various constituent plots. But Olrik does not appear to imply by this "Law" a narrative simplicity in the *Sage*, an oral narrative, because within the same paragraph he seems to be saying, rather, that the chronology of the *Sage* (oral narrative) is always progressive: it does not go back in order to fill in the missing details. If previous background information is necessary, then "it is given in dialogue" (Dundes 1965, p. 137).

This observation is valid; however, the issue seems to be not so much single-strandedness but an insight into a tendency of oral performance. Olrik points out that "each attribute of a person or thing must be expressed in actions" (p. 137); he notes that a great deal of information is presented through dialogue. Is this the same as "action"?

Oral narrative, more than most literature, which is fond of authorial description and revelation, likes to enrich the texture of the narrative through informational dialogue. People who are talking are doing something, and that is one kind of action. If Olrik cites Siegfried as an exemplar here, we may involve *Beowulf*: in the Old English epic the past is recalled more than a dozen times, and always in conversation. Upon his return home, Beowulf's retelling of his encounter with the Grendel family is so lengthy that it has been argued that this segment was at one time a separate, short heroic lay. *Beowulf* might well be used to demonstrate Olrik's point about filling in missing details, but only by allowing a great liberty in his meaning of "single-strandedness."

Olrik early wrote about the truth that oral narratives are efficient forms. His "Law of Patterning" has it that "everything superfluous is suppressed and only the essential stands out salient and striking" (pp. 137–38). Such "stylizing of life" has its own aesthetic value. Closely related is his idea of the "Law of Logic" which contends that "the themes which are presented must exert an influence upon the plot, and moreover, an influence in proportion to their extent and weight in the narrative" (p. 138).

But this is certainly true of literature as well. We demand that written narrative and drama present us with data as action within episodes that reveal character and advance the narrative toward its predetermined conclusion. Everything is purposeful and, we have the right to assume, has been carefully weighted for its role within the entire economy of our narrative. (Descriptions and metanarrative passages of course distend the written narrative way beyond comparable folk works.) This distinction between life and fiction — the randomness of reality and the methodical purpose of art — is one of the basic tenets of our aesthetics. Olrik is not wrong to bring logic-in-art to our attention; it is misleading to think that it is characteristic of folk narrative alone.

So too with Olrik's "Laws" on the "Unity of Plot" and of "Epic Unity." He wrote of the latter that "each narrative element works within it so as to create an event, the possibility of which the listener had seen right from the beginning and which he never lost sight of" (pp. 138–39). Similarly, Wayne Booth (1967, pp. 52–53) comments that "our entire experience in reading fiction is based . . . on a tacit contract with the novelist": "It is this contract which makes fiction possible. To deny it would not only destroy all fiction, but all literature, since art presupposes the artist's choice."

Thus, when the "Laws" of "Unity," "Epic Unity," and "Logic" are taken together, they are not very much different from Aristotle's prescriptions for narrative. Olrik had considerable training in the classics, but that is almost beside the point: educated people in the West have read or at least know some of the arguments of the *Poetics*. Olrik could have conceived his "Laws" independently — is likely to have done so — but he could just as easily have been writing an essay on literary criticism. What he has given us is an important introduction to the nature of narrative itself.

Narrative may well be (as Aristotle said) a representation of the events of individuals' lives; but that representation is artfully fabricated. Character and event must be developed episodically (unless our narrative is to be an isomorph of that life), and besides having significance for the composition of the global plot structure, each must carry along the reader's/listener's interest within itself. Nearly every writer in the great tradition of our literature has realized characters and plot through human interaction. Exceptions are rare; James Joyce (most of whose events are interior) is an obvious one, and Faulkner's narrators (rather then his characters) frequently bear much of the discursive burden of the tale.

To those who have thought at all about the way narratives are constructed, Olrik's "Law of Tableau Scenes" is hardly a surprise. Narratives—and not only *Sagen*—do rise to peaks in which the actors draw near to each other. Drama presents an obvious example. But, to take a familiar literary example, Chaucer's *Troilus and Criseyde* are shown to develop through tableau scenes: Pandarus convinces Troilus that Criseyde is not unattainable, and then persuades her that the prince loves her. The two lovers are brought together in Pandarus's home, and then drift apart, pulsatingly, in a montage of tableaux alternating between the Greek camp and the city of Troy. Character does not change during each scene, but during the interstices, so that when the narrator returns us to each one alternately, we immediately note the change because we know how differently the characters (particularly Criseyde) have just acted. In nearly all discursive writing, not only in oral narratives, the attributes of people and things are expressed in action. Again, Olrik is not wrong; he is, we think, too restrictive.

For centuries we have said of the epic, for instance, that it does not begin in medias res. Although seldom justified in aesthetic terms, the reasons are ultimately that we cannot move abruptly from our lives outside the frame of the narrative performance, with its machinery of the willful suspension of disbelief, into the frame of the narrative world. That transition from lifeworld to fictional milieu must be gradual; we must have some time to persuade ourselves that the actors in the fictional world we are hearing or reading about are not merely cardboard fictions. We need some time to develop belief. The performer/artist must win us to his/her side within the frame of each work, and that is not easily accomplished. Should a moment of high drama be presented immediately at the outset of any performance, it would most likely be lost on an audience that is not prepared for it, an audience literate or aural.

Once again, therefore, Olrik's "Laws" of "Opening" and "Closing" come as no surprise: "The *Sage* begins by moving from calm to excitement, and after the concluding event, in which a principal character frequently has a catastrophe, the *Sage* ends by moving from excitement to calm" (p. 132).

Hamlet does not end at the moment of the hero's death, but with the entrance of Fortinbras's army and removal of the bodies; *Othello* does not end with Desdamona's murder, but with the Moor's apologia and partial self-discovery speech; *Lear* does not conclude at the moment of Lear's expiration, but only after several minutes' speeches are given about the lamentable state of the world, Burgundy's defeat in the just-concluded battle, and Kent's decision to join his master. Similarly, the epos cannot end with the last breath of Roland. Before ending, it needs to relax the clenched fist of the sword-hand; it needs the burial of the hero, the revenge, the death through grief of the beloved, and the execution of the traitor. (p. 132)

The *Chanson de Roland* has come to us in manuscript and so should be treated as literature, however long its provenance in oral currency. That Olrik treats it as an example of the *Sage* is unintentionally important for the point here: the aesthetic informing the *Sage* is not much different from that of narrative prepared in writing for a print medium. Oral narrative and written narrative are united by the psychology of the audience which, in the aesthetic of Kenneth Burke, is the form of literature (Burke 1968, pp. 29–44).

Most often cited is Olrik's "Law of Threes," which has intrigued folklorists before his writing and intrigues them still (see Dundes 1980, pp. 134–59). Three is the number of choice in international folktales (Dundes claims it is also pervasive in American culture); but the form of Faulkner's *The Sound and the Fury*, Dostoevsky's *Brothers Karamozov,* even Le Carre's *The Looking Glass War* show that the number three is no stranger to written narrative. Scores of novel cycles have been written as trilogies; and if one wants to see triads in superabundance, *Moby Dick* has more than triple the number of any three narratives combined. The Pequod has a crew of thirty, including three mates and three harpooneers. It is a traditional three-masted schooner carrying three whaleboats; it meets nine other ships on its voyage; Ishmael has signed aboard for a three-hundredth share, Queequeg for a thirtieth. The final encounter with the white whale takes place during a three-day chase, and when the ship is finally destroyed it is under a three-starred constellation. All told, Melville's triads number in the hundreds.

One of Olrik's most astute observations is framed in his "Law of Contrast," one of the earliest comments on the inclination of narrators to polarize characters, events, and plots. This insight has been almost universally slighted; he does not himself consider this "Law" to be his greatest. He argues (in the "Law of Contrast") that

> a strong Thor requires a wise Odin or a cunning Loki next to him; a rich Peter Kramer, a poor Paul Schmeid. . . . the Danish King Rolf who is so celebrated in our heroic sagas because of his generosity . . . thus requires a stingy opponent. However, in this example, the identity of the opponent changes. Now it is a Skolding: Rorik; now it is a Swede: Adisl. . . . Some types of plot action correspond exactly to the Law of Contrast. (1) The hero meets his death through the murderous act of a villain. . . . (2) the great king has an insignificant and short-reigning successor. (Dundes 1965, p. 135)

The idea of dramatic contrast was au courant at the turn of the century—having been with us at least since the time of Aristotle—and so we should not unduly credit Olrik with developing it solitarily; nevertheless, it does anticipate much of the work of some structuralists. The principle is applicable to much of literature. When Olrik writes that "this very basic opposition is a major rule of epic composition: young and old, large and small, man and monster, good and evil," he is not talking about oral narrative alone, but all narrative. The law of contrast is so much a foundation of the fictive imagination that one is hard pressed to identify much narrative that is not so polarized.

We can barely imagine any dramatic or narrative form without conflict. Hamlet is not realized for us until he struggles—with himself, with his mother, with his father's ghost, with Rosencrantz and Guildenstern, with Claudius. Those conflicts and contrasts define his character; those struggles comprise the play. Troilus's helpless love-longing in book one is sharply set off by Pandarus's playful manipulation of him. Both men contrast with Criseyde at the beginning of the action, as they will, though in quite different ways, in book five. There Troilus's nobility emerges all the more in contrast with Pandarus's frustrations and occasionally ignoble suggestions. Beowulf is established as the man of action largely through his *flyting* (ritualized poetic insult) with Unferth, after which Hrothgar's *thegn* is silenced for the remainder of the poem. Significantly, Unferth is a man of idle words. Throughout this epic the *scop* recalls numerous rulers from days of yore—weak kings, strong-headed kings, feuding kings, and timid kings. When we have reached the end of the hero's life, we have a full and detailed understanding of the ideal of kingship in the early Germanic Middle Ages. We also have a very specific, though idealized, idea of the character of Beowulf.

Olrik has given us an aesthetic of oral and written narrative. He used the example of the *Roland* to illustrate the "Laws" of "Opening" and "Closing." To illustrate the frequency of the number three he shows us Hector and Archilles in their race around Troy. For contrast to Roland, Olrik used the *Rolfssaga Kraka* and the *Volsunga Saga*; and elsewhere the *Nibelungenlied*, Greek myth (known only in manuscript), the Old Testament, and *Hamlet* are cited. So for Olrik, *Volksdichtung* encompassed more than folktales. He cast his nets far wider than he realized, but in so doing he has for the better gone beyond merely oral narrative into the realm of narrative per se. To use one more of his examples, there is nothing essentially oral about the "Law of Initial and Final Position" (Dundes 1965, p. 136): "coming last, though, will be the person for whom the particular narrative arouses sympathy." Like nearly all of the other "Laws," this describes the best way to tell a story, recited or printed. The "disease of literacy" to use Albert Lord's infectious phrase, does not change that aspect of the aesthetic sense that we take with us to every encounter with narrative.

In American universities, aesthetic merit is highly valued and great artists are discussed reverently, as is appropriate for professors of literature. The concomitant of such judgments is that it is often better, professionally, to be a mediocre Shakespearean than a leading writer on the poetry of, say, Royall Tyler. And, as inevitably happens, professor/critics attempt to enhance their own academic standing by pumping up the value of a mediocre poet who might happen to be their interest. (Such activity has its positive side, of course; overlooked geniuses are brought to light.)

The literary critic studies the text, primarily. It is by nature fixed, and is studied as an inviolable, numinous artifact. The natural concomitant of such an understanding of the text as artifact is the study of the book as a physical object, the counterpart, though it is quite a dissimilar counterpart, of the folklorist's interest in the communicative medium. Literary scholars immersed in literature focus intellectually on such related interests as the technology and history — and consequently on the impact — of writing and of printing.

The folklorist studies the communicative event live. While it is happening, while he or she tries to reduce the impact of the experimenter's effect or Heisenberg Principle (the sceintist's own presence as measurable factor in the "natural" situation), the folklorist records the dynamics of artist, audience, and context. In tradition-oriented studies, the product (the text) is placed in its context. The camera and the tape recorder are aids in capturing such creative moments as precisely as possible. Few creative folkloric moments are never witnessed by the social scientist, whereas almost no literary artist has, or would allow, such a witness to his/her own creative experiences.

It will be useful at this time to distinguish among three critical components in artistic (here narrative) productions: the artist/performer, the medium through which the work is expressed, and the audience. The relationship among these intertwined components is symbiotic; and each of those culturally defined levels of literary production — elite, popular, and folk — can be profitably defined by describing this relationship in terms of components and of the distance between each element and the others.

The anthropologist's conception of culture has been assumed in these last few pages: that is, all of the produced items — the "things — physical and cognitive, of a society. Literature, drama, film, television, and comic books are only a minute segment of a people's culture, despite most critics' association of popular culture exclusively with movies, television programs, and trashy novels. The bottom line of popular culture study (often) is an evaluation of an item or a genre in society and a resultant statement about that society. Popular culture, so defined, contributed little (for example) to medieval life; folklore, on the other hand, was a major expressive medium for much that was deeply embedded in the medieval grain. Its evaluation reveals a great deal about medieval Europe and its collective life.

In contemporary artistic transactions, an important mediator, the producer, intervenes in the artistic chain of creator/performer/audience. This agent, single or collective, assesses the tastes and desires of the consumer of art and guides the creation as well as the performance of that art according to what are perceived as the current canons of taste. The producer — whether literary agent, gallery proprietor, film distributor, or the like — is, today, in the very important position of being able to support the artist by marketing his/her products to an audience. Thus the producer can also influence the taste of an audience though the control exerted over what is offered to them; and even more significantly, the producer can control what the artist produces because of his/her access to and persuasiveness over available markets.

The professional producer widens the distance between the artistic creator and the audience which, in the instance of the generation of folk art, is quite close. The folk artist performs for a community whose tastes and preferences he or she usually knows directly as part of the community. Commonly, such an artist lives among the community he or she entertains or instructs; the distance between artist and audience in such cases is slight and is closely interrelated; often the audience knows the artistic product as well as does the performer, because it is a part of their tradition as much as it is of the artist's. In such a milieu the creator/tradition-bearer is probably anonymous, even to the performing artist, who interprets his/her role more as perpetuating a tradition than as exercising an individual creative talent. Few medieval authors signed their works; they viewed themselves as perpetuators rather than originators. When this attitude wanes, the author not only seeks to be identified in the public's mind with his/her own original works, others are discouraged from exploiting his/her contribution to the tradition. Then the copyright is born.

In the late Middle Ages in England, literary artists appear to have been more distanced from their audience than would be the situation in a folk community; nearly all literature then was learned, aristocratic, and international in its traditions. The modern world's producer intervenes between artist and receptor community, in fact deciding how much distance is permissible. Much of the popular narrative six centuries ago — and earlier — was performed by minstrels who seldom were the creators of their texts and who had to judge for themselves what would attract an audience.

Today's explicator of literature most frequently studies the artist, who is usually focalized; when his/her literary tradition is studied, when the relevant political and cultural environment is re-created, it is to shed light upon the artist's creative abilities. The work, the text, the product, will be analyzed for its components and their interdynamics, but the end is an evaluation of the artist's abilities. The folk communicative/creative process is often analyzed for its group dynamics. And while the event itself is interesting, focus is not on the artist so exclusively that the audience and its context are blurred. Reader-oriented (literary) criticism is in one way close to folklore research in that it takes account of both subject and object (sender and receiver) in the literary communicative event. Reader-oriented criticism assumes an active role in this interaction on the part of the "passive" reader, who actually contributes actively to the creation of the text's meaning. Just as the folklorist studies the audience of live performance, the reader-oriented critic scrutinizes the book's audience. Both are interested in interactions between artist and audience, though the difference and the distance between sender and receiver may vary considerably in folk and learned art performances, and variations in media cause a correspondingly great divergence in goals and in methodologies of analysis.

By the nature of their concerns, then, folklorists and literary scholars have drifted apart. It has not been until quite recently that narratologists in literature departments have become interested (again) in the folktale. In their attempts to discover the basic components of narrative, literary analysts have sought what they consider the simplest, most basic narratives existing "naturally," and it is to the folktale that they have turned. Gerald Prince's *A Grammar of Stories* (1973) analyzes "Little Red riding Hood" in a demonstration of methodology; Barbara Herrnstein Smith cites Marion Cox's study of "Cinderella" to argue that the "basic story" does not exist except as a kind of Platonic ideal, and that all narratives are versions of each other. However short the duration of this remarriage, folklore and literature are reunited.

CHAPTER 2

The Oral Tradition

ORAL TRADITION IS STILL ENOUGH of an abstract concept to warrant defining its understanding and use in this book. This chapter outlines some of the complexities of this phenomenon so that we may proceed beyond it in the rest of this volume.

Although many Romantics were, for their own reasons, enthralled with the idea of savage nobility and its lifeworld, a world in which the complicating (and corrupting) products of technology had not yet been imposed, that simple (oral) society has not been easy to identify. In his *The Singer of Tales* (1965, p. 137) Albert Lord laments the rise of literacy in Yugoslavia, where he and Milman Parry did so much of their fieldwork, with the remark that printing had introduced the notion of the "fixed" text and that there were now very few singers "who have not been infected by this disease." Their performances are reproductions rather than creations, Lord continues, and "this means death to oral tradition" (p. 137). Anthropologists and folklorists would not agree, since much of their research on the subject indicates that rarely is a society entirely oral (nonliterate or preliterate) or literate. The truth, as is usually the case with truth, is mixed.

Ruth Finnegan reminds us that some degree of literacy has been a feature of culture nearly all over the world for thousands of years (1977, p. 23). In searching for a model culture in which to demonstrate the consequences of literacy, Jack Goody and Ian Watt (Goody 1968) had to reject nearly every society of their acquaintance, certainly those of the third world (see also Finnegan 1977, p. 23), before deciding on classical Greece. They found that initially they had to "reject any dichotomy based upon the assumption of radical differences between the mental attributes of literate and non-literate peoples" (Goody 1968, p. 44). Finnegan's point, followed here, is that oral and literate societies exist in a continuity, not a dichotomy, as do their lyrics and narratives.

The two kinds of society, if one can even speak of "kinds," are not purely separate (Finnegan 1977, p. 24):

> They shade into each other both in the present and over many centuries of historical development, and there are innumerable cases of poetry which has both "oral" and "written" elements. The idea of pure and uncontaminated "oral culture" as the primary reference point for the discussion of oral poetry is a myth.

Finnegan sagely warns that nearly all of the (oral) third-world cultures have been exposed, in varying degrees, to the influence of literacy (1977, p. 23); the line between oral and written literature, if there ever was one, is now hopelessly blurred. Linguists, measuring the amount of detail, direct quotation, sound and word repetition, syntactic parallelism, etc., conclude that written imaginative literature uses aspects of spoken language (Tannen 1982a p. 18) and may be qualitatively indistinguishable. Finnegan was writing to argue with the Parry-Lord enthusiasts (discussed in chapter nine of the present book), but the point must nevertheless not be disregarded. Purely oral folk probably cannot be identified and studied today; but certain conclusions about orality are nevertheless possible, and some descriptions of oral literature can be made.

A few philosophers have tried to re-create what the world of the nonliterate must be like; and though this work is necessarily speculative, some important conclusions have resulted. One difficulty is suggested, for instance, by the necessity of using the locution "oral literature." "Literature" means that which is written; the addition of "oral" makes the compound an oxymoron. The whole matter of orality is intricate anyway. Do we mean orally composed, orally transmitted, or orally performed? And "oral literature" denies the priority of orality as a communication mode. Just as the early typewriters were "writing machines" and the first automobiles were "horseless carriages," we have created the back-formation "oral literature." The difference between "horseless carriages" and "oral literature" is that the horse did occur first, while writing did not precede oral communication. The term "illiterate," only slightly more so than "preliterate," gives a primacy and a normality to "literate"; to be illiterate is to lack something. Literacy has become so much the norm that we no longer think of "oral tradition" as redundant, though "tradition" originally meant transmission by word of mouth or by custom.

To avoid the paradox "oral literature," I have coined the term "oralature," employing both "oral" and a suffix implying language ordered for an aesthetic purpose. This neologism, for whatever reason, has not taken hold.

Goody and Watt note (Goody 1968, pp. 58–59) that even in the most literate cultures "the transmission of values and attitudes in face-to-face contact" is oral. They find this desirable in some instances, citing the conservative influence of primary groups whose oral communication is more realistic in its attitudes than are commercial media, particularly television. It has long been appreciated that in literate cultures the most important aspects of life are communicated orally.

Melville Jacobs (1971, p. 212) tells us that, in the societies he analyzed, everyone participated in the tribe's "literary" heritage, unlike the situation in ours. Myths retold within the community contained many apostrophic pontifications which established the truth and strength of the community's convictions (Jacobs, p. 235). The goals of some folklorists in their study of oralatures is not distantly removed from the aims of some literary critics; oralature is the expression of a people — to some extent this is also true of the written art familiar to us — and not of a few genuises (p. 121).

All of the verbal elements in culture — literate and nonliterate, but especially the latter — are transmitted by a long chain of interlocking face-to-face conversations between members of the group. All beliefs and values are related orally, face-to-face, and are held in human memory. Writing, and other components of a material tradition, are ideal for preserving data but do not lend themselves so cogently to the assertion of a culture's values. Oral traditions are both more specific and less ambiguous communication because the speaker reinforces an intended specificity of meaning with gesture, espression, intonation, etc., and various self-correcting mechanisms of which fixed print is incapable. Conrad's narrator in *Under Western Eyes* comments that "words, as is well-known, are the great foes of reality (1963, p. 1). Nevertheless we can speak of print's stability; the fixity of print does give the relative stability of meaning to words (or tries to) while oral folk ratify the meaning of each word "in a succession of concrete situations" (Goody 1968, p. 29). The vocabulary of nonliterates is small, commonly around five thousand words, about seven or eight times less than that of a college-educated Western European or American; but in an oral society there is much less disagreement about denotative and connotative usages. Words acquire and retain their meanings from their existential setting (Ong 1982, p. 47).

While literature has made many aspects of culture available to a very great proportion of society's members, the impersonality of print has also made culture easy to avoid. Print removes a portion of learning from that immediate chain of personal confrontations. In an oral culture the aged are the repositories of a culture's wisdom, but they can be discounted in modern technological society, not so much because of rapid changes in successive waves of the "future," but because wisdom is available in books. Plato had argued that the wisdom of writing was superficial; no give and take of cross-examination and responses was possible. If the reader questions a written proposition, there can be no response, no defense. A book can be put aside; it may never be opened at all. Discussion, argument, oral deliberation, are not easily sidestepped in face-to-face situations. Some Indian philosophers (in Goody 1968, pp. 12-13) were suspicous of book knowledge (it is not operative and fruitful) and knowledge not acquired from teachers. Be that as it may, the impact of writing (and later, print) had been incalculable. It universalized the Italian Renaissance, helped to implement the Reformation, and made capitalism possible (Eisenstein 1979). Print established the grammarian's canon of correctness.

Objectifying words in print, and especially in dictionaries, makes them and their meanings vulnerable to intensive and prolonged scrutiny. Words are impossible to fix. Lawrence Durrell (1961, p. 65) has complained about "as unstable" a medium as words. But this is no more than Chaucer had done; language changes in time, across distance, shifting as does mood. Dictionaries eventually become obsolete, yet during the era of their viability, they foster individual thought. The solitary, introspective reader is the polar opposite of the gregarious participant in an oral culture, yet both are—in these extreme images— heuristically symbolic. Nevertheless there is much measurable truth in this abstraction; the conservatism inherent in oral cultures militates against the individuation that writing and private reading foster. Ties in traditional societies are between persons; in literate cultures the ties are complicated by abstract notions of rules, "by a more complicated set of complementary relationships between individuals in a variety of roles" (Goody 1968, p. 62).

When sociolinguist Tannen summarizes the results of research comparing the relation of events, as narratives, by ethnic group (cited in Shiffrin 1981, pp. 960-61), it is not the same thing as comparing literate with nonliterate groups. The ancient Greeks used verbal strategies associated with oral traditions whereas Americans invoke those of literate traditions. But the claim could never be made that Greece is a preliterate culture, or that even in its most remote fastnesses its citizens were untouched by print. One of the innately appropriate uses of literacy is the compilation and preservation of data sets: lists, as well as modern economic systems (capitalist or socialist), could not exist without literacy. Complicated accounting procedures (and ones not so complicated) and the storage of resultant data demand writing. So do records, files, bookkeeping, diaries, and the calculations stimulated by these procedures. Workers' wage and tax records stored by the hour, day, week, or year; chronology, as typified by our dependence on the calendar; precise dating — all such precise sequences require writing, if not print. So too with histories and other records of the past, in fact the very notion of the past as a series of datable events that happened *then* — all depend on writing. Walter Ong (1982, p. 99) notes that writing was invented largely in order

> to make something like lists: by far most of the earliest writing we know, that in the cuneiform script of the Sumerians beginning around 1500 BC, is account-keeping. Primary oral cultures commonly situate their equivalent of lists in narrative, as in the catalogue of the ships and captains in the *Iliad* (ii. 461–879) — not an objective tally but an operational display in a story about a war. In the text of the Torah, which set down in writing thought forms still basically oral, the equivalent of geography (establishing the relationship of one place to another) is put into a formulary action narrative (Numbers 33: 16 ff.): "Setting out from the desert of Sinai, they camped at Kibroth-hattaavah. Setting out from Hazeroth, they camped at Rithmah . . . ," and so on for many more verses. Even geneologies out of such orally framed tradition are in effect commonly narrative. Instead of recitation of names, we find a sequence of "begats," of statements of what someone did.

Such sets occur in oral narrative for several reasons. The narrator in oral traditions is inclined to use the mnenmonically useful formula, does not mind redundancy, is inclined to exploit balance (repetition of the simple subject-predicate-object sequence aids recall), and the narrative context is far more vivid than a mere list. As Ong neatly puts it, "the persons are not immobilized as in a police line-up, but are doing something — namely begetting" (p. 99).

Not to dispute those who believe that Scripture is literally true in a sense that would be comprehensible to a literate historian, but oral tradition is rarely accurate with the precision of those who keep written records. This is one of its strengths. Useless data are forgotten in an oral tradition while remembered phenomena are updated — made consistent with current beliefs and attitudes. Jack Goody tells the story (1968, p. 33) of Gonja myths at the beginning of the twentieth century which explained the seven political subdivisions in terms of the founder and his seven sons, each of whom succeeded to the paramountcy in turn following the father's death. Fifty years later, two of these subdivisions had been absorbed, for one reason or another, and British anthropologists collecting folktales in the area found that the myths now described the founder and his five sons. The geneologies were altered to fit the facts of political reality during a half-century of serial remembering of etiological legends. And, Goody concludes (p. 33), a similar process will transmute other elements of culture such as myths and even sacred lore.

Literate societies cannot alter their past as can an oral culture. At least not in the same way:

> Instead, their members are faced with permanently recorded versions of the past and its beliefs; and because the past is thus set apart from the present, historical enquiry becomes possible. This in turn encourages scepticism; and scepticism, not only about the legendary past, but about received ideas about the universe as a whole. (Goody 1968, pp. 67–68)

Hence the literate's suspicion of orality and oral tradition. Oral literature is respectable only if it has come down to us in manuscript form.

Much of the work of American linguists on orality has thus been necessarily on speech among Americans, none of whom have been non- or preliterates. It is not the same thing, but it is the only research that has been done. Deborah Tannen (1982a) summarized much of the work conducted to date in a recent article in *Language*; some of her observations are pertinent here since the similarities between written and oral discourse (of literature) are deomonstrated (Tannen 1982a, pp. 2–16).

Tannen found literary discourse not substantially different from "ordinary conversation" but actually quite similar to it. Using features traditionally felt to be literary — sound patterning, word repetition, etc. — she coincidentally argued against those who still believe that oral qualities are detectable when such a performance is fixed in text form. The speakers interviewed by Labov (1972) in his now seminal research used both oral and literate strategies in spoken discourse; one might well argue that, rather than being "natural," Labov's informants were probably influenced in their narrative constructions by the conventions of our literary heritage. The influence of literacy is impossible to excape in our society; in primary classrooms the discourse of children was analyzed and found to be a preparation for literacy.

Recent sociolinguistic research confirms that storytelling in conversation is based on "audience participation in inferred meaning" (Tannen 1982a, p. 4); among Clackamas Indian tales, episodic transitions are sparse — sometimes just a morpheme — the audience filling in details (Jacobs 1971, p. 213). The effect of conversation, and narrative in conversation, involves the auditor(s). Labov found that ordinary conversation "shows a much more complex structure" than oral narratives. In research that compared oral narratives with written versions by the same informant, the oral renderings were more expressive, the written stories more content-focused. Writing compacts narratives, integrating their verbal units better. Yet when informants were asked to write imaginative prose — a "short story" — the result was lengthier; written imaginative literature combines the facility of involvement of spoken language with the integrative quality of writing. Lakeoff has shown (cited in Tannen 1982a, p. 4) that many features of ordinary conversation are also in popular contemporary writing. Parallelism and intonations thought to be basic in poetry are also basic in face-to-face conversation. And further assimilating the two styles — if there are two — is the finding of researchers that informants' written versions of stories used alliteration and assonance, traits associated with orality. Yet, for our purpose — a description of an oral tradition in a nonliterate society — the above conclusions are at best tangential, useful mainly in discussing orally — derived text literature. They show how speech affects our writing and vice versa, and that is not the same as the situation in a traditional society.

Oral tradition is the transmission of cultural items from one member of a culture to another, or others. Those items are heard, stored in memory, and when appropriate, recalled at the moment of subsequent transmission. Several disciplines — anthropology and folklore, but sociolinguistics and psycholinguistics as well — attempt to describe a world, one that literates can barely imagine. In a casual line, Levi-Strauss comments that "ethnology is first of all psychology" (1966, p. 131).

Memory, to repeat, is a vital human process in transmission. Psychologists break this down to four functioning categories: verbatim, gist, episodic, and general memory. Verbatim memory is the least frequently used in the lifeworld, certainly in oral traditions, though it is not unheard of. Passages are remembered by piecing together retrievable data, and then by giving them coherence by filling them out with supplementary information; it has been shown that people listen for meanings — unless otherwise motivated — and not verbatim wording (Clark and Clark 1977, p. 134). We all assume that Albert Friedman was right when he wrote that memorization is the basic vehicle of oral tradition (cited in

Finnegan 1977, p. 53), but memory is not a simple phenomenon. It is not a reduplicative process but a creative reconstruction.

Memory for prose-written, alas, in Clark and Clark's cited experiment, and not transmitted orally—depends primarily on four factors: the type and style of the language to be passed on; the situation of the listener at input; the interval of retention; and the circumstances and purposes of the output. Though these conclusions about the influence on oral transmission were deduced from literate subjects, they seem to be largely true of verbal transmission in general.

Controlled experiments have demonstrated the ability of long-term memory to store verbatim forms alone. Clark and Clark (1977, p. 136) refer to those Hausa-speaking Nigerians who have memorized the Koran and who do not know any classic Arabic. Their ability is not rare. Somali poets commonly memorize their poems, even those that take several evenings for a complete recital (Finnegan 1977, 74). Finnegan also reports that memorization was centrally involved in the recitation of Cambian epics of Sinjata (p. 78); Ruandan and South African praise poems are also usually memorized (p. 79). When Finnegan leaves Africa, however, where she has done so much field work, she is on slightly less firm turf; the 40,000-line *Rgveda* is cited, composed more than a millennium before the birth of Christ, and is said to have been transmitted verbatim (pp. 122, 135). But this has recently been questioned, since it is thought that these transmitters may have occasionally consulted manuscripts for accuracy. This would bear out the report of Clark and Clark that memory for verbatim wording is rapidly lost, and over the long haul what is retained is the meaning (1977, p. 139).

But, though illiterates do try for verbatim repetition (Ong 1982, p. 62), they seldom achieve it, except in short genres and in the rare cases cited above. Jacobs reported that his informants probably transmitted their older myths with "something close" (1971, p. 268) to phrase and sentence memorization, in "some if not all episodes." But his diachronic experience with the Clackamas was limited, and he really could not be sure.

Milman Parry defined the guslar's formulas as "a group of words which is regularly employed under the same metrical conditions to express a given essential idea" (1930, p. 80). For many of his disciples the phrase "regularly employed" came to mean "repeatedly employed." For Lord, Magoun, and others, formalicity became an indisputable sign of oral composition (cited in Finnegan 1977, p. 69). We all now recognize that the most marked trait of oralature is repetition—of some sort. Yet there is no universality of opinion about those aspects of the formula that must be repeated to "qualify"; metrical, syntactical, semantic elements have all been considered, but vary in varying oralatures. Even the length of a putative formula is questioned: linguist W. L. Rogers (1966) questioned the failure of literary scholars to define with satisfactory precision any of the components of Parry's formula. Joseph Russo argues (1976) that a fuller and more rigorously analyzed sample of Homeric verse might not support the claims for a higher formulaic content in the epics, and that the overall level of formulicity might prove to be little higher than that assumed for literary texts. Further research has not borne out Russo's suspicions; and despite all the modifications and reservations expressed about the oral formulaic theory, Parry did make us aware of that characteristic of oral narrative, the repetitive formula, however and in whatever way repetitive. Repetition may not be the "touchstone" of oral poetry (Finnegan 1977, p. 130), but it occurs so often that Ong can meaningfully speak of "the oral drive to use formulas" (1982, p. 99).

Formulas, of whatever sort, are memory aids almost entirely. Too much has been made of the audience's liking for familiar language because of its comforting aspects; it is more likely that aural participants in oralature performances enjoy formulas and familiarity of plot because through these elements they can participate more than passively — not as active performers, but neither are they as merely receptive as modern hushed audiences at a poetry reading. Experiments have shown that listeners filter out what they consider to be errors (many traditional audiences will correct errors as they occur, aloud); the auditor stores in memory only what is thought to be correct, or what is thought was intended (Clark and Clark 1977, p. 138). Passages are relatively easy to memorize if they are meaningful and in the listener's native language. Grammaticality is also important, as is brevity; rhyme is an aid to memorization, as is metricality (Clark and Clark 1977, p. 141).

In memory people store kernel sentences and the necessary notation that will account for a transformation when the sentence is recalled; the process of output "makes note" of the necessary transformations and appropriately transforms the stored kernel sentence. American speakers — at least those from whom these results were observed — are biased toward active sentences in memory and to subject priority. There seems to be a preference for an "order-of-mention-contract," supporting Labov's thesis that recalled personal experiences are related with a chronology that matches that of the actual events. The comparative is easier to remember (over the equative), as are positive statements over negative ones.

Inferences are stored, and when recalled, people often mistake their inferences for the original sentence. A major source of confusion is people's inclination to integrate new information with that of their world knowledge before storing; at recall it is often difficult to remember which pieces of information were acquired when. All known facts regarding a single entity are clustered around a "single point," and that organization controls recall (Clark and Clark 1977, pp. 156–60), Thus, Jacobs found (1971, pp. 249 ff.) that his Clackamas stories and myths did not explain nature, people, or customs; explicitness was unnecessary because certain memory cues in the narrative would evoke the relevant message. In such a traditional society, just the titles of stories were sufficient to explain the plot to the audience. Everyone participated in the tribe's literary heritage (p. 212) so that the meaning of each narrative was effectively conveyed to all members briefly and without the sense of moralizing.

Information at the instant of input is made consonant with the listener's "global representation" of reality; and, as noted, in a traditional society that global representation will more closely represent group values and attitudes than in a literate one. Recall will reflect this construction, even if it is inaccurate or wrong. Memory is reconstructive in any case. But the individual's global representations, made at the moment of input, have already shaped the information according to his/her background and experience, so that the recalled product may be relatively divorced from the original source of information (Clark and Clark 1977, p. 164). The same phenomenon happens during the communicative process of stories. Listeners build global representations of elements of the heard narratives, with the results (sharpening, leveling, rationalization) described by Bartlett (1932).

A group of Finnish folklorists codified the kinds of "mistakes" ("variations" is closer to the evaluative truth of the situation) they found in their field experience. In songs, single verses or groups of them are displaced, while some segments are dropped altogether. Forgetting was increasingly frequent when the performer was outside his/her community or family, another evidence of the stabilizing role of an informed traditional audience. Details superfluous to "the main theme" (Krohn 1971, p. 66) are the first to disappear from a narrative. Specific traits may be generalized and specified, the result of partial recall loss; or details may be repeated or expanded (Krohn 1971, pp. 56–72).

All of these processes conspire to alter the details in the transmission of narratives (as of ordinary facts), to get it "wrong." Stories in our culture are goal-oriented (Clark and Clark 1977, p. 170), and even though many of the details are altered in transmission, the goals of the narrative tend to be preserved. That leaves a great deal of room for variation; and it is another demonstration of the fragility of interpreting traditional narratives from the text alone. Stories may be shortened by reducing causative agents, initiators, and enabling events with no loss of meaning to an experienced audience, as Jacobs found. Yet compared on the basis of transcriptions alone, such a truncated story would seem to bear little relation to an analogue distended with detail.

Rumelhart (1977) found that the listeners he observed structured their own hierarchies of heard stories, and their recall was determined by this structure. Those aspects so ordered were setting, event, action, change of state, the internal and overt responses of characters, etc. Listeners arranged these components when they formed, at input, their own global representations of the story. In recall, this hierarchy was reconstructed. The classic psycholinguistic study of the effect of memory on storytelling is Bartlett's, often cited by folklorists but always with appropriate qualifications since Bartlett's subjects were Cambridge University students, not the homogeneous group one finds in a traditional society. The narratives were transmitted to each student in writing, not orally. And the narratives used in these experiments were not native to the students, but — as nearly all have remarked — somewhat strange and exotic. Consequently, the Cambridge students made many more alterations in transmitting these tales than would be true of the native transmission of familiar material. For instance, Bartlett noted the tendency to rationalize certain magical or otherwise supernatural elements; but this is just what we would expect from students at Cambridge relating an unfamiliar story filled with magical elements in which they did not believe.

In recent years reader-oriented criticism has stressed the role of the receiver in the aesthetic transaction. In oral tradition the listener is even more important in several respects, certainly important in understanding the oral tradition itself. Since Lord we have all become aware of the oral poet's instant responses to his or her aural audience, and to his or her flexibility in reacting to them. If the performance is not going well, the reciter usually has several techniques for enlivening audience interest. The writer has no such audience awareness. In some societies the group involves itself quite actively, as in Hawaiian oral poetry where the composition is collaborative, ensuring a precise transmission of traditional materials (Finnegan 1977, pp. 85–86). Melville Jacobs likens an oral performer to a Western actor, the performance to theater (1971,

p. 211)—not a brilliant or original metaphor, but one that usefully describes the situation. It is in a theater where the audience is free to correct the performer. The older Clackamas listeners made corrections of phrases and even specific words during the recital of myths. And at story recitals a full discussion of the plot (both during and after recitals) is usual; interruptions were by a theorizing and fantasying audience (Jacobs 1971, p. 269). The same happens among the Somali, who feel free to correct "faulty" renderings of known poems (Finnegan 1977, pp. 74-75). Much more so than with written poetry, an oral audience's aesthetics reflect the purpose and effect of the poem (Finnegan, 1977, p. 236).

One of the American folk preachers I recorded in a domestic oral tradition of formulaic composition (Rosenberg 1970, pp. 103-4) was instantly able to correct errors he had just made in his own performance; the correction formulas of the Reverend Rufus Hays appeared to be spontaneous, not preformed like the one Finnegan notes during the singing of Yoruba hunters' songs. In that situation other expert singers may be present, and if they feel that a mistake has been made, they will interrupt the singer with some such formula as, "You have told a lie, you are hawking loaves of lies . . . listen to the correct version now. . . . Your version is wrong" (Finnegan 1977, p. 232).

Edson Richmond once remarked to me that folklore was everything that didn't get communicated when an oral performance is transcribed. The performance situation is vital; it throbs. Lord noted that when his *guslari* dictated their poems, the meter—the meter of the rapid oral communication—broke down and nearly all elements of the performance were affected. Jacobs noted the same among his informants (1971, p. 221). Linguists have found that, when subjects are asked to write out versions of stories they have been reciting orally, the written versions are different also: more compact and more integrated (Tannen 1982b, p. 8).

The best stories, oral as well as written (as many think), say the least while evoking the most. (Though linguists define literate strategies as supplying maximal background information and "connective tissue" [Tannen, 1982b, p. 3].) In oral traditions brief statements often evoke a substantial recall. Narratives that allow the audience a maximum of imaginative creativity are the most successful (Jacobs 1971, p. 21). In this way the auditors participate in the performance in a creative way; they feel as though they are a creative part of the performance in active, participatory ways that the reader is not. Repetitive language enables an audience to anticipate not only the narrative elements to come but the phrasing as well. Empowered to criticize, oral/aural audiences are genuinely part of the performance, creatively, and not merely passively. Tannen (1982b, p. 10) confirmed what folklorists have known for decades, that oral versions are more expressive. Written versions are more content-focused; Jacobs's (1971, p. 20) collected oral tales were contextualized.

Axel Olrik's "epic laws" of oralature have already been mentioned. In a more general way, thinking in an oral culture is in mnemonic patterns, "shaped for ready oral occurrence" (Ong 1982, p. 34). The oral style of discourse is more focused, slower-moving, frequently redundant. Oral poetry tends to be additive rather than subordinated (Ong 1982, pp. 37–40). The characters in such narratives are noticeably "heavy" characters types, rarely three-dimensional, and monumental (Ong insists that round characters are not possible, 1982, 152); their creators strive to make them memorable. Oral cultures do not organize long, climactic narratives; climactic plots are not natural, do not conform with events in the lifeworld (pp. 70, 143). Yet oral narratives can be lengthy (narratives quite aside from the *Odyssey* and the *Iliad*, whose "oralness" needs several pages of qualification and explanation); Stith Thompson singles out "vagabonds" as individuals who often "string out their stories to an inordinate length," while some tellers elaborate their tales to an extraordinary degree while keeping "the old general pattern" (1977, pp. 451–52).

Keeping to the "general" pattern is the best that nearly all oral transmitters are capable of. Precision, as already noted, is a product of writing. An oral culture cannot deal in geometric figures, abstract categorization, or formal logic; and illiterates cannot organize "elaborate concatenations of causes" (Ong 1982, pp. 55–57). It is print that fosters tight and intricate plotting (p. 133) such as we take for granted in the detective story and the spy novel. Goody similarly observed (1968, p. 54):

> The same process of dissection into abstract categories, when applied not to a particular argument but to the ordering of all the elements of experience into separate areas of intellectual activity, leads to the Greek division of knowledge into autonomous cognitive disciplines which has since become universal in Western culture and which is of cardinal importance in differentiating literate and non-literate cultures.

Inaccuracy and reduced intellectual performance (of certain analytic processes) occasionally deplored by cerebral literates is certainly present. Yet much of the contempt felt by literates for the unlettered is not justified. Levi-Strauss has shown how some of the most important aspects of "the savage mind" (1966) are merely differently coded expressions of the same fundamental thoughts of sophisticated cultures; "savage mind" (*la pensee sauvage* in the original) is in itself an ironic statement intended by the author, since savages are not, popularly, supposed to have sophisticated thought at all. Yet, not only do totemic societies evolve cerebrally intricate structures, they also reflect on the nature of poetry (Finnegan 1977, p. 236).

Neither economic development nor literacy seems to influence the flourishing of poetry; among certain Polynesian societies, praise poems are felt to belong to certain families, and at times a member's claim to rank may depend upon his power to reproduce, "letter perfect," his family chants and his "name song." Many oral poets are among their society's elite (Finnegan 1977, p. 202). Among the Clackamas, upper-class life is depicted in the poems of the oral tradition (Jacobs 1971, p. 176). Ong concludes *Orality and Literacy* by remarking that, while no one wants to advocate illiteracy, and while every oral culture of his knowledge wants to acquire the ability to read once it has been exposed to it, oral cultures have produced "creations beyond the reach of literates, for example, the *Odyssey*" (Ong 1982, p. 175). The list should be extended; and it could be extended to include those written works that have also enjoyed an extensive oral currency: Marlowe's "Come Live with Me and Be My Love" and Raleigh's reply were printed anonymously on broadsheets and were sung (as were many poems) by broadside street pedlars. The poems of Burns are still recited aloud today. Far from being its executioner, writing coexists peacefully with orality.

PART TWO

Historic Folktale Analysis

THE METHODOLOGY FORMERLY USED TO RECONSTRUCT folktales is not much used today by literary historians or by American folklorists. The Finnish folklorists developed the procedures. They assumed that the folktale was a relatively stable item that probably did not vary in its basic outline—whatever that might be—over the centuries. Further, they developed a methodology for decomposing the tale into its component parts, much as linguists had analyzed sentences into words, and words into phonemes and morphemes. If these assumptions were true, one could reliably speak of "types" of the folktales—narrative configurations which remained constant as the tales were transmitted over time and distance. And if types were discrete and stable, they could be catalogued (as they were) into dictionaries of folktales. Additionally, the Finns made further, and more detailed, dictionaries of the narrative components of folktales: the motif indexes.

But this logical chain has its weak links. While most tales seem to be stable, some folklorists have observed in several of them a tendency to change. We know that new tales are occasionally created; and several serious scholars of folktale transmission and form think it likely that several tales have changed over the years. We also know that most tales interact with textual versions, and are thus altered in some measure, quite apart from the conduits of orality. We can never be sure that a narrative, thousands of years old, is genetically related to one collected recently, even as "recently" as the nineteenth century. Was the tale substantially different then, but did it become fixed in its present form owing to textual transmission? Did a narrative come down to us by borrowing from a literary creation? And if so, in what way?

This methodology has been important to literary historical scholarship for nearly a hundred years. Medievalists especially, in the first four or five decades of this century, have used this methodology (or the results of those folklorists who used it) to make influential conclusions about the relations of narratives that we know about in manuscript form but which structurally resemble known folktales. And while American folklorists are not interested in the Finnish historic-geographic method (for their own reasons), in many cases it does still seem to have the promise to illuminate.

The three chapters that comprise this section summarize the methodology that has been used and mentions some of the more persistent conclusions, ideas that have shaped our reconstructions of literary history. Chapter five, "Embedded Folktales," takes the example of one literary narrative, the medieval English romance *Sir Degaré*, and demonstrates how it can be disassembled to show its folktale components.

The Finnish Method
and Its Assumptions

A CRITICAL ANALYSIS OF *Beowulf* published in 1969 argued that the character of Unferth was a necessity within the epic tradition of its culture; the author's methodology was not only that of the literary critic / historian but of the traditional folklorist. In outline, the argument proceeded as follows: narrative structural similarities between *Beowulf* and the folktale type designated by Aarne-Thompson as "The Three Stolen Princess" (A-T 301) invite comparison. Specifically, Beowulf's challenge by Unferth when he first arrives at Hrothgar's court has no counterpart in the known folktales. Similarly, while nearly all heroic folktales begin with an *enfance* of the hero (in the subtype, "The Bear's Son"), the old English epic introduces a youthfully vigorous but mature warrior and leader. Some form of the folktale antedates the epic (probably composed during the eighth century, written down around 1000 A.D.), and it is unlikely that the character of Unferth would appear in any of them. His (presumed) absence in the folktales suggests that he is the creation of the *Beowulf* poet; but since accounts of the hero's youth are absent from the epic, it is likely that, in replying to Unferth about his youthful escapade with Breca in the North Sea, Beowulf recounts in this analepsis his adventurous *enfance* which is in the folktales. To conform with Germanic epic tradition, the *Beowulf* *scop* relocated the story relating the hero's youth from the beginning of the narrative to a more convenient point when it can be evoked in retrospect (Rosenberg 1975).

This comparison between an epic, which has devolved to us in manuscript, and a folktale, which has never been collected and must therefore only be hypothecated, is predicated on several assumptions. They are basic ones to some folklore research, especially as it relates to literary texts. Much that will be discussed later in this chapter depends on an understanding of these folklore methodologies and how they are applicable to literary-historical criticism.

Preliminarily, it will be useful to define the components of folk narrative study. For much of the past century the system used has been the legacy of Finnish folklore; but the clearest definition is Stith Thompson's, "the smallest element in a tale having a power to persist in tradition" (1977, p. 415). The narrative elements meant are of three kinds: the actors within a tale, descriptive items in the background of the action, and, the most popular kind of motif, single incidents. By current standards this is nebulous; but despite all the problems inherent in this definition and the analytic system based on it, the influence of the Finns has been so pervasive that folklore narrative study is barely possible without reference to it.

A type, Thompson also has defined, "is a traditional tale that has an independent existence" (1946, 415). Though a type may occur in oral tradition with one or more other types, it does not depend upon them for its meaning. Independent existence is the sole criterion for the determination of a type. But, perhaps confusingly, single motifs exist independently in tradition and may thus be considered as types. The theoretical problems with these concepts are obvious enough, but as is often the case, the system has been manageable in practice—most of the time. And it may be, considering the directions being taken by American folklorists in the late 1980s, that the motif indexes (dictionaries of motifs arranged by content) are of more value to literary scholars who are trying to establish relations between oral and written narratives. The hero who encounters a monster, defeats it, and follows it to its lair in the lower world; the heroine who marries a nobleman and whose promise of constant obedience is put to the test when the husband pretends to have her children killed; and the husband who wagers with a stranger on his wife's chastity are all collected (and listed) motifs. The scholar desiring to know whether these aspects of *Beowulf, The Clerk's Tale,* or *Cymbeline* have folklore counterparts (they all do) can quickly make that determination by consulting Stith Thompson's *Motif-Index of Folk Literature* (1955–58).

In order to establish any relationship between a literary narrative (in this example *Beowulf*) and a tale-type, a paradigm abstracted from many authentic oral versions of the latter is compared with the text. Examples of oral variants taken from the geographic region of the manuscript's home are compared in detail, paying close attention to the great influence of versions in print. If the researcher is lucky enough to have a transcript of the precise oral narrative involved, the task is greatly simplified; but such good fortune is extremely rare. Folktales per se were not collected until the nineteenth century, and it has not been until this century that electric or electronic recorders have made collections very accurate. Almost always the oral narrative is not available; folklorists have therefore turned to paradigms, or composites, of a great many collected tales whose consistency in outline – in the nature and sequence of distributional elements – enables the researcher to group them as "types."

The following composite of type 301 (or A-T 301) is from the international index, *The Types of the Folktale*, by Aarne and Thompson, composed from folklorists' experience with such tales:

I. *The Hero* is of supernatural origin and strength: (a) son of a bear who has stolen his mother; (b) son of a dwarf or robber from whom the boy rescues himself and his mother; (c) son of a man and a she-bear or (d) cow; and (e) engendered by the eating of fruit, (f) by the wind, or (g) from a burning piece of wood, he grows supernaturally strong and is unruly.

II. *The Descent.* (a) With two extraordinary companions (b) he comes to a house in the woods, or (b[1]) a bridge; the monster who owns it punishes the companions but is defeated by the hero, (c) who is let down through a well into the lower world. Alternative beginning of the tale: (d) the third prince, where his elder brothers have failed, (e) overcomes at night the monster who steals from the king's apple-tree, and (f) follows him through a hole into the lower world.

III. *Stolen Maidens.* (a) Three princesses are stolen by a monster; (b) the hero goes to rescue them.

IV. *Rescue.* (a) In the lower world, with a sword he finds there, he conquers several monsters and rescues three maidens. (b) The maidens are pulled up by the hero's companions and stolen.

V. *Betrayal of Hero.* (a) He himself is left below by his treacherous companions, but he reaches the upper world through the help of (b) a spirit whose ear he bites to get magic powers to fly or (c) a bird, (d) to whom he feeds his own flesh; or (e) he is pulled up.

VI. *Recognition.* He is recognized by the princesses when he arrives on the wedding day. (b) He is in disguise and (c) sends his dogs to steal from the wedding feast; or (d) he presents rings, (e) clothing, or (f) other tokens, secures the punishment of the imposters, and marries one of the princesses.

Allowing for a number of variations from this basic type – itself incorporating a number of various possibilities – *Beowulf* is an analogue. Arguments to the contrary have not been very convincing. Beowulf is of supernatural origin and strength: his relationship to the bear, embodiment of strength for the Nordic Middle Ages, is seen in his name (Chambers 1959, pp. 365-81). With companions Beowulf does come to a house (an impressively royal house) in the woods, where a monster punishes the hero's companions but is, in turn, defeated by him. The hero follows the monster through "a hole" into the lower world and there slays the monster with a sword he finds on the premises. But he is deserted — treacherously in the folktales, by mistake in the epic — and has to reach the upper world without his companion's assistance.

Beowulf varies from the Aarne-Thompson paradigm in one important respect: the folktale hero's abduction and eventual rescue of the three pricesses is so important an element that folklorists identify the tale as "The Three Stolen Princesses." No such ladies have been distressed in the epic. Given the masculine quality of this heroic (and essentially martial) poetry, rescuing women — even princesses — would be out of place. The lady in jeopardy as a suitable stimulus for the hero's risk of life is a later development in European literature — late in the thirteenth century in France, a century later in England. It is almost beneath Beowulf's dignity to risk his life merely to save a princess. Consequently, inevitably, when there are no stolen princesses, part III, there can be no Recognition — part VI.

Yet, researchers familiar with this method of comparison insist that *Beowulf's* incorporation of four elements (I, II, IV, and V) of type 301 is sufficient to consider it a variant, and not a randomly similar narrative. The matter is not without controversy, even among folklorists (Sydow 1922). The type is based, necessarily, on tales collected during the past two centuries; it is theoretically possible that the tale changed during the millennium before that, and is not accurately definable by recent versions of type 301.

Finnish folklorist Kaarle Krohn, who helped develop the original methodology, wrote,

> Polygenesis [the independent creation of folktales, rather than the diffusion of a single tale] in the most extreme sense, that every variant was composed separately at innumerable sites, is unthinkable. Usually a single origin is assumed for the traditional forms of one ethnic or linguistic group. . . . But even one single independent reoccurrence of such a complicated form, for example, the Cinderella tale, as the result of the general similarity of human fantasy or pure chance is highly unlikely." (1971, p. 136)

In the case of "The Three Stolen Princesses," enough variants without princesses have been found to indicate a tradition of narratives similar (in outline) to *Beowulf*. Such narratives are nevertheless judged to be part of the A-T 301 tradition; they are subsets of it, or more technically, subtypes.

One of the characteristics of the folktale making indices of motifs (the smallest decomposable unit of narrative existent in oral narrative) and tale-types possible is stability. Stith Thompson remarks that "the examination of all versions of a tale impresses one with the remarkable stability of the essential story in the midst of continually shifting details" (1946, p. 437). This stability is accounted for, in part, by (the now somewhat arguable) "Law of Self-Correction" formulated by folklorist Walter Anderson. This "Law" is in two parts; both indicate reasons why folk narrative retains its "essential story" in travels across continents and over the course of centuries. First, most raconteurs have heard their tales many times, not merely once, from their sources. That repetition helps them to get it "right." Usually, in addition, the teller has heard a particular narrative from a number of different people, often in different locations; listeners in these various audiences often insure that the teller gets the story "correctly" and often will correct a "mistake." The internal logic of a narrative is an element not touched upon by Anderson, but nevertheless it seems to be a factor in maintaining consistency: if "A" happens, then "B" follows: before the horse can be stolen, the barn door must be unlocked. This logic cannot be violated.

So basic is the idea of the dogma of monogenesis (or the rejection of polygenesis) that when folklorist (and medievalist) W. Edson Richmond found two ballads whose "differences in phrasing are so great that it seems inconceivable that one could have developed directly from the other," he did not seriously consider the possibility of polygenesis but concluded that "one must, therefore, predicate a lost archetype in which the same plot as that found in our versions was developed, though the lost archetype need not have had phrases or stanzas common to either of our extant text" (1963, pp. 75–76).

The comparison of a literary text with folktales where none have been, or could have been, collected, is with a hypothetical reconstruction. We assume the existence of folktales of the type, "The Three Stolen Princesses," because the essential story (the chain of nuclei distributional elements) of type 301 is the essential story of *Beowulf*. The folktales cannot be dated exactly unless the collecting folklorist so documents his or her own experience; *Beowulf* suggests that analogous tales are at least as old as the composition of the epic. And because we assume the stability of the folktale, we assume that, in outline at least, "The Three Stolen Princesses" was in the eighth century much as it is today. To a degree, this is an article of faith.

On such assumptions certain otherwise puzzling aspects of *Beowulf* can be explained. Why do Beowulf's companions sleep in Heorot on their first night there when they have come to Hrothgar's land only to fight a monster known to attack its victims at night? No comment is made by the poet about these warriors, so self-possessed that they sleep on the edge of doom, nor about Beowulf's inactivity when Grendel does appear — having burst vigorously through the door — and proceeds to devour the hero's hand-picked warrior friend, Hindscio, while Beowulf permissively watches. Gwyn Jones, who knows as much about folk narrative as he does about medieval literature, puts it succinctly: these details are "gaunt and unassimilable folktale motifs which the *Beowulf* poet found he could neither reject nor rationalize" (1972, p. 24, n. 1). In the folktale, we should recall, the hero's friends are punished by the monster before the hero kills him (it?).

Friedrich Panzer's detailed study of *Beowulf* in relation to analogous folktales (1910), while making a number of points which are now in an intellectual public domain, had methodological weaknesses. One was Panzer's failure to give proper weight to those variants of type 301 found in Scandinavia, where *Beowulf* was recited and composed for the manuscript (Cotton Vitelius A XV). The *oicotype*, a term first borrowed from botany by the Swedish folklorist C. W. von Sydow, in folklore refers to a geographically or chronologically limited variant. Panzer's study was on the one hand admirable in that it accounted for nearly all the variants of type 301 that were available; on the other, it took into account variants that had been collected in regions far from Scandinavia where variants differed substantially from *Beowulf.*

A word about the Finnish historic-geographic method and its methodology is in order at this point. Perhaps the classic study in English is that Stith Thompson (first published in 1953, reprinted in Dundes, 1965), analyzing the American Indian "Star Husband Tale." Thompson sought a tale whose known variants were few enough to make the body of data easily comprehensible but whose geographic distribution was wide enough to allow the Finnish method full scope. A few folklorists in his day had argued that literary versions of any tale were so influential (because widely read and thus transmitted) as to render studies of oral tradition defective (Dundes 1965, p. 418). Thompson also chose for a model a tale that was current in a culture "with no possible or likely literary influences" (p. 418). The "Star Husband Tale" was ideal. Thompson presented the following outline (p. 419):

> Two girls are sleeping in the open at night and see two stars. They make wishes that they may be married to these stars. In the morning they find themselves in the upper world, each married to a star — one of them a young man and the other an old man. The women are usually warned against digging but eventually disobey and make a hole in the sky through which

they see their old home below. They are seized with longing to return and secure help in making a long rope. On this they eventually succeed in reaching home.

All of the versions of the narrative under examination are collected and grouped according to the location of their discovery. In practice, literary versions would have been handled separately; the Finns paid special attention to them in their own analyses owing to the much greater influence exerted on the tradition by tales in print. Thompson did not deal with literary versions; his grouping of Amerind tales was by region, e.g., Eskimo, North Pacific, California, Plains, Southwest, Woodland, and so forth. All of the variants were then decomposed into variations within the narrative that offered significant possibility for differentiation. For instance, since the number of women occasionally varied, Thompson symbolized that trait as "A" and used subscript numbers to indicate the number of women present: "A_1" indicated that the tale had only one woman, "A_2" indicated two women (the most common variation), etc. Trait "B" designed the "Introductory Action," the means or motivation of transportation of the women to the upper world; trait "C" designated the "Circumstances of Introductory Action" — what the women were doing when the action begins; trait "D" signified the method of ascent, and so forth.

Once all of the tales have been thus decomposed into constituents, and the major narrative elements coded, the entire corpus of tales is compared. Each trait is evaluated according to its frequency of occurrence, distribution, and content. Thompson remarks of trait "D" that "it seems clear from its frequency and distribution that . . . the translation to the upper world during sleep is the normal form" (p. 439). Some interpretation is often necessary, as in the case of trait "F" (distinctive qualities of the husband): of the eighty-six tales used in this model demonstration, Thompson found that only twenty-seven described the star husbands as an old man and a young. But in several other versions the star husbands were contrasted in some way: in two tales the husbands wore different-colored blankets, in two others they were initially seen as a "red star sun" and "white star moon"; and in one plains version, the dim star is a chief, the bright star his servant (p. 440). Thompson, interpreting, concluded that, since all of these versions have "contrasting husbands," they "may well be variants of" the old man/young man polarity.

On the assumption — to simplify but not to distort through over-simplification — that, if a raconteur tells a particular tale to several different listeners, the chances are extremely remote that they will all "get it wrong" in the same way, or that they will all make the same changes or all have the same memory lapses. Therefore, in order to determine the "basic tale," the archetype from which all the others derive, the folklorist employing the historic-geographic method counts each variant of each trait to decide, statistically, which versions dominate. The composite of the predominant traits produces this archetype. For the "Star Husband Tale," Thompson concluded that the archetype had the following traits (p. 449):

> Two girsl (65%) sleeping out (85%) make wishes for stars as husbands (90%). They are taken to the sky in their sleep (82%) and find themselves married to stars (87%), a young man and an old, corresponding to the brilliance or size of the stars (55%). The women disregard the warning not to dig (90%) and accidentally open up a hole in the sky (76%). Unaided (52%) they descend on a rope (88%) and arrive home safely (76%).

The actual tales may then be examined to see if their traits match those of this hypothetically reconstructed archetype. Thompson was fortunate in this regard, as about a dozen of the collected "Star Husband Tales" did conform to the statistical model. The tales were then examined according to their geographic distribution to identify subtypes and *oicotypes*. This procedure can now be performed by computer (see Rosenberg and Smith 1974). In this model study, Thompson found that changes in the archetype came about through the addition of a single item or a narrative unit that required additional changes to maintain consistency. The husband's descriptive polarities, he noted, were found in several groups of tales on the periphery of the main area; he concluded with a basic assumption of the Finnish method, the rationale for the identification of ancillary rather than basic traits: "it seems inconceivable that any one of these versions should have originated the story, for it is beyond all probability that any one trait should be consistently forgotten, and never recur elsewhere" (Dundes 1965, p. 450).

To return to *Beowulf*: when a comparative analysis of those analogous folktales (the appropriate subtype of type 301) in Scandinavia depict the hero's childhood, the methodological assumptions of the Finnish historic-geographic method indicate that the epic is "unusual" and that the statistical norm is to present such a subset of narrative units (the *enfance*) at the tale's beginning. The indication is also that this folktale tradition was antecedent to, as well as coexistant with, *Beowulf*, or else the *enfance* would appear with much greater frequency; if *Beowulf* was the original, then several hundred tellers of the collected versions of type 301 "got it wrong," and all of their tellers deleted this portion of the hero's life. But the epic does have a recounting of the hero's youthful adventures, of sorts; it occurs when Unferth challenges him about a swimming match in which he had reportedly earlier engaged, and Beowulf replies with the true account of that contest. If the folktales were available to those *scops* who rendered the discourse we know as this Old English epic, and the customs of Germanic epic tradition militated against the strictly chronological placement of the *enfance*, it is not unlikely that such a narrative portion would appear, only later. One of the common features of the Bear's Son's youth is his unpromising conduct; that aspect of Beowulf's early years is not mentioned until after two thousand lines have been recited.

These conclusions concerning *Beowulf*'s relation to the type 301 tales are valid if the Finnish method is valid. But that intricate and elaborate methodology is not without its critics. The primary complaint of folklorists is that a full historic-geographic study commonly takes between ten and twenty years to complete, dealing as it does with several hundred variants of a single tale (sometimes more than a thousand). Very few researchers have completed more than one in their lifetime; only a few have attempted even one (Thompson 1977, p. 444). Most American folklorists, if they work with this kind of material at all, much prefer to deal with a limited number of *oicotypes*, facilitating a cultural statement that is, after all, one of folklore's prime objectives. Not even the development of a computer program to speed up the comparison of decomposed folktale abstracts and to identify — almost immediately — subtypes, has increased the popularity of the Finnish method in the United States. But the objection to the excessive time necessary to complete such a project is not entirely relevant to our study of folklore and literature.

More to the point are two assumptions on which the Finns, and most other European scholars, have founded this methodology: we should ask whether folktales are as stable as the Finnish method seems to imply, and whether polygenesis is possible. As has long been recognized, it is the nature of material in oral transmission to vary; this is especially true of folk narratives. Antti Aarne has even made a list of the most likely changes (listed in Thompson 1977, p. 436): details are forgotten or added, two or more tales are strung together, incidents are repeated (usually three times), narrative material from other tales is substituted, animal characters may be replaced by humans (and vice versa), etc. Vladimir Propp was to complain, as early as 1928, that these constant changes and shifts made the tale impossible to define by current standards (1968, pp. 3 ff). Yet, despite all these doubtful expres-

sions about the folktale's stability, it is consistent enough for our purposes — and in the geographic areas that are the concern of literary
scholars of a European tradition. It has long been believed that European tale-types evolved clearly and that they are usually relatively fixed
in form, like — to use Thompson's metaphor — inert crystals (1977, pp.
390, 447).

Is polygenesis possible? Certainly, but in the main only in certain
circumstances, with certain genres, in international contexts. Single
motifs, it has long been acknowledged, can arise independently of each
other. And across cultural boundaries, certain tales seem to have analogues where direct diffusion cannot be demonstrated. For instance,
some European tales seem to have analogues among North American
Indian tales:

> The interesting parallel between the adventures of Lodge-Boy and Thrown-
> Away and the medieval romance of Valentine and Orson, both concerned
> with twin heroes, one brought up at home and the other abandoned at birth,
> is certainly nothing more than a coincidence. That the American Indians
> should have known the chivalric romance is almost inconceivable, since it
> has never been told by Europeans as a folktale. (Thompson 1977, p. 337 n. 21)

And polygenesis is the likely explanation of the great similarity of dozens
of hero tales and heroic legends (such as the defeated heroes Saul,
Leonidas, Bjarki, Byrthnoth, Roland, Gawain, *et al.* detailed in my
Custer and the Epic of Defeat [1974]); heroic legends differ from folktales in respect to the belief of the tradition-bearers, the "facts" upon
which the legend may be based, and so on, all of which may cause it
to behave differently in oral transmission. Polygenesis is a common occurrence; the problem is to find out when it occurs, and where.

On net, then, taking into account the major flaws of the historic-
geographic method, it is nevertheless workable in most of the cases that
would concern the literary scholar. The folktale is often enough unstable in structure in oral transmission, but in the case of type 301, for
instance, it has been shown to be satisfactorily constant: it has been
recently collected in Latin America in a form immediately recognizable
as of a type with *Beowulf* (Barakat 1965); and it has been quite stable
in the Baltic region, where the *Beowulf scop* performed and heard
others perform. And, while some genres appear to have spread polygenetically, the ordinary folktale (A-T types 300–750) has not yet been
shown to be subject to independent creation. To return to the argument
outlined at the beginning of this chapter: given several folkloric assumptions about the nature of oral narratives in transmission over the course

of a great length of time, it can be reasonably argued that the *flyting* between Unferth and the newly arrived Beowulf is a repositioning and enhancement of the hero's *enfance* commonly found at the beginning of tales of type 301.

This discussion of the Finnish method's applicability to literary studies cannot conclude without reference to one of the most important of such studies in recent years, one that is in several ways a model of such approaches. "New Light on the Origins of the Griselda Story," by Francis Lee Utley and William E. Bettridge (1971), compares about fifty variants of "Griselda" (Aarne-Thompson type 887) with the literary versions of Chaucer, Boccaccio, and Petrarch, and arrives at new—and rigorously argued—conclusions.

The first step in their demonstration was to show that the striking similarity of both episode and even phrasing of some contemporary folktales (of type 887) with literary versions marks the oral narratives as reflexes: "we cannot doubt that the provenience is ultimately literary" (p. 157). This folktale—that is, one of its type—cannot therefore have been the source of Boccaccio's *Decameron* tale. The authors next demonstrate that "Cupid and Psyche" ("The Monster/Animal as Bridegroom" Aaarne-Thompson type 425A) is hardly likely to be the source tale either, despite the claims of Griffith (1931) and Cate (1932); the argument at this point does not depend entirely on the Finnish method, though Utely and Bettridge maintain that the Griffith/Cate argument is weakened greatly because the subtype of A-T 425 in which the children are taken away has not been found in Italy or the Mediterranean. Again, *oicotyping* argues against Boccaccio's using this tale (425A) as a source. "No romance oral variants," they remind us, "of the stolen children subgroup exist" (p. 150). Utley and Bettridge insist upon precise *oicotyping* methods in their literary analysis (p. 168):

> One is reminded [by guessing at the origin of Griselda's name] of nineteenth-century folktale study, where scholars like Clouston, Frazer, or Lang could take a fragment from India, another from Australia, and another from the Faroes, and from them construct a flourishing tale. . . . One major difference between folklore research a hundred years ago and now is that today the folktale is a recognized set of identifiable and identified documents, most of them well-attested from scientific and accurate collectors, rather than a few exemplars "liberated" like those of the Grimms with many a hypothetical "lost source" as intermediary between them.

The positive conclusions of this research tentatively suggest that Boccaccio's source was a Turkish folktale similar to a complex of Aarne-

Thompson types including type 894 ("The Ogre Schoolmaster"), type 707 ("The Three Golden Sons"), and some version of type 425. In the final stages of their deliberations, Utley and Bettridge located nine Mediterranean versions of their tale, listed in the Turkish archives as type 306 ("The Patience of a Sultaness/Princess"). A composite abstract of this tale readily shows its similarity to the Chaucer/Boccaccio/Petrarch versions:

1. A Padishah wants a wife, who has great patience and looks like him.
2. He marries a poor girl and takes away three of her children under the pretext that he will eat them.
3. Then he announces that he will marry another wife.
4. The wedding turns out to be that of his eldest son, and the Padishah explains everything. (Eberhard and Boratov 1953, pp. 33–43).

But how would Boccaccio have heard a Turkish version? The last element in the Utley-Bettridge research was historical—though with a smattering of theology. Corresponding with folklorists in Turkey and Greece, Utley and Bettridge were able to reconstruct a fourteenth-century cultural bridge "from Turkey to Greece to Italy"—and in the reverse direction, though one way might have been sufficient (p. 192). The (suppositious) route of transmission then suggested that the tale, of Turkish origin, was picked up by a Greek in the fourteenth century or earlier, and brought across the Aegean to Zákinthos, whence it found its way to Italy and to Boccaccio (p. 193). What does such a suppositious cultural route demonstrate? If no such commerce existed between Turkey and Italy, the case for the argued relation of tales would have been critically damaged. Finding that such a route did exist allows the Utley-Bettridge hypothesis to continue to exist, but it is in itself a feeble element of proof, coming as it does after the fact of the comparative study of narratives.

Narrowing the search down to nine tales not only gave these scholars an easily grasped corpus of material but made statistical analysis very risky; the composites, the paradigms thus possible, necessarily have to be constructed from a scant data base indeed. Nevertheless—or perhaps because of that fact—it is one of the most piercing and learned analyses of this narrative and its analogues; given the paucity of collected tales available, it is difficult to foresee how this research will ever be methodologically surpassed.

And while that may be true—the next several decades will be the test—larger questions remain about the methodology as an intellectual entity. The objection of some folklorists that the Finnish method is superorganic can be appropriately asked by literary historians: the principles governing the behavior of folktales in transmission over time and through space seems to proceed regardless of human or cultural considerations. The teller of tales is almost incidental to the hydraulic laws of folktale transmission whose manifestations we observe and analyze. The form—the structure—of the folk narrative is essential exclusively, dominating symbolic or semantic or hermeneutic considerations. All source studies, and not only the reconstruction of the folktale as source or analogue, tend to become ends in themselves; interpretation, meaning, significance are commonly neglected, though this is not an insurmountable flaw in the methodology. And source studies such as those described in this chapter cannot deal with stylistic features of narratives, those qualities of narrative that distinguish the performed tale from its telegraphic outline in the tale-type indexes.

The Utley-Bettridge conclusions are only as sound as their methodological assumptions and the corpus of collected tales of the A-T 894/707/425 matrix. More thorough collecting in the western Mediterranean may someday uncover narratives that undermine their argument. And more rigorous analyses may one day fatally question the Finnish method, throwing the whole mountain of argumentation onto that academic slag heap where now repose those nineteenth-century theories of solar mythology and of the unitary source of folktales. It just might happen; for just as the folktale can be seen, over centuries, to be evolving, so folktale research is spinning, and at a much faster rate. Utley and Bettridge analyzed *The Clerk's Tale* according to the procedures of a time-honored methodology, but that methodology is not for all time.

Is it even for our time, let alone for times to come? In the United States the prognosis is not encouraging. To begin with, folklorists are hesitant to commit so much of their time and labor to historic-geographic studies, and they are dubious of the results. And most of the present generation of folklorists is wary of literary studies; certainly they are not congenial to any analysis that highlights the text—as opposed to the live performance—as communicative event. The folktale of (scholarly/analytical) choice is the urban legend. Among literary historians, the Finnish method seems to be of greatest interest to medievalists, as the folktale is so frequently an analogue or a source of the narratives they study.

The Finnish method incorporates many of the inherent weaknesses and shortfalls of structuralism and of source studies as a critical mode. Historic-geographic researchers may have difficulty dealing precisely with narrative material that is thought to have existed before the first folktales were collected, since tales from ancient times may have been different from their present configurations and textures. Propp thought that, just as astronomers could hypothecate the existence of stars never seen, so folklorists could postulate the existence of tales never collected (p. 114). This assumes a great deal about astronomers and their discipline. Is such optimism transferable to the study of human-generated stories? That issue may lie at the core of the matter of the Finnish method; we are more skeptical today about our potential to understand human behavior.

CHAPTER 4

Sources or Analogues?

FOR THE STUDENT/SCHOLAR OF LITERATURE, folklore is usually studied as a source. And the final goal of source studies should be an evaluation of the studied work. Often enough, though, source research ceases after the source has been located or hypothecated, and such hypotheses and identifications become ends in themselves. This is also true of folklore sources, which are in several ways subject to the same principles as other source data, though by the nature of folklore distinctive problems may arise.

André Morize's study of source materials and their use in literary research is one of the most exhaustive such compilations to date, and is still useful (1922, pp. 96–127). His taxonomy includes six categories. (1) Direct "borrowings" by an author may be from the work of another, or even from his or her own productions. (2) Documentary sources are more common in the nature of the historian's (and the lexicographer's) research, though authors frequently refer to a great variety of documents for a variety of reasons, background being only one of them; Flaubert's extensive research into the flora, fauna, topography, climate, etc., of North Africa preparatory to his writing *La Salammbo* for example. (3) Composites, epitomized by Lowes's findings in *The Road To Xanadu*, seek to establish the multiplicity of sources which are the author's heritage. (4) Sources of detail are used to identify portions — or language, plot, technique, characterization, description, and so forth — of literature to determine an author's inspiration. (5) "Oral and indefinite" sources for Morize, as for most literary scholars, are of no greater importance than the others. Folkloric sources most commonly fall into this category. The oral source is almost always "indefinite." As Father Ong has most cogently pointed out (1982, p. 32), "sound exists only when it is going out of existence. It is not simply perishable but essentially evanescent, and it is sensed as evanescent." (6) Sources of inspiration may have provided ideas, subjects, characters, settings, plots, and so forth, but the category probably overlaps one or more of the others. (7) The graphic and plastic arts have been the prime mover of much literature.

Several quite distinct kinds of folklore may appear in literature, any specimen of which, when explicated and appraised, may be of interest and value to the literary scholar/critic. Customs and habitual practices may be so much a part of the reader's culture that he or she does not recognize them as behavior that may be isolated and studied: crafts and innumerable products and processes of material culture, from bows and arrows to wooden buildings; beliefs, rituals, superstitions; gestures; and verbal lore, this one category having scores of subdivisions such as riddles, proverbs, jokes, legends, songs (of many kinds), anecdotes, personal-experience stories, poems, fables, and folktales. This list of genres of verbal lore is merely the skimpiest beginning of the variety of forms in oral currency.

Writers and authors may "use" folklore in their works for any of several purposes. They may wish to impart verisimilitude to their depiction of a regional setting, as does Turgenev in several of the short stories in *Fathers and Sons*, as does Chaucer when he has John the carpenter mouth several naive superstitions in order to dramatize his gullibility and simplicity, thus preparing us for the ease with which he will be tricked (in *The Miller's Tale*). We may also include among the conscious "users" of folklore such novelists as D. H. Lawrence (especially in *The Plumed Serpent*), John Steinbeck (throughout the novels, but also the screenplay of *Viva Zapata*), and Gustave Flaubert — all of whose knowledge of such lore, which appears so prominently in their writing comes from library research. Contemporary novelists and short-story writers, notably Isaac Bashevis Singer and Chaim Potok, portray the very lush texture of their own ethnic legacies through the incorporation of their "native" lore that includes customs, beliefs, and stories, but include them in a totally unself-conscious way. William Styron was able to capture some of that ethnic flavor in his *Sophie's Choice*, though Styron is himself an outsider to Jewish culture, and was inspired by the liefstyle he saw in others — more to his credit.

A second use of folkloric materials is symbolic, folkloric nature of the materials having little to do, per se, with their use in literature. Citing an often-read critical essay by Q. D. Leavis, Daniel Hoffman (1961) cites Hawthorne's "The Maypole of Merry Mount" as a literary product in which pagan rituals are juxtaposed with the austerity of Puritan attitudes in order to highlight the ethos of these two cultures. The

New Englanders are criticized at the same time that they are shown to have attained a more difficult though a more worthy state than Eden.

A third major literary usage of folkloric materials by literary narrators has been the absorption of a narrative's story, recomposed (in writing) for a literate audience (See Utley 1964). "The Celebrated Jumping Frog of Calaveras County" by Mark Twain is a folktale rewritten. Gottfried von Strassburg incorporated a version of "The Dragon Slayer" folktale (type 300) in his *Tristan,* and the *Parzival* of Wolfram von Eschenbach imbeds some version of Aarne-Thompson motif J2450 ("The Literal Fool") and tale-type 1696 — "What Should I Have Done or Said." *Culhwch and Olwen* are based on the popular international tale "Six Go through the Whole World" (type 513A). The source of Eudora Welty's *The Robber Bridegroom* is not a hidden matter; scarcely less obvious is the dependence of Geoffrey of Monmouth (and Shakespeare after him) on the popular "Love Like Salt" (type 923). And this list, too, only begins to approach the barest outline of literary works based on extant folktales.

More than three decades ago, Richard Dorson (1957) proposed a tripartite methodology for the identification of authentic folklore in literature. Dorson first wanted to show biographically that the author in question had in fact been exposed to the folklore in question: if it is claimed that the *Beowulf* poet, for instance, based the Old English epic on some oral version of type 301 then current, we will want to provide evidence that tales of this kind were current in the Baltic region. More positively, if a modern poet such as William Butler Yeats were being analyzed for his knowledge of a specific body of lore (as in Rosenberg 1967), we would require a demonstration of his knowledge. As it happens, Yeats collected lore in the field and discussed Irish traditions at some length with Lady Gregory and others before he used these materials in his "Celtic Twilight" poetry. And Washington Irving's exposure to Germanic traditions can be shown to have inspired the plot of "Rip Van Winkle."

Secondly, Dorson insisted that the folklorist (he was not interested in the researches of the literary historian) examine the work itself for evidence of the author's knowledge of lore. While Irving's attention to detail in "The Legend of the Sleepy Hollow" has many touches of verisimilitude, Irving's knowledge of folklore — like that of many other writers — may well derive from his reading. For instance, T. S. Eliot's varied use of Arthurian legendary materials in *The Waste Land* reflects his reading of Jesse Weston's *From Ritual to Romance,* Frazer's *The*

Golden Bough (and other works), as we know from the facts of his life. Steinbeck both wrote from his experience and used information gained from his reading for backgrounding. Thomas Pynchon's *The Crying of Lot 49* seems to be based, in outline, on the idea of the grail quest; but that is a vaguely defined plot structure with many analogues, and Pynchon's scrupulous privacy has discouraged investigation into a biographical approach to the question.

Finally, Dorson recommends—in addition to biographical and internal demonstrations—that the researcher seek for corroborative evidence, by which he means a demonstration that the folkloric item which we seek to demonstrate (folktale, proverb, ritual, etc.) has had an independent existence in an authentic oral tradition. Unlike the first two elements of proof, this last one is concerned with the folkloric material itself rather than with the author's knowledge of it. An independent existence in an authentic tradition is an important issue in the Ossian epic, as is the background to some of Robert Graves's poems and his *The White Goddess*, and for a few of the poems of Robert Burns. Folkloric antecedents have sometimes been claimed for the Old Russian *Song of Igor's Campaign* (as the title is usually translated)—despite Nabokov's vigorous insistence that its composition "attests to deliberate artistic endeavor and excludes the possibility of that gradual accretion of lumpy parts which is so typical of folklore" (Nabokov 1960, p. 6).

Dorson, as noted above, was interested in gathering ethnographic data—a folklorist's concern. The literary scholar approaches the same problem from another perspective entirely. Sources, folklore included, are studied for what they may reveal about the author (Sanders 1952, pp. 162–67). The results may produce further knowledge about the author's learning, working methods, relation to contemporaries, nature and extent of originality, and artistic intention in a particlular work. Most critics today would place a greater emphasis on the last two.

Many of these aspects of an author's craft can be deduced when the source is the entire plot of a narrative, as happened commonly in the Middle Ages and Renaissance, and occasionally today. Francis Lee Utley's work has been the most important in this regard. (It is difficult to see any future research that will move substantially beyond the ground he prepared; to a great extent this book is a continuation of his thought.) Utley had to combat, unceasingly, the bias of his medievalist colleagues against the very nature of folklore. When Roger Sherman Loomis denounced as absurd the idea that Arthurian romances were acquired by their authors "in the huts of plowmen or the haunts of peddlars" (1958a pp. 1-25) but admitted that *The Violent Death of Curoi* did closely resemble certain folktales common to most of Europe, Utley replied that

> all kinds of men tell folktales; literary men of past and present, nomadic Arabs and sedentary Kurds, pre- and post-revolutionary proletarians, primitive and acculturated tribes, bards, *filid*, and college students. (1964, p. 603)

"Folklore," Utley often used to insist (as in 1964, p. 601), "implies no diminution in art over written literature; it is simply another kind of art with its own rules, the rules of the oral process."

Utley was primarily a medievalist, having studied under Kittredge at Harvard. Chaucer was his main literary interest; consequently, Bryan and Dempster's *Sources and Analogues of Chaucer's Canterbury Tales* (1941) was an important book for him, mainly because of its omissions. He had to continually combat the prejudice that a medieval literary version of a narrative was closer to the Chaucerian tale than a folktale, even one collected during the last one hundred years (Utley 1965, p. 589). In a paper read at the MLA's Chaucer Group session in 1963 and at the International Congress for Folk-Narrative Research (Athens, 1964), and later published in the journal *Leographia* (1965), he noted that twenty-two of Chaucer's twenty-eight tales (including prologues and the frame) had folktale analogues, yet Bryan and Dempster printed their texts in only four cases: for *The Miller's Tale, The Franklin's Tale, The Merchant's Tale,* and *The Shipman's Tale.* But, he argued, and as the present book has demonstrated, the recently collected tale might well be closer in "content and motivation" to Chaucer than a contemporary literary text, and could thus make a greater contribution to understanding Chaucer's art (1965, pp. 589-90). Fifteen of the *Canterbury Tales* have "clear" Aarne-Thompson analogues.

Chaucer's borrowing from Boccaccio is usually discounted for three reasons. (1) Those tales whose plots they share (in the *Canterbury Tales* and the *Decameron*) are dissimilar in language and in narrative detail. (2) Other sources or analogues have been found for the English narratives. (3) Since Boccaccio renounced his vernacular work in 1360 or shortly afterwards, he would have worked against their circulation in 1370, the year of Chaucer's visit to Italy. Nevertheless, in at least five instances (not including the idea of the frame), these two men shared the same narratives. It is thus only when one assumes the existence of oral tales, in circulation in Europe (specifically in Italy and England) at the time, that one can explain the commonality of these five tales with their similar nuclei though quite individual integrational units, style, and language.

Beowulf's relationship to analogous folktales (of type 301) has in
one way not been so controversial. Chambers (1959) noted that a "vast
store of old wives' tales" had been collected in the nineteenth century,
but they "certainly go back to a very ancient period" (p. 62). In particular, he noted that one tale, the Bear's Son (a subtype of A-T 301,
"The Three Stolen Princesses") had been "instanced" as "showing resemblance" (p. 62) to the *Beowulf* story. And, as Chambers summarizes several arguments, as the Ur-tale common to both *Beowulf* and
the *Grettis Saga* is reconstructed, it is apparent "that it must be something extraordinarily like the folk-tale outlined above" ("The Bear's
Son"). As will be shown below, Chambers did not want to admit the
likelihood of a folktale source for the epic, but such a possibility did
offer convenient solutions to at least two interpretive problems: all of
the Geats sleeping on the night of the expected attack of Grendel, and
the hero allowing some of his companions to be eaten before springing,
himself, into counteraction; and the departure of his comrades from
the edge of the mere when they see blood bubbling to the surface (which
they assume to be Beowulf's). Both are explained as elements in the
original folktale which the court poet was unable (or did not bother)
to rationalize (pp. 64 ff.). Chambers concluded that, while one might
disagree with Panzer's (1910) comparison of the epic with over two hundred folktales in certain particulars,

> he can hardly rise from a reading of his book without being convinced that
> the story of Beowulf's adventure with Grendel and his mother is a story of
> a type akin to those folk-tales which the research of the nineteenth century
> has collected. This does not of course mean that, at the time when these
> stories were attributed to Beowulf, they belonged solely to "the folk," as
> against the nobler classes.

Chambers takes care not to attribute this court poem to smiths,
goosegirls, or yokels of any kind; *Beowulf* belongs to the noble classes.
It may have analogues among such collections as the Grimms,' "but this
does not mean that the main story of Beowulf's adventures is trivial
or childish, nor that it belongs to the folk, as opposed to the aristoc-
racy" (p. 484). Earlier (p. 379), Chambers had cited a French-Flemish
tale found in "a somewhat sophisticated collection; to be more convincing, he would have preferred that the tale had come "from the lips of
some simple-minded narrator as it used to be told at Condé on the
Scheldt."

Surprisingly, Chambers's conclusions about the folktale connection
with *Beowulf* were reached with only slight understanding of folklore
methodology. To be fair to him, it wasn't until the publication in Eng-

lish of Thompson's *Motif Index* (1955-58) and the Aarne-Thompson *Types of the Folktale* (1961) that rigorous methodological tools became generally known to scholars, however unprofessional their attitudes toward the "simple-minded" folk. And ironically, literary critic Chambers was convinced by Panzer's comparative study, while Stith Thompson, expressing a representative folklorist's opinion, found his conclusions "dubious" (1977, p. 33).

Chambers's primary lack of sophistication with the apposite folktales — and he was by no means distinctive in this shortfall — had to do with his failure to understand the genre's (relative) stability. Again, his failure was typical of literary scholarship in his time; in quoting Andrew Lang — a folklorist to be sure, but one whose theories had long since been questioned — Chambers thought that folktales (in Chambers's words) "consist of but few incidents, grouped together in a kaleidoscopic variety of arrangements" (1959, p. 483). The metaphor describes a continually shifting concatenation of narrative elements (motifs, or distributional elements we would now say), which situations, Chambers concluded, "seem to place us at the mercy of chance" (p. 483). Had the premise been correct, the conclusion would have inevitably followed.

And yet, some of his flashes of insight are illuminating, particularly since *Beowulf: An Introduction to the Study of the Poem* was first published in 1921. That was before Sydow had published his theories on the principle and value of the oicotype; nevertheless, Chambers was somewhat skeptical of the importance of variants of type 301 (he never uses the Aarne-Thompson type numbers) which had been collected in such far-flung areas as India, Mexico, even North Italy. And rightly so. "Panzer's theory," Chambers concludes, "must stand or fall by the parallels which can be drawn between the *Beowulf-Grettir*-story on the one hand, and the folk-tales as they have been collected in the countries where this story is native; the lands, that is to say, adjoining the North Sea" (Chambers 1959, p. 374).

Oicotypes (though not by that name) he understood, but not subtypes. Folktale study was not commonly enough known for Chambers — or the many scholars whose work he summarizes — to appreciate that "The Bear's Son" could be a subtype of "The Stolen Princesses." "The stories just seem[ed] too dissimilar: despite similarities, the essential difference remains. . . . the Bear's son rescues princesses in the underworld, and it is *because* they wish to rob him of his princesses that his companions leave him in the lurch. There is nothing of this in *Beowulf*" (p. 477). This same interpretation has more recently been presented by Jones (1972, pp. 10 ff.); since he does not have to struggle mightily with the idea of so grand an epic deriving from so humble a narrative, Jones's conclusions and observations seem sensible.

Parallels and analogues have been the bane of many medievalists. How to know which were important, which contingent or coincidental? The folktale hero's companions were treacherous, leaving the hero helpless in the mere or waterfall (or so they thought) while they made off with the rescued princesses; but Beowulf's companions were by no means perfidious. Why? Not allowing the poet enough leeway to change the character of these minor actants, Chambers assumes (not necessarily incorrectly) that the *comitatus* could not be acceptably portrayed in this manner, and so an excuse had to be found for their early departure: "and the blood-stained water was the nearest at hand" (1959, p. 64). The reason such parallels presented such problems was founded in a basic misunderstanding of the folktales' life history; literary critics were led to believe that, "since there are many features of popular story which float around and attach themselves to this or that tale without any original connection, . . . it is easy for the same trait to recur in *Beowulf* and in a group of folk-tales, without this proving that the stories as a whole are connected" (Chambers 1959, p. 65).

In yet another surprising judgment — given the bias of literary historians for textual evidence and a concomitant suspicion of oral data — Chambers cites Krappe's argument (p. 483) that a line from the folktale collection, *The Ocean of Story*, expresses "exactly the same moral" as does a line from *Beowulf*: "For even destiny takes the part of men of distinguished valor." But the hero is Indian; therefore the folktale cannot be connected with the Anglo-Saxon epic; therefore, this verbal parallel (allowing for the language differences) "*can* only be an accident" (p. 483). The correctness of this methodology is often overlooked, even today.

The evidence of *Beowulf*'s relation to the folktale was cogent. Yet it appeared to be important to many medievalists of an earlier generation to dissociate their courtly epic from the tales of the "simple-minded." No serious scholar would contend that *Beowulf* was a folktale, but it appears today to be important to specify the ways in which it is not. Orality does not demonstrate much about this poem's genre; although the epic is known to us through its surviving manuscript, recent scholarship has often stressed its oral performance (see especially Lord, 1965). And if it was performed orally — its usual mode of presentation — its transmission was in large measure oral as well. Of its compositional mode little is known, but nothing of what is known of oral poets today indicates that oral composition is unlikely (Finnegan 1977, pp. 52–87). In what demonstrable sense, then, is *Beowulf* not a folktale?

It has been transformed from a folktale in style, form, and content. So well understood are these transformations that it will be necessary only to list them. The stylistic emphases, the learning, the concern with history and ethics (which are of an aristocratic class) have not been found in folktales; and while we have no idea of the details of folktale performance during the early Middle Ages, no evidence today of such performances suggests a product anything like the Old English epic. The form and content of *Beowulf* is unlike what we know of most folk narratives; the Serbo-Croatian heroic material, made famous in the West by Parry and Lord, is comparable in length (occasionally as long as the Homeric poems) and in their heroic subjects. But little in them would ever lead a Schücking to claim that they were composed to instruct rulers on the ways of kingship.

R. W. Chambers, then, though one of the most erudite of the Old English scholars of his generation, arrived at a number of *Beowulf/* folktale conclusions which are held to this day, though folklore science was insufficiently developed for him to make the necessary connections with rigor. The folktale is not a loose concatenation of freely floating episodes, conjoining in particular tales almost at random. And again, like his colleagues, Chambers had a disturbingly contemptuous idea of "the folk" and their creative abilities. Nevertheless, Chambers and his contemporaries did persuasively establish the folktale–literary tale relationship, with Panzer's help, though that work was itself sometimes misleading.

The debt of Shakespeare's *Cymbeline* to the cognate folktale, "The Wager on the Wife's Chastity" (A-T type 882) presents different problems of sources and attributions. An oversimplification has it that the bard's idea for the main plot came from Boccaccio (*Decameron* II, 9), perhaps by way of William Painter's *Palace of Pleasure* (Clements and Gibaldi 1977, p. 77). Stith Thompson remarks that this and similar tale-types — stories of the wife who perseveres in the face of misunderstanding and abuse and finds her lost husband after many adventures — were very popular in the late Middle Ages and on through the Renaissance, and that they appear not only in romances but in novellas and drama as well. But, more importantly, he comments that, in general, "eventually these literary tales were adapted to the purposes of an oral story-teller, though they have never become popular [as folklore] and cannot in any sense be thought of as a product of folklore" (1977, p. 109).

Type 882 has a wider distribution than Thompson's general remarks suggest, having been collected throughout the Baltic region,
Middle Europe, the Iberian Peninsula, Italy, Sicily, the Balkans, Turkey, Greece, and the United States. In *The Types of the Folktale* (p.
299) Aarne and Thompson give the following composite:

> A ship captain marries a poor girl. Makes a wager with a merchant on
> the chastity of his wife. Through treachery, the merchant secures a to-
> ken of unfaithfulness (ring). The captain leaves home. The wife follows
> him in men's clothing. They reach home again and everything is explained.

By a comparison of plots on this level of abstraction, one would be
hard put to identify type 882 in Boccaccio, and its relationship to *Cymbeline* is obscure. Yet they do appear to be related; and while it would
not be wise to disregard Thompson's observations on the age of this
class of tales, we can nevertheless be certain that type 882 is at least
as old as 1360, the date of the *Decameron*, and so could chronologically have been an influence on Shakespeare's writing of *Cymbeline*
(1609–10).

If Shakespeare's primary source was some version of type 882, or
Boccaccio, he has made of this story — by no means an uncomplicated
one to begin with — a very rich and intricate, multifaceted tragicomedy,
by far exceeding either of those two narratives — what we expect, in
short, from Shakespeare. Blended together with the story of the wager
on the wife's chastity is that of the banishment of Belarius, and his
consequent abduction of the king's sons, Guiderius and Arviragus;
the strained political relations with Rome over Cymbeline's withold-
ing of tribute, and eventually war between the imperialist and its col-
ony; Cymbeline's queen's unscrupulousness; Cloten's boorish wandering through various scenes; the husband's altered status in Shakespeare's play, where he is an adopted son of the king, and not merely
a merchant.

A diagram of the nuclei of all three narratives will illustrate their
differences clearly. (See table 4.1.) A few items need further elucidation.
We are not told of the wealth or poverty of Boccaccio's heroine, though
by implication, considering her many skills which could only have been
acquired by someone with a great amount of leisure, she does not appear to have been poor. Bernabo does not leave home, disconsolate,
followed by his wife in disguise; just the reverse, Ginevra finds employment with a merchant and sails with him for the Middle East, settling
in Acre. Later she arranges for her husband to be brought, unawares,

Table 4.1. Comparison of Traits in Aarne-Thompson Type 882, Cymbeline, *and the* Decameron

Cardinal Traits	Type 882	Cymbeline	Decameron
1. Marriage to poor girl	X	—	—
2. Husband on journey	?	X	X
3. Wager on wife's chastity	X	X	X
4. Merchant's treacherous "proof"	X	X	X
5. Wife ordered murdered	—	X	x
6. Husband leaves home	X	X	X
7. Wife follows in disguise	X	X(?)	X
8. Reconciliation	X	X	X
9. Seducer punished	?	—	X

to her new home. Shakespeare's duped husband, Posthumus Leonatus, leaves home to spend his banishment in Rome; Imogen has set out in the world, in disguise, but it is not with the intent of following him, and their eventual reconciliation is by chance.

The peregrination of the husband in Boccaccio is one of the major ways in which he differs from Shakespeare. Ginevra's adventures in Acre comprise a major portion of the narrative; in the analogous slot Shakespeare develops a few of his subplots, particularly Cymbeline's defiance of Rome's demand for tribute, and the exiled life (and character development) of Belarius and his two captives/sons.

If Boccaccio was Shakespeare's source, more than just the narrative element of the slandered wife's fortunes in Acre were altered. Shakespeare's couple exchanges gifts (which will function subsequently as identifying tokens): she receives a bracelet, he a diamond ring; Boccaccio does not have the gift-giving. Nor does he permit the husband to confront the duplicitous "seducer" as in *Cymbeline*. The king, in act V, grants a boon to Imogen (disguised as "Fidele") which will enable her ("him") to demand of Iachimo where he got the diamond ring he wears. And, by no means of least importance, while Boccaccio's heroine is more the victim whose death had been ordered by her momentarily demented husband, Imogen is so distraught that at one point she orders her servant, Pisanio, to kill her. But throughout, Imogen's sensitivity and perspicacity are highlighted; Ginevra is much more the actant, proceeding through the inevitable steps which are the assigned elements of her narrative destiny.

It would seem safer to assume that *Cymbeline* is modeled on some now lost chapbook or play, possibly even on some oral version of type 882, rather than on the *Decameron* tale, given these major dissimilarities. As well, the names of Shakespeare's characters are different. The elements of the wager are not the same: gold florins in Boccaccio, a diamond ring against ducats in Shakespeare. The proof of the alleged seduction differs: Ambrogiuolo takes a ring, a girdle, a purse, and a gown during the course of two nights in the wife's chamber while Iachimo makes note of the decorative details of Imogen's bedroom and steals only her bracelet. As a final touch, Boccaccio's "seducer" reports that he has seen a few "downy hairs" under the wife's breast, "bright as gold"; his counterpart in *Cymbeline* has seen a mole with five red spots. All the locations are different. A distraught Imogen asks Pisanio to kill her as her husband has ordered; Ginerva thinks of a feigned death herself at the same time that she contemplates her future disguise. Posthumus is a poor man, not a merchant as in the Italian story; and he is banished, not merely on a business trip. Boccaccio has no counterpart for Cloten, whose rejected suit has angered his mother, the queen. To give specificity to Imogen's pretended murder (though she is allowed to escape in disguise), Shakespeare dramatizes the motif of the "Compassionate Executioner" (K 515.2). And, *Cymbeline* ends in reconciliation (for several of the characters, not merely the estranged couple) while the *Decameron* story concludes with the punishment of the would-be seducer.

Now all of the above details might have been effected by Shakespeare, to suit his own dramatic instincts, or to meet the requirements of a staged drama. Many of the variances between the two stories are minor; underneath them the core story, "The Wager on The Wife's Chastity," is clearly identifiable. And other changes in the narrative — as it is transformed from prose to dramatic poetry — can be accounted for by a difference in perspective: the endings, for instance. Type 882 allows for a concluding motif (or cardinal distributional element) to be either one of reconciliation or vindication. But on the basis of all of these differences, and only the essential plot lines being analogous, it hardly seems reasonable to assert that Shakespeare got the story from Boccaccio. Some other source, regrettably now lost to us, seems more likely.

All of the scholars mentioned above agree that type 882 is present in *Cymbeline*, though it also embeds another folktale, the well-known "Snow-White" (A-T 709). Thompson's paradigm (1977, p. 245) lists five components:

I. *Snow-White and her Stepmother.* (a) Snow-White has skin like snow, and lips like blood. (b) A magic mirror tells her stepmother that Snow-Shite is more beautiful than she.

II. *Snow-White's Rescue.* (a) The stepmother orders a hunter to kill her, but he substitutes an animal's heart and saves her, or (b) she sends Snow White to the house of the dwarfs (or robbers) expecting her to be killed. The dwarfs adopt her as a sister.

III. *The Poisoning.* (a) The stepmother now seeks to kill her by means of poisoned lace, (b) a poisoned comb and (c) a poisoned apple.

IV. *Help of the Dwarfs.* (a) The dwarfs succeed in reviving her from the first two poisonings but fail with the third. (b) They lay the Maiden in a glass coffin.

V. *Her Revival.* A prince sees her and resuscitates her. The stepmother is made to dance herself to death in red hot shoes.

Cymbeline embeds this narrative with some modifications, of course. The queen (Cymbeline's second wife, thus Imogen's stepmother) is not given any lines to indicate her jealousy of her stepdaughter, but the latter has angered her by her rejection of Cloten's suit, preferring her own choice, Posthumus. And it is not the stepmother who orders Imogen to be murdered; her husband, Posthumus, does so in a fit of pique when he thinks she has accepted Iachimo as her lover. The servant Pisanio has been ordered to kill her, but he cannot bring himself to execute the gracious Imogen, allowing her to escape (in a man's disguise), while he volunteers that "I'll give but notice you are dead, and send him / some bloody sign of it" (III, iv, 125–26). Imogen does quickly find her way in the woods to the cave of Belarius, Guiderius, and Arviragus; they are neither dwarfs nor robbers, as in the folktale composite, but they are outlaws from the jurisdiction of the king, and considered dangerous felons. The stepmother has sent poison (in a box instead of in lace, a comb, or an apple) and her three hosts — for whom Imogen does housework — at first give her shelter, but she finally succumbs to the queen's poison. It is not a fatal dose; Imogen revives to be reunited with her husband (not a prince who chances upon her in the woods); and the wicked stepmother is punished.

The "Snow-White" portion is no minor subplot within *Cymbeline*; it ranges throughout the play, from the first scene to the last, supplying several of its most important episodes. The climax of the folktale, with its motifs of the "Compassionate Executioner," "Calumniation," and residence in the house of the robbers, all occur in the pivotal third act of the play. Table 4.2 illustrates the enmeshed conflation of both folktales within the total economy of Shakespeare's scene sequence.

Table 4.2. Comparison of A-T Types 709 and 882 with Cymbeline

Type 709	Cymbeline		Type 882
Jealous stepmother	I, i	I, i	Husband leaves home
		I, iii	Wager on Wife's chastity
		II, iii	Duplicitous "proof" of seduction
Compassionate executioner	III, iii		
Calumniated maiden	III, iv		
		III, vi	Wife in man's disguise
House of robbers	IV, II		
Poisoning attempts	III, iv;		
	IV, ii		
Aid from robbers	IV, ii		
Resuscitation	IV, ii		
Reconciliation	V, v	V, v	Reconciliation

One can even imagine Shakespeare linking these two tales through the association of the calumniated wife (maiden) which motif both tales share, and the eventual satisfying marriage/reunion with the husband.

That Shakespeare coincidentally invented this narrative sequence independent of the analogous folktale, or that it accidentally developed within *Cymbeline* is extremely unlikely. Advocates of the Finnish method would say impossible. But demonstrating the presence of this tale-type within this drama, already acknowledged to embody "The Wager on the Wife's Chastity," is easier than suggesting where it may have come from. *I₁ Pentamerone* of Giovanni Batiste Basile (1634: 1943 rpt.) includes an analogue (Day II, tale 8) which is, however, not much like Shakespeare's narrative: a young girl, Lisa, is born out of wedlock when her mother swallows a rose petal, and she is raised by fairies. Her mother does not seek her death, but a deathlike sleep is brought on by a curse placed on the comb she uses. She is given over to her uncle and aunt — a baron and baroness — and these foster parents eventually revive her. The aunt keeps little Lisa in menial servitude until one day a favorable marriage is arranged for her by her uncle.

Basile's use of this tale shows that the type was roughly contemporary with Shakespeare; and while it has been located — with little variation — throughout the Mediterranean, and from Ireland to Asia Minor (Thompson 1977, p. 124; Opie and Opie 1975, p. 175), Jackson believes he has found it in the medieval *Peredur* (p. 114). Walt Disney's animated version derives largely from the Grimms' (tale #53), which so closely describes most of the variants that the Thompson paradigm is in effect a synopsis of this version. "Snow-White" has not been included in the multivolume *Dictionary of British Folktales* (Briggs, 1970), though type 882 is not either. No literary analogues (other than Basile's) are given by *The Types of the Folktale*. Thus, Shakespeare's source or sources remain a mystery. The evidence of the text argues that he used this folktale as part of *Cymbeline*, but corroborative evidence positively demonstrating a source is missing.

Of at least equal uncertainty is the relationship of Chaucer's *Franklin's Tale* to its alleged source, Boccaccio's *Filocolo*. Chaucer's other sources for this tale, Geoffrey of Monmouth, and a Breton setting, are of slight import. From them he got the names of at least two of the characters, and the atmosphere of the Breton romance (Bryan and Dempster *Sources and Analogues*, pp. 377 ff.). But of greater consequence, is that Chaucer is said to have taken the plot of the *Filocolo* for his Franklin (specifically *Questions IIII*, posed by Menedon in the *questioni d'amore* section). Nothing is known of Boccaccio's source for this narrative—it is "the blind promise" or "rash boon" story, motif M 223—though he undoubtedly had one. As an autonomous tale, M 223 has been found as far from Britain as Asia, but not in Italy.

While Bryan and Dempster (*Sources and Analogues*, pp. 377 ff.) found that it was "highly probable" that Chaucer got the story from Boccaccio, a closer look clouds the issue. In Boccaccio's narrative the wife, in order to be rid of her pesky suitor, Tarolfo, makes the rash promise that she will submit to his lust if he can make a garden bloom and grow fruit in January as though it were May. But if he cannot, he is to stop pestering her. Accordingly, Tarolfo sets out around the world, vowing never to rest until he can effect such a transformation. In faraway Thessaly he comes upon Tebano, who is at the moment collecting roots. During their conversation the latter reveals that he can make January gardens bloom as though in May, and in return for such a secret Tarolfo pledges half of his "castella" and all of his "tresori." They both return to Italy and perform the magic fructation, and a shocked wife has to confess to her husband the fateful bargain she has struck. The husband is the noblest character in the story (according to Fiammetta) and insists that, since honor is more precious than either wealth or pleasure, he must counsel her to comply with Tarolfo's desires. Accordingly, she offers herself to Tarolfo, but he, respectful of the husband's generosity, declines. Finally, Tebano also refuses payment, insisting that he, too, cannot do less than the acts of noble character he has just witnessed.

Chaucer's *Franklin's Tale* differs in several respects: the impossible tasks set by the wife are different; Tarolfo sets out on a aimless quest, not knowing where or how he can accomplish his botanical transformation; he meets Tebano by accident, whereas the Franklin's young lover is directed to a particular magician by a mutual friend; the magical formula is entirely different, the Italian version (Boccaccio's) using a magical liquor which is poured over the garden flora; and the payment for the magician differs. We should note other variations: Chaucer's husband leaves town, while Boccaccio's remains, making it more convenient for his wife to confess her rash promise to him (also heightening her guilt since she is not allowed to feel the pangs of loneliness as does Dorigen). The Italian's wife is concerned far more with her reputation than is Dorigen — who seems something of a moral drifter — and her fear is one of the prime motivations in her setting the supposedly impossible conditions. Word is sent to Tarolfo of the wife's stipulations, while Dorigen confronts Aurelius directly.

Once more, several of these changes are for the most part superficial; that is, after allowing for them, the cardinal distributional elements of the story remain. For Bryan and Dempster these elements were so contingent that they could claim a genetic relationship between these stories. But one should not argue, unless tentatively, that these discrepancies between *The Franklin's Tale* and *Il Filocolo* are irrelevant to establishing a direct relationship between these tales; certainly it is not "highly probable" that Chaucer used Boccaccio for his source. One cannot argue for such a relationship given such differences in detail.

Analogous to both stories is the folktale "Which Was the Noblest Act?" (Aarne-Thompson type 976), but it is not close enough to either to encourage an argument for a genetic relationship. As Stith Thompson describes it in outline (1977, p. 343), a bridegroom permits his bride to fulfill an earlier promise to visit her lover on their wedding night. On the way she meets robbers; when one of them hears the story, he escorts her to her lover. On hearing her complaint, the lover takes her back to her husband, chaste. The tale ends with the question, "which was the noblest act?" (motif H 1552.1). Unless some specific version of type 976 that closely resembles *The Franklin's Tale* can be found, we have to conclude that Chaucer's inspiration did not come from this type as we have it in paradigm form today. Not only are the folktale's characters different (they are robbers), so is the focus because the Franklin has been able to shift his sympathetic perspective from one character to another inconspicuously. Unlike the (hypothetical) teller of the folktale, the Franklin does not have one of the noble acts performed on the wedding night. And while it might be argued that Boccaccio and Chaucer (or their sources) changed this crude detail so that Dorigen's virtue is tested after marriage and that the other variations are of the kind likely to occur in a literary redaction, the discrepancies, however rationalized by the critic, hardly constitute proof of a close genetic relationship between folktale and *Canterbury Tale.*

The evidence that either Boccaccio or some version of type 976 was Chaucer's source is not really persuasive in either case, despite the optimistic claims of Bryan and Dempster. Boccaccio is assumed to be the source (rather than to have provided merely an analogue) of *The Franklin's Tale* because of Chaucer's use of other plots of the Italian's, and in the absence of more likely analogues, we have always assumed Chaucer's borrowing of this story. This assumption is not untenable.

However, one of the legends of Saint Nicholas, that of the widow of Bari (appearing in MS 3151 in the *Catalogue des manuscrits de la Biblioteque Royale de Belgique* 5, ed. J. Van den Ghehn [Bruxelles, 1905]), written down some time after 1087 (when the saint's relics were translated to Bari), is provocatively similar to tales of the "Rash Boon" matrix. The date is uncertain; the narrative's setting in Bari proves only that this locale became the story's locus after 1087 but says nothing about either the exact date of the tale's origin or the moment of its entry into Europe (other analogues of Boccaccio's narrative having been found no closer to Italy than Asia). To summarize the legend (Rosenberg 1980):

> A wealthy and beautiful widow in Bari was the object of a clerk's lust, but always managed to avoid him. However, one day, while dining with several priests of the town, she remarked what a pity it was that no one had written a suitable poem or canticle of praise for her favorite saint, Nicholas. When word of this reached the languishing clerk, he applied all of his talents to write such a song of praise, and a few days later presented the lady with a copy of his labors. She, who had promised any gift to the one who should compose such a piece, now had to plead to be excused from her (rash) promise. Nevertheless, the clerk persisted in his lusts. Finally she relented, though first obtaining a day to herself in which she prayed for deliverance to Nicholas. That good saint, ever indefatigable to the pleas of his devotees, visited the young clerk, lifted him by the hair and dropped him to the floor, and then whipped his frightened victim. When the clerk begged for forgiveness, Nicholas directed him to the widow, whom he beseeched for mercy. When they made their peace, each departed for their home.

The author (or authors) have made certain adjustments appropriate to a saint's legend. Here the object of the widow's desires is neither the return of her husband nor to be rid of a peskily aggressive suitor, but a suitably reverent and lovely song to honor her favorite saint. And it is not the ethical nobility of the pivotal characters that keeps the story's morality tidy but the widow's prayers to Nicholas and his direct intervention. Nevertheless, the important motifs are in the legend of the Bari widow, and in the "correct" sequence. A chaste and beautiful woman provokes the lust of a young man of her town; it hardly matters to the framework of the tale that Dorigen is not a widow. In the functions of the characters, the woman's marital state is not as important as her appeal to the suitor. The husband has to be present in both Chaucer and Boccaccio to perform one of "the noblest acts," of course; he would be contradictory in the legend of the *widow* of Bari. The eleventh-century tale will have a similar ending — the woman remains chaste — as in the fourteenth-century narratives. And, most importantly, all three women get into trouble because of the "Rash Promise." That promise (motif M 223) differs somewhat in each story. The Bari widow pledges "any gift to the one who should complete" words of praise in a hymn to Nicholas, "if he should do it well." In *The Franklin's Tale*, it is some form of the folkloric motif "Never" (Z 61) which as folklore often takes the form of "when black sheep turn white," or something of the sort. Related motifs include "reward: any boon that may be asked" (Q 115), and "religious personages tested" (H 1573.2).

The conditions of "Never" or the challenge to compose an appropriate hymn are met in both narratives: "Tasks performed through cleverness or intelligence" (M 960). In both stories the rash promise, in one way or another, is avoided. Dorigen is rendered ethically helpless when caught up by the literalness of her foolish, rash promise. She creates the dilemma which she cannot solve by herself, subsequently turning over that responsibility to her husband. It is human behavior with moral and ethical implications. The widow of Bari prays to her most revered saint; her rashness had been on behalf of his glory to begin with, and had been turned to a lecherous purpose by a clerk whom she should have had every reason to trust, and so she appropriately turned to Nicholas for salvation. With perfect consistency he rescued her and punished her tormentor. Chaucer's ethical tale is set in pagan times so as to free him from a strict Christian application to his character's actions; and Aurelius is not a clerk. He does not exploit the pious worship of a saint for his own lecherous ends. He is, it seems to me, morally less culpable. Consequently, the Bari clerk's punishment is appropriate, even necessary, given its narrative context. Aurelius must not be punished; his is one of the noble acts, and his role in *The Frank-lin's Tale* is also concluded appropriately.

The same sequence of motifs occurs in Chaucer's tale and in the ear-lier legend, as we would insist upon in claiming a genetic relationship, however remote, between these two narratives:

I.   The Blind Promise (Rash Boon), M 223; Reward: Any boon that may be asked, Q 115.
II. Never, Z 61.
III. Religious personages tested, H 1573.2; Tasks performed through clever-ness or intelligence, H 960.
IV. Attempted seduction punished, Q 243.2.1.

I am not arguing that *The Franklin's Tale* came from an oral nar-rative, though that is certainly a possibility. But the evidence for a liter-ary or an oral source is murky at best; we have Boccaccio's analogue and Chaucer's known predilection for the work of his Italian colleague, and no known oral analogue close enough to undeniably challenge the assertions in *Sources and Analogues*. But, given the difference between the analogous tales of Chaucer and Boccaccio, neither can we argue with certainty that Chaucer was oblivious to any other influence— specifically, that he had not heard tales of the A-T 976 matrix, or that he had not heard an oral legend of the widow of Bari, or some other similar legend which had become attached to the cycle of another saint. Neither can we be certain that Boccaccio did not derive his inspiration from one of these oral sources.

The Bari legend appears to be in the early tradition of that story which eventually came to Boccaccio and appears in the *Filocolo*, and to Chaucer, by whatever oral or literary route, and appears as *The Franklin's Tale*. The presence of this story—some version of type 976, though the legend cannot be accurately dated—places the "Rash Promise" story in Europe, sometime during or shortly after the eleventh century. If this legend and *The Franklin's Tale* are related—demonstrations of this kind are never as positive as one would like—then we have not only established its tradition in Europe prior to the fourteenth century and suggested an (indirect) source for Chaucer and Boccaccio, but we have also demonstrated how a pious tale has been taken from its course in the stream of oral tradition and put to a somewhat different purpose by authors who found in it something that spoke to their own interests and artistic needs.

Chaucer's intentions in his tale (the Franklin's intentions?) induced him to alter the prime cardinal episode, the "Rash Boon." In a pious legend it is not as central as in *The Franklin's Tale* because the widow's character and motivation are never in question. Her grant of the boon functions solely to provoke the lustful response of the clerk. It is piously made in her enthusiasm to honor her beloved saint. In Chaucer's (the Franklin's) hands, this motif becomes the very symbol of Dorigen's shallowness, foolishness, and frail reason. And, as such, it emerges as the central narrative element of the story, foregrounded because it must function as a delineator of character as well as a narrative crux—which it is, simply, in the other analogues.

We have already examined literary works with differing relationships to analogous oral narratives. *Beowulf* is unmistakably related to type 301, though a number of questions of interest to the literary historian (particularly chronological priority) arise from the establishment of that relationship. *Cymbeline* is widely understood to have been based on some version of type 882 ("The Wager on the Wife's Chastity"), but also appears to embed type 709, "Snow-White." In what form Shakespeare would have heard of or read these narratives is unclear. And while it is relatively easy to show that Chaucer does not seem to have taken Boccaccio's *Filocolo* as inspiration for his *Franklin's Tale*, the actual source is (once again) an uncertain question. The legend of the Bari widow may or may not be analogous, but in any event it does little more than establish the presence of the "Rash Boon" stories in Europe prior to Boccaccio's and Chaucer's use of such narratives.

Similarly, an analogue has been claimed for Chaucer's *Miller's Tale* and one of the Milesian episodes (VIII, 5–7) from Apuleius's *Golden Ass*. In a 1971 study, *The Literary Context of Chaucer's Fabliaux* (Benson and Anderson), the editors print analogues to several of Chaucer's *Canterbury Tales*. *The Miller's Tale*, they correctly point out, should have one or more (they hope all) of three motifs: the prophesied flood, the misdirected kiss, the hot iron. *The Types of the Folktale* gives prominence to the motif of the tub, in which the duped husband is persuaded to sleep while a priest (or some other character) "dallies" with his wife, and from which he falls at the tale's end—an equally important component. This is tale-type 1362, "The Flood." Benson and Anderson admit that one of the tales they have included in the chapter on "*The Miller's Tale* and Its Analogues" is not an analogue because "it has none of the three characteristic motifs" (p. 3). Nevertheless, the tale (from the *Golden Ass*) has been included because "it makes an equally novel use of a tub to deceive the husband" (p. 3).

The editors are quite right in their reluctance to claim that Apuleius's tale is an analogue for *The Miller's Tale*. In the second-century story an ingenious wife received her lover shortly after her husband left one morning for work. However, when he returned home shortly thereafter and knocked on the door, his wife quickly hid her lover inside a tub in the corner of her bedroom. The husband proudly announced that he had just arranged to sell the useless tub sitting in the corner for five *denarii*; would she help him drag it off so that it might be readied for the buyer? With astonishing quickness the wife retorted that she had just sold it for seven *denarii*. When the husband, overjoyed at the prospect of so much found money, asked where the buyer was, the wife indicated the tub, where he was at the moment inspecting its soundness. The lover, who had heard all this, called out from the barrel that it was old and full of cracks. Emerging, he asked the husband for a candle to examine it more closely, but the husband insisted on inspecting it himself. When he was inside the lover "stretched the worker's wife on the tub and, throwing himself upon her, fearlessly gave her a barrel of fun." The wife then put her head down into the tub, indicating various places which needed cleaning, keeping up her pointing out of places in need of care "until both jobs were finished" (Benson and Anderson 1971, p. 9). The money was given over and the worker carried the tub on his back to the lecher's house.

Superficially as well as genetically this "Tale of a Poor Fellow's Cuckoldry" is barely like Chaucer's *Miller's Tale*. The wife in Apuleius is at least as clever and quick-witted as she is lecherous, and it is she who makes the narrative "work." The lover merely follows her lead. In Chaucer's story it is Nicolas, the "hende" clerk who invents the ruse that will enable him to sleep with the carpenter's wife. Alisoun is willing enough, but in scheming she is passive. The stories do not share a single motif; the flood, the misplaced kiss, the hot poker struck in revenge—all are, as the editors point out, not in Apuleius. The situation is different in each: the lecherous wife entertaining her lover in the morning, surprised by the early return of her husband, has no relation to *The Miller's Tale*. And neither does the inventive use of the tub. In the earlier story it appears actually to be a barrel, since the lover hides inside it and needs a candle to examine it closely. When the husband has volunteered to go inside to inspect—he has not been duped into doing it— and the lover stretches the wife over it, the kind of "knedyng tubbe" (or "kymelyn") in Chaucer's tale cannot have been meant. A tub is not a barrel, even if other motifs in the tales were similar. But they are not; these two tales are in no way related, except, perhaps, through a willingly imaginative association.

So too with Benson's and Anderson's listing of Jaques de Baisieux's "Tale of the Priest's Bladder" (1971, pp. 344–59). In Chaucer's *Summoner's Tale* a priest's fart is divided among friars, and—as Utley remarks (1965, p. 595)—"if ever a tale looked like a folktale it is this one," but no analogous folktale motif has ever been found; perhaps (as Utley guesses) its obscenity has masked its collection or its appearance in the indexes. In de Baisieux's fabliau a dying man bequeaths his bladder to greedy and expectant clerical heirs. In this case a stronger argument for an analogous narrative would seem to be possible—given the similarity of setting, of actants and their social roles, and the at least metonymic association of bladder and fart—though Utley passes by such a temptation, including *The Summoner's Tale* with those of Chaucer's narratives that have no folktale analogues and (only) possible literary analogues (1965, p. 598).

As in all of the demonstrations above, establishing a relationship between narratives based on a comparison of their narrative distributional elements, or motifs, is a cumulative matter. The elements of proof are rarely as positive as a letter from an author in which he or she discusses his or her source—even if that could always be trusted—or extended passages of verbatim copying. Nevertheless, by a judicious adaptation of folklore methodologies, likely relationships between (or among) impressionistically similar narratives can be established. The folktale is, after all, a narrative too, just as the short story, the novel, or the fabliau; and many of the methodologies worked out during the past century and a half for establishing its genesis, its life history, its kinship to similar tales, are useful for similar analyses of literary tales.

CHAPTER 5

Embedded Folktales

THE METHODOLOGY USED TO IDENTIFY a folktale that has been incorporated within a literary narrative is common enough for researchers who wish to demonstrate the relationship between literary and oral tale, for whatever reason; when the manuscript under examination contains more than one constituent tale, the analyst's tasks are greatly complicated. Yet this situation is not unusual; it is true of many of the medieval romances; an incoherence, a random assemblage of episodes, is assumed. Once that assumption is made, other conclusions are unlikely. In this respect the Middle English *Sir Degaré* may serve as a model. Conventional criticism holds that it is a "composite of motives found elsewhere in medieval romance" (Severs, ed. *A Manual of the Writings in Middle English*, p. 141). Yet, a comparison of this narrative with those outlined in the *Types of the Folktale* indicates an intricate relationship between this romance and three folktales.

Though *Sir Degaré* has been said to be "not without power" — hardly lavish praise — and is a story "deftly handled" (*Manual*, p 141) whose "dramatic tension plays an important part" (Mehl 1967, p. 42), it has not been carefully examined. This chapter will argue that one of the most interesting aspects of *Sir Degaré* is its structure, that it is an excellent example of what a talented romance writer can do with shorter stories that come to his or her hands (or ears). Source studies of this romance so far have not been satisfying; but it does seem that this romance, found with so many others in the Auchinleck MS, is not a redaction of a now lost French original. Such a hypothesis, in any event, with no evidence that such a French story ever existed, tells us nothing about *Sir Degaré*. Even if such a hypothetical manuscript (or oral narrative) existed, the most critical issues concerning *Sir Degaré* are not answered. Where did this French original come from? What were that poet's sources? Was it, too, a "composite of motives"? Does any narrative exist — or persist — if it is a random composite of motives?

One is provoked to search for folktales that might be embedded in this romance because of several obtrusive motifs, salient because they occur not only in other romances but much more frequently in folktales: the maiden is ravished by a knight from fairyland; the boy born of this encounter grows up and eventually marries his mother; he wins this right because he has been victorious in a martial contest; as an infant he had been raised abroad; he possesses two recognition tokens, one to identify each parent; and he enters, unawares, into a fight with his father.

Many of the Middle English romances share motifs and tale-types with folktales and ballads. Before commitment to paper the romances were performed in the same milieu as those other forms, and a great deal of borrowing of motifs has taken place. (See Lindahl 1987, pp. 159–72, for a discussion of oral communities). Some romances—possibly most, to put the matter more controversially—derived from narratives in oral currency, despite Loomis's strictures that such lofty stories could not possibly originate in the imaginations of "plowmen, goose-girls, blacksmiths, mid-wives, [or] yokels" (1958a, p. 2). What we would recognize as plot outlines are borrowed; a court poet, for instance, may make a number of changes in both the distributional elements (the episodes) and in the integrational ones, tailoring the narrative to the tastes of listeners.

Sir Degaré is the adventurous attempt of a young man to find his mother and father; as he discovers them he also finds a wife for himself, and the story that began with the young bachelor's quest ends as he discovers his parents' identity and begins his own nuclear family. Several folktales, almost assuredly known to medieval Europeans, describe the search of a youth for his parents; two of them bear a particularly close resemblance to this Middle English romance.

Sir Degaré is infrequently read or studied, though it is in the widely inclusive French and Hale edition, among twenty-seven romances; the more popular and more available paperback editions of Sands and Rumble do not include it. A summary at this point is not, therefore, superfluous; and rather than risk distorting the relation of the narrative elements in a précis of my own, which, however unconsciously, might favor certain events, that printed in the *Manual of the Writings in Middle English* (pp. 140–41) is given below:

In Brittany a king unsurpassed at arms has offered his only daughter and heir to whatever suitor overcomes him in tournament; during the years no suitor succeeds. While on her way to the abbey where the deceased queen is buried, the princess becomes separated from the royal party and lost in a forest. There as her attendants rest under a chestnut tree in the heat of the morning, she moves off alone and is ravished by a knight from fairyland. On parting he leaves a pointless sword with her for the son she will bear; the point of the sword the knight himself keeps to identify his son later on. When the son is born, the mother, fearing for her reputation, secretly abandons him, but leaves in his cradle gold, silver, and a pair of gloves together with a letter informing the finder that the infant is noble and should love only her whom the gloves fit. A hermit, who finds the infant and christens him Degaré ("the one almost lost"), entrusts him to his sister until his tenth year and thereafter educates him himself.

Given the gold, silver, and gloves and informed of the letter Degaré at twenty begins to search for his parents. With only a sapling as weapon he saves an earl from a dragon's attacks and is forthwith knighted. Since the gloves fit no one present, he continues his travels. Meeting a king offering his only daughter to any suitor who can overcome him, Degaré unhorses him and so is married. Only later, when he gives her the gloves, does he discover that he has married his own mother, who at once confesses to her father her meeting with the knight from fairyland and Degaré's secret birth. Armed now with the pointless sword, which his mother has kept for him, Degaré sets out to find his father. He travels far in the forest where he was begotten, and reaches a castle, but then occupants appear, four huntresses, a dwarf, and a beautiful lady with attendants. Degaré conducts himself courteously, yet no one speaks to him. He is refreshed at a banquet and then reveals his love for the lady of the castle. Following her to her chamber, he lies down and is lulled to sleep by the music of a harp. Next day, after he learns that her father's death has left the castle undefended, he fights off a neighboring suitor and is promised the lady's love and hand in marriage. But this he puts off until he has found his own father.

His search leads him now to a forest, where he is challenged by a knight for poaching. Though Degaré protests his innocence, he accepts a fight and readies his pointless sword. But sight of the pointless sword moves his challenger to break off fighting and, by means of the missing point, which he has with him, to identify Degaré as his own son. Joyfully the two then seek out Degaré's mother. As soon as his marriage to her is dissolved, the knight from fairyland, to the king's satisfaction, marries her. Accompanied by his mother, father and grandfather, Degaré returns to the castle on the island and is joined to the lady to whom he earlier promised his love.

Nearly a dozen folk motifs delineating the major contours of this romance can be identified. The following listing of them will provide a shorthand of narrative analysis as well as establish the criteria necessary before proceeding with a folktale comparison.

A marriage test is posed to any adventurer who would wed the daughter of the king of Brittany (H 1310). But the ravisher of the princess does not bother with a tournament: "Prince Finds Heroine in Woods" (N 711.1). A sword token is left for the future son (T 645), who is soon abandoned—"exposed" (R 131). When Degaré grows up, he defeats in tournament a king offering his daughter to a superior knight—the "Suitor Test: Tournament" (H 331.2). Degaré quickly realizes that his newly won bride must be his mother because of the gloves she had left with him when he was an infant (S 334). He now begins his search for his father, along the way saving a beleaguered maiden whom he can marry if he chooses (T 68), but whose affection he puts aside for the moment (L 225). Shortly thereafter, he encounters his father as they prepare to fight one other, each unaware of the other's identity (N 731.2); a parricide (N 323) is avoided through the identification of the recognition token (N 731). Father and mother are then married (L 161), and Degaré returns to the island in the forest to claim his own bride.

Three folktales, all of them quite old and widely distributed, contain nearly all of the salient motifs in *Sir Degaré*. The most striking concerns Degaré's relationship with his mother, the folktale, "Oedipus," Aarne-Thompson type 931 in *Types of the Folktale*: "As foretold by the prophecy, the hero kills his father and marries his mother." The most commonly found motifs among the variants of this tale are parricide prophecy (M 343); mother-incest prophecy (M 344); exposure of child to prevent fulfillment of parricide prophecy (M 371.2); compassionate executioner (K 512); exposed or abandoned child rescued (R 131); exposed infant reared at a strange king's court (S 354); parricide prophecy unwittingly fulfilled (N 323); and mother-son incest (T 412).

Both Degaré and the folktale hero are abandoned as children. The folktale Oedipus is reared at an alien court, Degaré in a hermit's hut. Incest is accomplished in the folktale, as in the myth; Degaré avoids it at the last minute. Neither is the romance hero allowed to commit parricide, though the narrative has residue of it: Degaré encounters his father and is challenged to a fight, and though protesting his innocence, he consents to battle. This sin is also avoided at the last minute. Degaré had earlier fought his grandfather and had unhorsed him in the tournament in which he "won" his mother/bride. This earlier fight with the father (the grandfather, actually) is positioned correctly for the Oedipus story, occurring before his (near) marriage to his mother.

"The King Discovers His Unknown Son" (A-T 873) is the story of a father who has never seen his son until he recognizes him through the agency of a token left with his mother. Relevant motifs include: A king in disguise leaves a token with a girl to give to their son if one is born (T 645); the boy is twitted with bastardy and goes on a quest for his unknown father (H 1381.2.2.1.1); the folktale's king later orders the boy's execution, which element may or may not be present in Degaré's near fight with his father in the woods; the son is identified by the token (N 731, H 80); and the king marries the boy's mother (L 162).

A third folktale, "The Maiden without Hands" (A-T 706), shares several other elements with this romance, though one is in euphemised form. As *The Types of the Folktale* condenses this tale:

I. *The Mutilated Heroine.* The heroine has her hands cut off, (a) because she will not marry her father.

II. *Marriage to the King.* A king finds her in the woods (garden, stable, sea) and marries her in spite of her mutilation.

III. *The Calumniated Wife.* For the second time she is cast forth with her newborn children, because [various people] change a letter to the king.

IV. *The Hands Restored.* (a) By a miracle in the woods she gets her hands back again. (b) She is restored to her husband.

The most famous literary treatment of this story is in Chaucer's *Man of Law's Tale*; his source is the *Chronicle* of Nicolas Trivet. In Chaucer's tale the heroine is not mutilated (as in Trivet), and consequently does not get her hands miraculously restored. This is just the sort of alteration that more sophisticated authors make when they retell tales garnered from oral transmission; of course, a subtype of type 706 may have flourished during the thirteen and fourteenth centuries, a significantly retold variation in which no mutilation / miraculous restoration was involved. It is therefore not incredible that the adventures of Degaré's mother are functionally quite similar. The heroine of *Sir Degaré* does not have an explicitly lecherous father (depending upon how line 21 is read: "ꝑbis maiden he loued als his lif"), but neither do a great many of the folktales. Medievalists have long recognized that the father, or stepfather, who will not let his daughter marry because no one is good enough for her is merely another form of the lecherous father: Laura Hibbard (1960) found analogies in the related motifs of the father who married his own daughter because no one else was beautiful enough. In the romance *Emaré*, for instance, the father-daughter incest is explicit (Hibbard, pp. 302–3). Emaré's father, the emperor, is so taken with his daughter's beauty that he begins plans for their wedding. When she refuses such a union, he casts her adrift in an open boat.

Sir Degaré's mother is not cast forth, and the "joly knight" who ravishes her is not her father. Nevertheless, her father functions as the lecherous parent in that other important respect, preventing her marriage except to anyone who can defeat him at arms. And, like Chaucer's Custance, Degaré's mother does not have her hands amputated, but this crude detail does have its residue: a glove is given as a token. In the folktale versions the king recognizes his wife because of her missing hands, and at the end of the story fails to recognize her because they have been restored (e.g., Ranke 1966, pp. 84–89). In this romance the lady's gloves are taken off and left with the infant; they will later become the sign by which he will identify his mother. That the crudeness of the peasants' versions should be altered in this way is a common phenomenon, all the more plausible because of the metonymic relation of gloves to hands. (Table 5.1 illustrates the suggested way in which *Sir Degaré* embeds these three folktales.)

In the folktale "Oedipus," as in the classic myth, the young hero is sent to a foreign court to be reared; in *Sir Degaré*, as already noted, the hero's childhood home is a hermit's hut. His bride, his mother, is not won in a tournament in the folktale, but it is at that point that mother-son incest does nearly take place. And, the fight with one's father is not in the ninth position as shown on table 5.1 (but with a "?"); it occurs as part of number five, "Bride Won in Tournament." Nor does that element occur in type 873 ("The King Discovers His Unknown Son"), but it does correspond to the son's quest to discover his father;

Table 5.1. Comparison of Sir Degaré *to Three Folktales.*

Sir Degaré	"Oedipus"	"King Discovers Son"	"Maiden without Hands"
1. Marriage test	—	—	x
2. Forest rape	—	x	x
3. Glove as token	—	x	—
4. Infant given away	x	—	—
5. Bride won in tournament	x	?	—
6. Glove as token	—	—	x
7. Maiden in castle	—	—	—
8. Hero refuses princess	—	—	—
9. Hero fights father	x (?)	—	—
10. Sword recognized	—	x	—
11. Family reunited	—	x	x

Degaré has also embarked on a search for his parents when he wins the right to his mother's hand at a tournament.

The suggestion that a single narrative is genetically related to three briefer tales is only the first step in demonstrating their relationship. Similarities of motifs is also a beginning, and a risky one. In criticizing those scholars "who could slip one tale type to another on the wings of a single motif," Utley (1964, p. 605) warned that:

> Motifs do not float independently, but they undergo transfers from one tale type to another; we must therefore be careful, when pleading genetic relationship between two widely separated parallels, to trace complexes of motifs rather than single motifs, however central they may be to the main story. Arthurians will surely be interested in this warning, since their study has been plagued with those who turn such catenae of varying but overlapping motifs into the pseudo-history of a tale. Motifs ABCDE in Ireland may well equal motifs AB-DEF in France, but ABCDE and DEFGHI give us mere illusions of Historical connection. The basic axiom of international folktale science is that the tale can be shown to have been diffused and not independently created, because it is complex and coherent enough to make independent origins unlikely.

The folklorist looks for independent narratives, not individual motifs. No less distinguished a scholar than Kittredge once claimed that the Middle English *Sir Orfeo* derived from the Celtic *The Wooing of Etain* based on the overlap of only one detail: in both stories the king is abducted from amidst a company of armed protectors (1886). And the detail was a relatively trivial one at that.

To establish a genetic kinship, more proof is needed. Specifically, we will want to know whether oral narratives are ever conflated in the form just suggested, whether the indicated motifs occur in the same order in oral tradition as hypothecated in the manuscript narrative, and whether the tales in question could have been, historically, available to the writer.

To answer the first question in relation to *Sir Degaré* and Aarne-Thompson tale-types 931, 873, and 706, a recent, popular edition of translated German folktales (Ranke, 1966) contains a narrative (Ranke's number 29) which is a conflation of A-T 303 ("The Twins"), 304 ("The Hunter"), and 300 ("The Dragon Slayer"). This complex tale, called "The Three Brothers" by its teller, begins when three brothers set out into the world but soon part at a crossroads. The first receives magical aid from an old man he meets in the woods; he finds a princess imprisoned in a castle, and with the aid of the received magic slays the giants who hold her captive. The next morning, when everyone and everything in the castle have disappeared, he sets out in the woods again, shortly meeting another brother, who tells of his wanderings into a town whose inhabitants were in mourning because of three beseiging giants and a dragon; the second brother slew the dragon and exposed the false hero who tried to take credit for the deed. After some adventures the brothers again walk deep into the forest — where they become lost. Meanwhile the third brother is experiencing similar adventures: the woods, an old man, magical assistance, and enchanted castle. Because the youngest brother has been the most generous to the old man, he is given the ability to disenchant the castle.

Table 5.2 shows the relationship between these three folktales and the complicated narrative of which they are constituents. At this point — the originators of this narrative being inaccessible — one can only guess

Table 5.2. Tale-Types in "The Twins," "The Hunter," and "The Dragon Slayer"

Life token (E 761.14.1)
Parting at crossroads (N 772) — 303

Magic object from old man (D 823)

The skillfull marksman (F 661.1)

Hero finds maiden in castle (N 711.2)

Princess rescued (R 11) — 304

Giant decapitated (K 912)

Lowly hero marries princess (L 161)

Dragon-tongue proof (H 105.1) — 303

Castle's occupants asleep (F 771.14.4)
Magic object from old man (D 823) — 304

Dragon (B 11)

Dragon fight (B 11.11.1)

Imposter claims reward (K 1932) — 300

Dragon-tongue proof (H 105.1)

Castle's occupants asleep (F 774.14.4)
Child begotten in magic sleep (T 415.2) — 304

Disenchantment (D 700) — 303

These motifs also found in 300

why this combination was created, by Ranke's teller or one of his sources. Similar adventures, and especially motifs, overlap the tales. One brother fights giants, the other a dragon; and several narrative portions of Aarne-Thompson types 300 and 304 are identical. The similarity of episodes and of the tales' trajectory makes combinations plausible; their similarities are further indicated, though by no means infallibly, by the proximity of their numbers in the Thompson index.

The order of the motifs is important. In the German folktale the motifs, though occasionally separated by interrupting episodes from the other tales, nevertheless retain the same sequence in "The Three Brothers" that they had in their simpler, component versions. The motifs are not scattered throughout the narrative in a random or haphazard order; stories in oral tradition are not constructed along principles of chance episodes.

The final test of plausibility concerns the availability of the proposed folktales, in this case to the medieval writer or minstrel who performed *Sir Degaré*. The most obvious is Aarne-Thompson type 931, "Oedipus," which can be dated several centuries before the genesis of the romance. We also know that "The Maiden without Hands" has considerable antiquity dating from at least the very early thirteenth century. Prominent literary treatments subsequent to Trivet have been by Gower, Chaucer, and the romancier of *Emaré* (see Schlauch 1927; Bolte-Polivka, I: 198 ff.) Its distribution all over Europe, the New World, and the Balkans further suggests (but does not prove) its age as well as its popularity. As for A–T 873, "The King Discovers His Unknown Son," there is little evidence to demonstrate antiquity. The tale has been collected in Scandinavia, central Europe, Russia, the Balkans, India, and the New World, but it has not been collected in the numbers one would hope for when arguing for a medieval genesis. The age of type 873 cannot be demonstrated one way or another.

This cumulative evidence allows for the hypothesis that *Sir Degaré* owes its fourteenth-century form to three otherwise independent folktales, joined together by its composer or one of his or her sources. The romance's salient motifs, as well as several relatively minor ones, are found in these tales. And within the romance the motifs appear in the order in which they occur in oral tradition. At least two, and probably all three, were available to medieval constructors of narrative. Only the artist who first invented *Sir Degaré* knows the components used with any certainty, as is usually the situation with medieval literature, but on the evidence of episodic residue and the assumption that theories of monogenesis apply, the construction suggested above seems likely.

One portion of the narrative, however, is not explained or accounted for by the three folktales. In this episodic set Degaré journeys far into a forest and finds an enchanted castle on a river island. Occupants magically appear — four huntresses, a dwarf, and a lovely lady with attendants — but they ignore the stranger. At dinner that evening, Degaré professes love for the lady of the castle and is subsequently lulled asleep by her magic harping. On the following day he defeats a suitor, is promised his beloved, but declines until he has found his father. Degaré goes on to encounter his father, unrecognized, further on in the forest, and the folktale parallels resume.

This interruptive portion of the romance does not conform to any folktale; and it does not display the uncomplicated plot development of most folktales. The encounter with the lovely lady in her enchanted castle could be deleted from *Sir Degaré* without devastating its coherence: this is essentially the account of a young man searching for mother and father, and not for a wife. When he discovers his mother, in mid-story, and later his father, his quest has been satisfied. The parents are reunited. The lovely lady is an extra blessing.

But an important one. So many narratives of this type conclude when the single hero acquires a wife, and commences his own family, that this idea is de rigueur in this genre. To suggest that the enchanted maiden interlude is "added to" the narrative instead of being one of its original components is not to say that it is trivial; rather, it is the mark of a very skillful yarn-weaver adroitly able to integrate such an important thematic portion into the narrative. It is not likely that a minstrel or jongleur would have as the core story this brief episode — a common enough element in Arthurian romances, but not known to have an independent life in oral tradition — around which he or she wove that complex web of three folktales. They are, when blended, coherent and autonomous, and can easily stand without the enchanted-maiden interruption. It is more likely that the episodes related to the maiden's rescue were added after the major portions of the story had been formulated. Degaré is motivated to find his parents; the story begins and ends with this dual search. Had marriage been the privileged quest, Degaré would not have postponed his betrothal until after he had found his father. In the end he achieves all of the principal goals: the narrative has required that he discover his father (the psychological significance of this quest should not be slighted: see Ramsay 1983), and cultural assumptions of the genre impel his inventor to have him marry.

Priority cannot be assigned to any of the three constituent tales; none seems to have semantic or chronological priority. It can be asserted, however, that at least portions of this romance had been in circulation for many years before *Sir Degaré* was fixed in writing; whether the narrative in the Auchenleck MS form had existed prior to this particular manifestation cannot be determined. Hibbard thought that the name of the hero indicated its "ultimately popular character" (1960, p. 302). This is not to suggest that *Sir Degaré* is merely, in its present form, a folktale altered and euphemised.

We can argue that *Sir Degaré* is a well-constructed story, and that as narrative art its obscurity owes much to the inability of its critics to come to terms with it. Like nearly all of the other romances in Middle English, the imagery of *Sir Degaré* is meager; to the modern reader its rhetoric is often unimaginative, its meter boring and irregular, its episodes stereotyped. Nonetheless when these evaluations are levied against it, we should remember that such are the criteria used for reflexive literature, for works which can be read at leisure, reread and mulled over, worked and meticulously reworked by the author. Such are the criteria one would use to judge the careful precision of such poets as Keats, or of the prose of such neurotically meticulous writers as James Joyce.

Narratives meant, at least in part, to be performed should not be judged by literate criteria, as Albert Lord demonstrated in *The Singer of Tales* and as I confirmed in *The Art of the American Folk Preacher*. Other criteria must be found. The manipulation of narrative units — here nuclei and catalyzers (Barthes 1982) — rather than the sophisticated use of rhetoric — is among the most important aesthetic considerations. *Sir Degaré* would rate high on such a scale. Three separate, originally discrete tales have been blended to form another, new, unique story surpassing its constituents. This blending is not a casual operation, nor are the results casual. *Sir Degaré* is an autonomous narrative with reasonable consistency within itself. Like most romances, and nearly all folktales, it begins with the hero's quest and concludes when that quest has been fulfilled. The sequence of nuclei involves Degaré's attempt to attain the goal of his quest, the discovery of the identity of his parents. During this procedure he overcomes hostile agents (dragons) and rescues the oppressed from peril; then he marries his princess. He receives aid from the charitable, surpasses obstacles, makes traditional conquests.

This narrative's balance has not been hidden: the battle with the dragon occurs before the first climax — the discovery of his mother — and the combat with the giant follows. During the course of this narrative Degaré matures; having found his mother and his father, he leaves their home to found a new one, and a new family, for himself.

As a young man, Degaré was "of swich power" that no one "him mi3t astond" (lines 287–90). When he sets forth into the world on his dual quest, he refuses the offer of horse and armor; instead he arms himself — appropriate to the warrior who will prove his worth with deeds and not rely on the advantage of his birth — with an oaken staff. Medieval studies, rather than medieval literary criticism, would hold that the aim in examining such a narrative is to make a cultural statement. The Middle English romances, among other narratives, are best appreciated for what they say about society.

Aesthetically, this chapter suggests a new criterion: an appreciation of the working of two or more otherwise autonomous tales into a new one, coherent and autonomous itself, yet retaining the interesting aspects of its constituents — the near mother-son incest, the fight with the unknown father, the rescue of the innocent maiden and her eventual marriage. Centuries have demonstrated the interest these elements have for Western audiences, and the minstrel was wise to retain them and to maintain their salience. In other words, the poet did much that was right in this kind of art, certainly accomplishing the important goals of the traditional fabulator, much more than merely to "combine an astonishing number of folklore and romance motifs" (Hibbard, p. 302). They are combined with great skill.

PART THREE

Structuralism

PERHAPS NO IDEA OR METHODOLOGY has had a greater influence on literary criticism since the end of World War II than structuralism. It has been the coagulant for an entire literary school, though many different practictioners have worked within its borders, each with his/her own demonstrable notion of structure. For more than two decades structuralist critics dominated literary analytical thought, certainly making it one of the most influential literary approaches of this century. Structuralist philosophies have permeated a number of humanist disciplines — anthropology and history, for instance. Few scholars in any of these fields realized (or cared) that the impetus for this "movement" derived from analysis of folktales.

Russian scholar Vladimir Propp was not himself primarily a folklorist; and he was not the first to dissect folk narratives. Yet his work, published in Russian during the late 1920s but remaining practically unknown until its translation into English in 1958, would stimulate scores, perhaps hundreds, of literary critics. Thus an idea for folkloric analysis was found to have a great many uses — many of them valuable — for the analysis of literature as well.

The following section on structuralism, composed of three chapters, discusses "the history of the problem" — what Propp considered to be at fault with the Finnish historic-geographic method and its principles of destructuring — and then summarizes Propp's place diachronically within the context of Russian structuralist thought. His intellectual progeny are also considered.

Chapter 7 examines in detail a more recent structural analysis of literature, that of Eugene Dorfman, whose structural application was formulated to deal with the Old French epics and romances. Interestingly, Dorfman pays no tribute to Propp for his ideas, but this slight is typical; well-known to and admired by folklorists, this father of modern literary structuralism is only sparingly acknowledged by his intellectual children. A conclusion of this chapter is that every narrative has several conceivable structural foundations, more than one of which may fruitfully describe the subject work. The student/reader must decide which of several valid analyses is the most useful.

Chapter 8 concentrates on a single narrative, *Beowulf* (claims having long been made both for its literariness and for its orality), and what I believe to be a misleading structural analysis recently performed on it. The imPropper structural analysis of *Beowulf* thus has an entire essay devoted to it, but the subject is important enough to command this much attention. Professor Daniel Barnes, of Ohio State, whose assertion regarding *Beowulf* is attacked, still believes in the truth of his analysis; more importantly, he has been generous-spirited enough to overlook our scholarly disagreement and to be a conscientious and constructive reader of this manuscript.

CHAPTER 6

Propp's Progeny

As HIS INITIAL CHAPTER, "On the History of the Problem," tells us Propp's interest in writing *The Morphology of the Folktale* was limited to a structural description of that oral genre (1968, pp. 3-18). Yet his critics, modifiers, and extenders occasionally seem to forget the limited nature of his objective, leading them to subvert his system or to ask it to carry an additional burden, as though it were an attempt to deal with all narratives. Literary critics, for instance, are more interested in novels and short stories than in folktales; and those literary forms differ significantly from oral tales. Literary forms are (relatively) flexible and varied in their narrative configurations and they are not as rigidly bound by the (culturally determined) rules to which the folktale is subject. Roman Jakobson (cited in Dundes 1964, p. 40), was one of the first to urge that folklorists discover the structural principles of their material, for "the folk-tale [is] subject to much stricter and more uniform laws than fields in which individual creation prevails."

The publication of *Morfológija skázki*, but especially of its translation as *Morphology of the Folktale* in 1958 was a momentous event in the history of folkloristics and of narrative theory scholarship; it was, in the exuberant exclamation of one of my students, "the mind-blowing book of the decade." Nearly every scholarly article on the structure of narrative—even if that structure is semiolinguistic or the product of computational analysis (e.g., Kahn 1973)—begins with tribute to the great Russian pioneer, even if that tribute is tinged with criticism and snideness. Many critics thought that Propp had succeeded in his intention of raising the study of the folktale to the level of botany (1968, p. xxv), and some still do. Propp's appeal to that generation of folklorists who began their professional careers in the early 1960s must have been what it was to Propp's colleagues in 1928; dissatisfied with the nebulous and elusive outlines of the Aarne (later Aarne-Thompson) classificatory indexes, Propp offered the hope of a precise, objective method of analysis. And he offered, optimistically, an infallible means of predicting the form of any folktale the researcher might encounter. Though most structuralist folklorists have moved on to new areas of research (Alan Dundes has recently complained that morphology takes the "folk" out of "folklore"), Propp's stature is such that no responsible work on a structuralist analysis of narrative or of narrative theory can begin without first citing him and his seminal work.

The situation that Propp addressed, and hoped to redress, in the mid-1920s was Finnish murkiness. Several theories of narrative were floating about aimlessly, competing with each other for acceptance — none, however, gaining a clear-cut supremacy. None was very satisfying; all were merely descriptive of content. No description of narrative adequately depicting the process of storytelling had as yet been developed. Propp began by taking several extant theories to task. Wundt's *Volkerpsychologie* (Propp 1968, p. 6) proposed — typical of the state of the art in the 1929s — a classification according to the following categories: (1) mythological fables, (2) pure (*Reine*) fairy tales, (3) biological tales and fables, (4) animal fables, (5) geneological tales, (6) jokes and fables, and (7) moral fables. Propp correctly paralleled this contentual classification with Antti Aarne's index of the Finnish School's ideology (1968, p. 8).

Propp objected that the several contental classification systems then current did not adequately describe the target narratives. Speaking of Wundt — though the same objections would apply to Aarne and others — Propp regretted that the means of differentiating among major categories was impressionistic and not scientifically precise. For instance, he noted that many tales substitute animals for human characters, and vice versa, and the same tales give the same actions and characteristics to humans, objects, and animals as well. Animals frequently appear in "fantastic tales," yet according to the indexes of Propp's day, those tales were undifferentiated. Wicked humans were "replaced" by demons in other versions of the "same" tale; some narratives treated the identical character heroically or comically, depending on the wont of the teller, the preference of the region or the audience. Propp asked, rhetorically, whether "pure" fables couldn't be moral as well; and what was a "pure" tale anyway? He noted that some indexes classified their tales by the character of the hero, others by plot complication, still others by the number of heroes, or by one outstanding narrative feature of the tale's action.

To the Finnish method Propp addressed other, though often related, questions, since its motif lexicons and tale-type indexes were gaining favor, conceptually, among European folklorists. Comparative folktale study had demonstrated that, as tales migrated geographically, so their constituent motifs migrated and adjusted to their new environment, sometimes changing entirely, thus blurring the outlines of tale-types. Wesselski argued that written versions, powerfully influential, should alone be studied (quoted in Thompson 1977, p. 441). He questioned the basic premises of the Finnish method: that the motif is the smallest, indivisible unit of narrative; was it really, as claimed, an organic whole, an autonomous entity? Tales were frequently placed into different categories by different folklorists, all using the Aarne index as the basis of classification. Twenty percent of the A. I. Nikiforov tales could not be placed with certainty (i.e., tale-type) and had to be ambiguously identified. Characters shifted shapes and roles; plots blended and melted together; an objective isolation of themes was not possible with the existing methodologies.

Not all theories of narrative structure derive from Propp's system, of course—the linguistic model he discusses elsewhere—but his more enthusiastic followers have occasionally succumbed to the temptation of claiming that the *Morfológija* is the fountainhead of all such analyses of narrative. In her preface to the first English edition of the *Morphology*, Svatava Pirkova-Jakobson claimed that "Claude Levi-Strauss applies and even extends Propp's method in his study of myth and in the interpretation of the meaning of myth from its form and structure" (1958, p. xxi). But the French anthropologist's seminal essay on his own variety of structural analysis, "The Structural Study of Myth," was published (in English) in 1955; and it is significantly different from the approach of his Russian forebearer. Levi-Strauss would subsequently criticize, among other things, Propp's syntagmatic approach. But such has been the Russian's fame and influence that, like heroic motifs to illustrious heroes, ideas became identified with him.

Linguistics has provided more models to narrative theorists than has any other discipline. Greimas (1971) divides narrative features into the now familiar classification of dynamic and static predicates; Todorov's three "primary categories" correspond to "proper name," "verb," and "adjective" (cited in Culler 1977, p. 204). Todorov's title, *Grammaire de Decameron*, indicates the source of his model (in Culler, p. 215). Pierre Guiraud's foreword to Eugene Dorfman's intriguing book, *The Narreme in Medieval Romance Epic* (the "-eme" of the title alone denotes the linguistic source of its inspiration), asserts that "we must not be surprised if today literary criticism approaches this problem [structural analysis] in the light of linguistics" (1969, p. vii). Even Alan Dundes, called by many European folklorists Propp's "disciple" in America, devised his own narrative analytic scheme (in *The Morphology of North American Indian Folktales*) using the "motifeme" as the basic unit of narrative, a concept borrowed from the linguistic system of Kenneth Pike (Dundes 1964, pp. 59 ff.).

Claude Brémond begins his essay "Morphology of the French Folktale" with an acknowledgment that "the subject of this study" is to test a method derived from the one V. Propp used in his analysis of Russian folktales (1970, p. 247). Brémond had hoped, he says, "to establish certain constant relations of implication or exclusion in order to isolate sub-types of the fundamental pattern." But his expectations were thwarted, in both Propp's work and that of Alan Dundes: "these hopes were deceived for no specification appears from the study of Russian folktales. Propp has pointed out the similarities in all Russian folktales but he did not succeed in specifying the differences" (p. 248). Brémond thus chastises Propp for doing what he set out to do and not what Brémond thought he ought to have attempted.

Brémond proceeds from an entirley different notion of the relationship of parts within a narrative than did Propp (see Culler 1977, pp. 208 ff.). Propp defined a narrative's functions as the acts of the characters understood from the point of view of their "significance for the course of the action" (1969, p. 21). The conception is teleological. It assumes that the author — to extend this application to a literary author as well as folktale tellers — knows how he or she wishes the narrative to end and directs all the elements in the story toward that end. This view assumes also that, in those instances in which the author does not know in advance how the tale will end, he or she will have the time to revise those earlier portions composed in ignorance of the final choice of an ending. The situation is not quite the same for the folktale teller, who presumably knows very well how his tale will conclude and, unless he is in a particularly playful or perverse mood, will direct his narration with that end in mind.

Brémond wants a structural system that will allow for alternatives to the courses of action actually chosen by the characters. Since Propp defines all functions in terms of their ultimate consequences, his system does allow for choice. When we read a story we often feel that the characters are free to choose among several courses; and Propp's system does not take these options into account. But a narrative is fixed; once composed its characters are not free in the same way that people have a relative freedom of choice in their lives. And certainly the folktale is even less free than prose fiction in its possibilities. Once the author has decided what will happen to the characters, they are frozen. The folktale's characters are, by and large, fixed by tradition. A narrative is, by its nature, an expression whose characters are determined by their creator. There are alternatives open to the dramatic personae within this closed system, and in fact Propp accounts for some of them: after the hero/ine has set out upon the quest (↑), a donor may be encountered who may be willing or unwilling to impart the information necessary to get the hero to the desired place. The hero's response may be positive (DEF) or negative ($\frac{DEF}{neg}$). Within Propp's system the pivotal character may be a questing hero or a victim; the tale may involve a struggle with the villain (an eventual victory over him/her/it), H–I, or the imposition of tasks and their accomplishment, M–N, or both, or neither. Propp defines subtypes according to these structural phenomena.

The dendrogrammatic flowchart that Brémond proposes (see fig. 6.1) does account for alternative courses of action, the difference being that his accounts for the possibilities within a general narrative frame, whereas Propp "charted" the course of the individual tale. Beside each function, Brémond wrote, there is a possibility of a contrary choice. (Some of the most unlikely terminology in the history of literary criticism emerges from such attempts as Brémond's: "Nefast procedure,"

Fig. 6.1. Brémond's Flowchart.

		Success (objective reached)
	Actualization (procedure in order to reach the objective	
Potentiality (objective to reach)		
		Failure (objective missed)
	Lack of actualization (inertia, prevention to act)	

"Dupery to do," "procedure of degredation," "Danger to prevent," "re-fused harmfulness," etc. No doubt this results either from problems inherent in translations or because Brémond is not a native speaker of English.)

Brémond succeeds in the task he has assigned himself: his chart does clearly depict the options confronting the hero of a narrative — or, more accurately, the creator of the story. With an objective to attain, understood by the hero, the quest can actually begin — potential can be activated — or the opportunity can be denied, either by the pivotal character or by some restraining external force. If the quest is undertaken, it will either succeed or fail. The chief virtue of this diagram is its clarity. But is it needed? Does it clarify the possibilities more than does, say, Dundes's Lack–Lack Liquidated? Or Propp's A–K? How real, in terms of narrative, is the option, "Lack of actualization"? If the hero chooses not to proceed or is prevented from doing so, the narrative ends right there. We might still have a story of sorts, but the upper branch of Brémond's tree becomes extraneous. Very few folktales end with the hero's decision not to embark on a quest (Brémond was constructing a "Morphology of the French Folktale"). Nevertheless, as a graphic representation of the tale's entire economy, charting its thrust, this is successful. But when Brémond attempts to describe portions of the tale which are, in detail, more complex, his commendable clarity breaks down.

For instance, in another chart (see fig. 6.2), he has attempted to illustrate a triply embedded sequence (the accomplishment of a task which reveals an obstacle which, when overcome, reveals a new task which, when accomplished, reveals another task with further obstacles, etc.). The pheonomenon is common in folk literature. The portion of narrative that Brémond sets out to describe is from one of the tales of *Le conte populaire français*. The hero must rescue a princess held captive by a giant. But in order to do so he must destroy an egg (repository of the giant's soul). But in order to get the egg he must capture a pigeon which is within a black bear — which the hero must also kill. Consequently, the hero transforms himself into a white bear and kills the black, then into a hawk in order to kill the pigeon, and when he has secured the egg he smashes it. Propp would have indicated this sequence as DEF^3 or $M\ N^3$ depending upon the relation of the sequence to its results within the tale; in this case, since the accomplishment of the several tasks enables the hero to kill the giant and thus to free the princess (and marry her?), the functions involved are $M\ N^3$. Not wonderfully detailed or explicit, but concise and clear. Brémond, on the

Fig. 6.2. Brémond's Chart of Embedded Tasks.

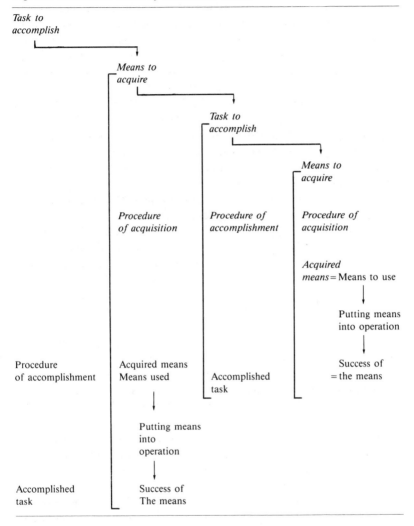

other hand, has constructed the chart shown in fig. 6.2 to depict the same sequence of embedded tasks.

Brémond criticized Propp's "UNILINEAR series of functions" (1970, p. 250), and while charts (typically represented by figs. 6.1 and 6.2) certainly account for a wider range of possibilities, clarity is no longer one of Brémond's virtues. Graphic representations are supposed to facili tate understanding, but Brémond's narrative summary is far more comprehensible than his chart. We all would have been helped had he demonstrated how a specific tale would be charted. As it is, hours may be spent figuring out the illustration in fig. 6.2. My guess is that the "task to accomplish" (upper left of fig. 6.2) can be rewritten as "to rescue the princess." The "means to acquire" are the hero's magical powers, and the "task to accomplish" is to slay the giant. The "procedure of accomplishment" (middle of left-hand column) is the breaking of the egg which contains, or is, the giant's soul. The "accomplished task" (bottom of left-hand column) is the slaying of the giant — or is it the effected rescue of the princess? Even after the reader has puzzled through this chart, what more is known either about this tale or about any narrative with this embedded sequence?

One of Brémond's major conclusions is that all stories proceed from a satisfactory state through a degredation of that state back to one that is satisfactory (1970, pp. 251ff.). But this is hardly new; it barely, if at all, alters Todorov's assertions (1977, p. 111) that the minimal complete plot consists in the passage from one equilibrium to another (passing through disequilibrium, and allowing that the second equilibrium will not be the same as the initial one). It is hardly different from Dundes's description of the North American Indian tale's progress from "Lack" to "Liquidation of Lack," a modification of Propp by way of Pike (1964, p. 75). Propp himself had pointed out that the Russian tale always began with "A" or "a" and ended with "K" or "W," and that if the tale was told properly (!) the solution would match the initial villainy and the object of the quester's search (1968, p. 648). All of these definitions are, after all, confirmations of Aristotle's earlier formulation of beginning, middle, and end.

Brémond began his critique of his Russian forebear with the statement that, although he did "not definitely repudiate formalistic orientation," he found its foremost practitioner wanting: "we consider that the essentials of Propp's project may be saved, in spite of Propp himself" (1970, p. 248). In this one respect Brémond reflects the most fundamental truism of any system of literary criticism: no one methodology is exhaustive, none is definitive or completely satisfying. Brémond finds fault in Propp's lack of flexibility, in his inattention to the details — the alternatives open to the characters. For Dundes, who reduced many of his tales to the simple code, L-LL, Propp must have seemed too complicated, too detailed to account for Dundes's Amerind material.

Alan Dundes's contribution to structural analyses of narrative begins more modestly. For him, the situation among folklorists and narratologists was much the same as that which Propp confronted. Because the *Morfológija* was not accessible to Western readers until 1958, Dundes found nearly all of the old, inadequate classificatory systems still in place, perhaps even more firmly entrenched than ever. He too begins his book (originally his dissertation at Indiana University — where Propp was translated and published in English) with a chapter on the history of the problem and proceeds through the (now) familiar list of inadequate attempts to describe and classify the folktale. And while Dundes's own system is not purely Russian formalist but instead his own adaptation and application to the particular body of material at hand, he became with the publication of his own *Morphology* the "father" of American formalistic approaches to narrative.

Dundes took for granted a number of Propp's assumptions, not always (I shall elaborate later) to his advantage. Propp had declared that he had analyzed one hundred fairy tales from the Afanas'ev collection, but that "such a limitation" was "theoretically justified" (1968, p. 24). Dundes agreed that in a morphological study it was not necessary to analyze "every single version" (1964, p. 11); for support he used the analogy of the linguist (unlike Propp who was thinking like a botanist) who "can make a perfectly valid structural statement about a language without knowing every single lexical item in that language" (1964, p. 11). (I presume that Dundes meant every single syntactic structure, not every lexical item.) It would not be necessary *if* the folktale structure were as lawfully regular as grammar. At another place he repeats the assertion that the linguist cannot describe language processes through an extensive study of words and sentences, though this time Dundes does admit that this analogy is not a "true" one but merely illustrative (1964, p. 40).

In taking Levi-Strauss to task for his concern with all versions of a particular work, Dundes again insists that one of the advantages of synchronic analysis is that not all of the versions of the tale (or myth) need to be examined. But if not all, which ones? "Structural analysis of just a few typical versions of a tale would presumably be just as accurate as an analysis of a few thousand versions of the same tale" (1964, p. 46), contra the Finnish method. Dundes takes Levi-Strauss to task also for failing to define narrative units as precisely as the linguist has defined the phoneme (1964, p. 44).

Propp, and Dundes after him, was contemptuous of the attempt to construct tale-type indexes when those tales could not even be defined, let alone classified, with precision. They both hit upon a fundamental weakness of the Finnish method: surely, if the folktale is not stable, if it does not retain more than its skeletal form through centuries of transmission, an index can hardly claim to establish a genetic relation among variants, let alone enable the researcher to decide what is and what is not a variant. In a headnote to Stith Thompson's essay on "The Star-Husband Tale," a demonstration of the historic-geographic method in America, Dundes accuses the older folklorist of a superorganic approach in which tales alter lawfully, regardless of any human factors in the transmission process (1965, p. 415).

The structuralist approach is superorganicism par excellence. On the basis of the examination of an admittedly limited sampling of data, the structuralist assumes that all other specimens will conform to the model. "It should be obvious that structure is more likely to remain constant over a wide geographical area than content" (1964, p. 80), Dundes wrote, probably accurately, though the premise has not been seriously examined. Stith Thompson and Franz Boas decided that they could not distinguish folktales from myths; Propp found that the fairy tale "in its morphological basis represents a myth" (1968, p. 90). The conventional folklorist, differentiating one genre from the other by content analysis, can make the distinction; the structuralist often cannot. But is the folktale as stable as structuralists have to assume? Dundes notes that while some tellers are quite consistent in their narrations—the Tellamooks and Eskimos for example—others such as the Zuni and Isleto narrators vary their tales considerably (1964, p. 23–29). Their traditions encourage individual creative freedom, just as other cultures demand that stories be told in the old, traditional ways. Dundes himself provides the most telling demonstrations against the folktale's stability: while in most of the North American Indian "Eye-Juggler" tales the pivotal character loses his sight, an Indiana University M.A. thesis has shown that in about 80 percent of the tales Eye-Juggler regains his sight (cited in Dundes 1964, p. 81).

Another of the assertions Propp made about the structure of Russian folktales concerned the invariability of the sequence of functions. Brémond grants that, while each folktale does not contain all thirty-one functions, "the remaining functions follow each other in immutable order, and so every particular tale may be considered as an incomplete realization of that ideal sequence" (1970, p. 247). Dundes accepts this principle (1964, p. 50) although his own research has shown that Propp's function number eight, "Villainy," can occur initially or after the seventh function (1964, p. 58). That turns out to be more of a problem for Propp's system—to be discussed shortly—than for Dundes's. The American's system is sensibly broad enough to account for, to assimilate, such transformations. If a tale's initial function is a villainy or one of several possible "preparatory actions," it might matter for the former; but Dundes's "Lack" is sufficiently encompassing to subsume several preliminary features. He loses in specificity but gains in his description of the folktale's overarching trajectory.

One of the inclinations of both these structuralists is to assume the existence of narrative phenomena, even if they are not present in the tale itself. This sometimes makes it possible, or at least easier, to postulate an event when it is not present in the tale. The failure is thus assigned to a faulty teller, and not to the system. Dundes quotes Propp to the effect that if a violation occurs — a tale relates an episode which has detrimental consequences — even though a prior interdiction has not been stated, it may be implied (Dundes 1964, p. 53). Pursuing this methodological assumption, Dundes annotates certain tales in the same way; an interdiction may be understood and need not be explicitly stated. Stealing, for instance, is to be taken as a violation of an implied interdiction (1964, pp. 75, 82). This procedure may well be legitimate, though we would feel more secure about it if more specimens of the tales in question were examined and compared with the one under examination, as the Finns would do with variants of the same type. But, as the structuralist premise has it, a limited sampling is enough to demonstrate morphological consistency. But what does this say about the role of the individual teller in the process of tale composition and transmission? That subject shall be touched on in a moment.

The tendency of morphological analysis is to make all folktales look structurally alike. The same would be true of any corpus of narratives described by a similar system. To a certain extent this was what Propp was trying to do; and to a certain extent this was inevitable, given the units of description employed in morphological analysis. The Finnish method foregrounds differences between tales more distinctly. Yet, however unavoidably regreattable, the structuralist inclination toward leveling exists. Representatively, Dundes observes that the Zuni tale "The Little Girl and the Cricket" is structurally similar to the classical Greek Orpheus, "though the motifs are different" (1964, p. 84). This is interesting if we are trying to show a genetic relationship between these narratives, or if a cross-cultural comparison is the researcher's intention. In this instance neither is the case. Morphology gives us a fairly precise means of describing and defining narrative, but it cannot reasonably be employed to solve all of the questions we have about narratives. One of the most ingenius and potentially useful of Dundes's observations is the comparison of the interdiction/violation folktales with superstitions, which also "punish" violators of interdictions (pp. 106 ff.). (If a mirror is broken, seven years bad luck will result.) This may tell us quite a lot about the cultural function of certain folktales and myths, but it is not especially helpful in our role as narratologists. Dundes criticizes Stith Thompson for claiming that there didn't seem to be any "actual relationship" between the North American Indian "Star-Husband" tale and the Eskimo "Eagle and Whale Husbands" (1964, pp. 89–90); Dundes found them morphologically similar: both have Int/Viol/AE (attempted escape) motifeme sequences. But a genetic relationship between them is not thus demonstrated, and that would have been Thompson's concern. Morphology is a very powerful procedure, but it is not omnipotent.

For every gain there is some loss, as the old maxim has it. If all folktales can be subsumed under a single morphological umbrella, a great deal of important particularizing detail will be lost while important gains are being made in other areas. One of Dundes's most important contributions, as already noted, was his ability to compare folktales with other genres and in other cultures; further raising the level of abstraction in his descriptive process, however, caused him to lose even the particularity of Propp's system. Genetic relationships cannot be established; as Dundes admits, two myths having the same structure in different cultures may not be related (1964, p. 47). For Dundes's purposes that is not important. But for the folklorist employing the historic-geographic method, for the literary critic concerned with the meaning of narratives in different cultures, for Levi-Strauss, for Ovid, the relationship was/is crucial. Quoting linguists Voegelin and Harris, Dundes believes that "structural compatibility of languages [and folktales] may be stated independently of their genetic relationships" (1964, p. 97). Such is the manifesto of the synchronic researcher; but the approach cannot be extended to have it both ways—diachronically as well. Morphology cannot be used—contra a later statement—to formulate hypotheses of archetypes (1964, pp. 108–9). Historical relations and cultural ties are not demonstrated by morphological analysis; because of its innate limitations, it can do only so much.

Some of the most interesting aspects of "The Morphology of North American Indian Tales" may not even have been intended. Certainly Dundes does not foreground two interesting conclusions in any obtrusive way. The first concerns his definition of the (structural) movement, or economy, of his narratives. And the other is his (properly) modest claim for what he has identified as the Amerind folktale's nuclear motifeme sequence. Theoretical narratologists often seem not to have specific narratives in mind, and certainly many of them refer only to a very limited corpus. Dundes is more convincing here; he is working with a relatively large body of material which he cites frequently for his proofs. Brémond's failure in this respect has been noted. So too Gerald Prince rarely refers to existing narratives, making up his own sentences for his examples. Aristotle formulated his aesthetic principles based on not more than the Homeric corpus; and Genette has relied almost entirely on Proust. One wishes that those critics who have defined the minimal narrative as moving from equilibrium through disequilibrium back to a second, not identical, equilibrium (Prince, Todorov, Aristotle, etc.) had cited a wider range of data. A large number of North American Indian tales begin with a disequilibrium ("Lack") and move toward the implementation of an equilibrium ("Lack Liquidated") (Dundes 1964, p. 61). Is an initial "Lack" to be understood as implying a preexistent equilibrium? If so, it is an implication of narrative that has not been adequately discussed. Working from his material inductively, Dundes's findings must be counted as an important caution on widely accepted narrative theory.

The contemporary attempt to isolate and identify the minimal narrative apparently derives from Chomsky's definition and elaboration of the kernel sentence and its role in the generation of all other sentences. The analogy, however, does not really hold. Narrative expressed through language is composed of sentences, but sentences are not narratives. The same rules do not satisfactorily describe both. Dundes concludes, interestingly, that the nuclear motifemic sequence—the nuclear tale— "Lack–Lack Liquidated," is for North American Indians a minimum folktale (1964, p. 75). It can be combined with other motifemic sequences (i.e., Int/Viol; dct/dcpn), usually appearing in a medial position to form more complex tales. But, wisely, he does not claim a historical or a psychological priority for the nuclear tale. Again, his observations are convincing, based as they are on a number of actual tales.

The amount of data necessary to be examined is a major methodological point with Propp as with Dundes after him. The earlier work declared that a limited sampling, one hundred folktales from the Afanas'ev collection, was theoretically justified (Propp 1968, p. 24). Neither, Dundes insisted, was it necessary for him to analyze "every single version" of a tale, or group of tales, to arrive at valid conclusions (Dundes 1964, p. 11). Propp, it is most important to remember, wanted to analyze the folktale with the precision and certitude of the plant pathologist (1968, p. xxv). After explaining what morphology means to the study of plants, Propp asks why we don't have a morphology of the folktale. "Scarcely anyone has thought about the possibility of such a concept" (1968, p. xxv). But is the folktale like a plant? Are its components as fixed in their relations to each other and to the whole? Only God can make a tree; are tale tellers so careful in their constructions, so rigid, so lawful, that a morphology based on the model of the botanist's can be validly constructed? This is no facile metaphor in Propp's rhetoric. Among his concluding remarks he compares the means of tale differentiation not only with that of the botanist (again) but with that of the biologist (1968, p. 101). The system of classification must be consistent, uniform, and logical. Fair enough. Propp considered that his system was so powerful that it could also correctly reconstruct the existence of folktales never collected, on the model of astronomers' hypothecation about stars no longer seen:

> Just as we conjecture on the basis of general astronomical law about the existence of those stars which we cannot see, it is also possible to assume the existence of tales which have not been collected. (1968, p. 114)

The assumption here has to be of a stability in the transmission and performance of folktales that not even the Finns ever dreamed of. Levi-Strauss wanted to study all of the known variants of a myth before he could arrive at a conclusion. Dundes attacks this on grounds that a synchronic analysis does not require an examination of all of the variants (1964, p. 46), but if not all (again), then which ones? If the folktale's structure is as stable as that of plants, if its existence can be predicted with astronomical certainty, then a limited sample is enough.

We would feel more confident of Propp's assumption—a very basic one from which so much of his methodology springs—if he had been more meticulous in his analysis of individual tales. But all too often Louis Wagner, the editor of the second edition, has to footnote inaccuracies. Propp notes, for instance, that in a certain tale "a dragon kidnaps the tsar's daughter," which Wagner has to correct: "more accurately, the dragon suddenly kidnaps the tsar's three daughters (1968, p. 31). "The 'uncomely chap' seized the magic coffer," Propp wrote, but Wagner noted that "in the text cited, the fellow does not steal the coffer himself; he has his mother steal it and bring it to him" (1968, p. 31). A surprising number of tales are misnumbered, and Wagner has to correct Propp, as, for example: "this does not occur in tale 142. However, it may be found in tale 145." Or, Propp's reference to a tale is incorrect (#209) and must be properly identified (as #120) (1968, p. 34). Of the first eighty-nine tales cited by Propp in the *Morphology*, fifteen are incorrect or inaccurate in some way or other. That is a disappointing

16.85 percent of the tales referred to erroneously. In the best, established morphological tradition, my tabulation was concluded after eighty-nine examples were counted, as it was assumed that further investigation would only reveal further inaccuracies, probably at the rate of approximately 16 percent.

One of the tales Propp (presumably) did not examine is the matrix of Aarne-Thompson type 425M. It is not primarily a Russian folktale (and so Propp may be excused on that count, since it would not be in the Afanas'ev collection); type 425M is most at home in the Balto-Slavic regions — though that is close enough to pre-1945 Russia to merit looking for it. *Types of the Folktale* summarizes the composite:

> *Bathing Girl's Garments Kept* until promise of marriage. Husband usually serpent or water-being. After reunion; visit home after performing tasks set by husband. Formula for calling on him learned by others, who kill him.

Ms. Egle Zygas, who pointed out this traditional tale to me, is Lithuanian. In the versions known to her, the serpent-husband, the hero of the tale, dies at the end.

One wishes, therefore, that Propp had investigated a larger corpus of material, if not initially then at least subsequent to the intital formulation of his theories. They would then, perhaps, not have been stated with the assurance that they were tantamount to the laws of the biological and physical sciences but as working hypotheses. For the collecting and analyzing processes it is essential to continually reassess one's provisional conclusions in the light of new data: "it is by daily processing one's data, that is, collating and analyzing it, that one learns what more he needs for his corpus" (Samarin 1967, p. 128). Samarin's *Field Linguistics* clearly sets out the essentials of scientific analysis, and though he is writing here about linguistics, the principle applies to folktale analysis as well.

> But even after he has begun morphological analysis, he [the field worker] will have to determine, for example, if the variations of a particular morph are linguistically significant. The most important purpose of checking is to test the validity of analyses. . . . Checking is therefore an important part of field work, but it is one of the dullest parts. (p. 129)

If Propp is right in his assumptions — leaving aside all the inaccuracies about citations of individual tales — then the folktale is an autonomous entity whose form exists independently of the personality of the teller, whose role in re-creation and transmission is reduced to that of an automaton who must inexorably pass along, lawfully, the narrative with no creative participation. No asteroid is free to depart from its orbit, no maple may choose to become a fir. No folklorist that I know of would make such an assertion; as Dundes has himself put it, the folk would have been removed from folklore.

The evidence, within Dundes's own study, is to the contrary. We have noted, in "The Morphology of North American Indian Folktales," that Zuni and Isleto tale tellers often vary their tales as did the collected versions of the Eye-Juggler stories. And Propp rather tantalizingly cites some "transformations" from his material, as when Ivan sets out after a steed but returns with a princess (1968, p. 110). These mutants do not, however, contradict his established morphology but rather should become valuable in the study of transformations: "the storyteller has either changed the exposition or the denouement" (1968, p. 110). The tale, independent and immutably law-abiding, is unchanged. Other functions may alter as to their position within the tale. Yet, for Propp, "these deviations do not alter the deduction concerning the typological unity and morphological kinship of fairy tales. These are only fluctuations and not a new compositional system or new axes. There are certain cases, as well, of direct violations. In isolated tales the violations are rather significant (#164, #248), but a closer examination will reveal these to be humorous tales" (1968, p. 108).

The matter of the inflexibility of the sequence of functions, a conclusion universally accepted by disciples and critics alike, is also curiously presented. Propp insists that, though the "sequence of functions is not always the same as that shown in the total scheme," a "careful examination" shows that this is not a new, but "an inverted [obraščěnnyj] scheme" (1968, p. 107). What is the difference, then? If departures from the established order of tales are merely to be called inverted schemes and still counted as belonging to the original structure, we may feel that our good will is being tested. When is a departure from the established order not a new sequence? What is the margin between "new" and "inverted"? Propp does not say.

We see, then, that a number of questions should have been asked of the *Morphology* before it became enthroned in our most honored shrines. The serious philosophical and methodological assumptions, which are at least open to dispute, were never challenged, perhaps because the professional folklore community so eagerly welcomed the conclusions of structural analysis. And, as has been cited, we have also taken, unquestioningly, the expedient of assuming the "existence" of portions of a narrative even though they do not occur in our texts; the assumptions of this practice—that the tale is a permanent, unalterable entity, the ultimate superorganic form—have not been challenged explicitly, though superorganicism has been denounced by no less an authority than Dundes.

Nevertheless, despite these and other, minor, difficulties with the system, Vladimir Propp has made one of the most important contributions to our understanding of the ways in which narratives—not only Russian folktales—function, the way their components relate to each other and to the whole narrative. Though Propp's literary extenders and critics usually choose to overlook his working with only a certain kind of narrative, one relatively uncomplicated and possesing its own set of peculiarities, they almost always proceed along the basic methodological lines he established. His most serious errors are theirs also, and no one after him has established an alternative to his system. And it may well be, as in Brémond's snide phrasing, that Propp succeeds in spite of himself.

CHAPTER 7

The Structures of Narrative:
The Narreme

No will be surprised to read that structural analyses can be made of several aspects of narrative: phonemic, syntactic, thematic, functional, episodic, and so forth. In this chapter I want to discuss two of the variations that are posible when the same aspect of narrative is under scrutiny—large, salient features which folklorists have termed "motifs," and analogous constituents that Eugene Dorfman calls "narremes." Of course other analyses of similar or even identical narrative units may produce even other results, from which other and in some instances contradictory conclusions may be drawn. The limited sample of analytic systems presented here does not aim at exhaustiveness but rather, hueristically, at presenting a sampling of what has been done, while implicitly acknowledging further possibilities.

The victim of this dissection is the twelfth-century (ca. 1175) romance of Chrétien de Troyes, *Yvain*. W. Wistar Comfort complained (in 1914) that few people other than students of medieval literature read the narratives of Chrétien (p. viii), and even though that situation has somewhat changed since, one would be hard-pressed to claim a runaway popularity for his romances. It is the plot, rather than Chrétien's discursive features, that interests us here; Comfort found in the French poet's stories "monotony, lack of proportion, vain repetition, insufficient motivation, wearisome subtleties" which were among his "most salient defects" (1914, p. viii). Why did Comfort spend such a large portion of his life translating Chrétien's works?) The succeeding seventy years have seen an almost complete denunciation and reversal of that position; but Chrétien de Troyes is studied here not because he has now been reclaimed to a position of respectability but because his narratives, especially *Yvain*, offer excellent opportunities for structural analysis. The structure of *Yvain* is intricately and inextricably related to Chrétien's sources.

The Old French romance shares several salient motifs with medieval

Welsh narrative, found in the collection now called the *Mabinogion* (trans. Jones and Jones 1949), and the relationship between them has been the source of considerable scholarly argument. The controversy is one part of the larger galaxy of disagreements between those who hold that Celtic literature and folklore have been the source of much continental medieval poetry and those who maintain that the continental literature that survives today originated there among poets like Chrétien. Analogous motifs in the Welsh *The Lady of the Fountain* argue for a common tradition, but whose? The differences between the Welsh and Old French romances also argue that one was not a redaction of the other, further indicating a mutually inspirational wellspring. Jean Frappier believes that this common source was continental, some *conte d'aventure* now lost (pp. 182–83). According to this theory, this *conte d'aventure* must have contained several elements of "faery lore" from several sources. Gwyn Jones and Thomas Jones, who translated the *Mabinogion*, think — also in the absence of any demonstrable proof — that Chrétien's sources were Welsh, probably folkloric (1949, p. xxix). Comfort could not decide whether these lost sources, which everyone agrees must at one time have existed, were either from some Romance-language narrative or from Celtic folklore (1914, p. x). We have barely gone beyond that summation in the last seven decades.

Unashamedly deriving his analytic method from a linguistic model, Professor Dorfman uses as his basic components a constituent of his own devising, the *narreme* (1969). A narrative is "a progressive chain or string of incidents, organized to tell a story" (1969, p. 5). Following Propp (although he doesn't say so), Dorfman conceives of stories as linear, each incident or event following necessarily from that preceding and mandating a succeeding unit. In this respect his system corresponds with that of Barthes, though Dorfman's major distinctions are between core (or central) incidents and marginals while Barthes's taxonomy groups together "Distributional" and "Integrational" units. The latter, we may remember, are also connected by a chain of logic, but their meaning is derived at a "higher" level — other than episode. Integrational units relate to description, to characterization, to philosophizing. Dorfman does not deal with such elements as they appear on the surface of narratives: his concern is with what he terms "substructures." An event, in his definition, is "anything that happens, an incident of some kind, particularly if some importance is attached to its occurrence" (1969, p. 5). This is not as precise as one would wish: is Chaucer's description of Alisoun (in *The Miller's Tale*) an incident? Nothing "happens" during these twenty lines or so, but they establish her character, and that becomes a predictor of her behavior in the tale. The core incident, for Dorfman, cannot be eliminated from the episodic inventory of the story without interrupting its continuity (1969, p. 6). Those incidents are marginal if their deletion from the inventory of narrative episodes would not "affect the basic story line" (1969, p. 7).

The chain of core incidents within the structure of the narrative are called, by virtue of their centrality, *narremes*. And a narreme is demonstrated by its "organic" dependence — logically established — on the preceding narreme and its causality upon the succeeding one. Initial and terminal narremes are, for obvious reasons, exempt.

Dorfman's primary interest is in the medieval Romance epic, as his title indicates, primarily the *Chanson de Roland* and *Cantar de Mio Cid*; the Arthurian romances (of Chrétien de Troyes) and a few *chansons de geste* are analyzed primarily to support his main thesis concerning those more famous and more important works. Having established the narremic chain in those two Romance epics, Dorfman investigates the substructure of *Yvain* as follows (1969, p. 68):

I Expansion: Prologue
   a/ Insult, the remarks and blows against Calogrenant.
   b/ Quest, Yvain, Calogrenant's champion, seeks revenge.
   c/ Test, the victory over Escalados the Red.
   d/ Initial Reward, the love and hand of Laudine in marriage.
II Autonomous Core System: Main Plot
   1/ Lover's quarrel, between Yvain and Laudine.
   2/ Insult, the doubt of one, and the forgetfulness of the other.
   3/ Acts of Prowess, the deeds in defence of the helpless.
   4/ Reward, the reunion with the lover, Laudine.

Yvain may thus be seen an analogous — so far as its narremic chain is concerned — with other Arthurian romances of Chrétien. All begin with quarrels within the family, either between lovers (as in *Yvain*, the *Lancelot, Cligés*, etc.) or within the family (as in the *Roland*). An insult or some villainy (to borrow Propp's word) follows which is either punished, or some act of prowess achieves a desired result.

Now, while *Yvain*'s relation to folklore is commonly acknowledged, the correspondence of the entire economy of the plot to a known tale-type has not been explored. But it does appear to be similar, in its episodes, to the type listed in *Types of the Folktale* as "The Man on a Quest for His Lost Wife" (A-T 400). The folklore composite lists six major elements in the type: the hero (on a quest or hunt, or other journey away from home); the enchanted princess; the hero's visit home; the loss of the wife; the search for her; and the recovery.

Type 400 is part of a complex of several closely related tales, most famously the "Swan-Maiden" (the motif D 361.1 occurs in several tales), "Cupid and Psyche" (type 425A), and (type 313) "The Girl as Helper in the Hero's Flight." Stith Thompson groups them loosely under the rubric, "Lovers and Married Couples: [subgroup] A. Supernatural Wife" (*The Folktale* 1977, pp. 87 ff.). Of this complex he remarks:

> Occasionally we are merely told that a prince is on a hunt and encounters the supernatural woman. A somewhat more complicated introduction tells of the hero's voyage in a self-moving boat to a foreign castle, where he finds the heroine. . . . In any case, the hero marries the supernatural woman and lives happily with her. On one occasion he wishes to go home on a visit. She consents, and gives him a magic object, usually a wishing ring, or else the power to make three wishes come true. But she warns him in the strongest terms against breaking certain prohibitions. . . . When he goes home he tells of his adventures and is induced to boast of his wife. . . . Sometimes it is another one of the prohibitions which he breaks, but in any event she does come, takes the ring, and disappears, giving him a pair of iron shoes which he must wear out before he can find her again. . . . In whatever way the wife is lost, the narrative now proceeds with his adventures while he seeks for and eventually recovers her. . . . With the help of the north wind and by means of his magic objects he reaches the castle and finds his wife. Sometimes she is about to be married to another man. A ring hidden in a cake, or some other device brings about recognition, and the couple are reunited. (1977, pp. 91–92)

This overview describes *Yvain* in outline, but not always in the particulars. Yvain is not really on a "hunt," but that is a minor variation. The important point, pace Propp, is that he get to this other, mysterious, alien land. And that land is magical, as the wondrous fountain indicates and as crossing a stream to get there confirms. Another minor variation: the folktale taboo is different. Often the hero is prohibited from speaking of his mistress's beauty (as in Lanval in the *Lay* of Marie de France), but in oral tradition this trait varies widely. The acts of prowess required to regain the wife's/mistress's good will differ greatly, and this is more important. On the one hand, these acts fill the same specific slot in the narrative. The folktale hero meets people who rule over animals and fish; he gets advice from an eagle, then from the sun and the moon, and finally the wind shows him the way home; he meets an old woman who sends him to her sister who sends him, in turn, to an older woman still, who gives him the necessary information to reach home. His tasks may involve climbing a slippery mountain, or obtaining magic objects from their quarreling owners. One can easily imagine these folktale details being replaced by the fight with the giant, the rescue of the lion from a serpent's clutches, and Yvain's other adventures. Yet, Thompson observes that, as loosely organized as this tale is, details of the quest are remarkably consistent, and they enable the researcher to identify it as belonging to the type (1977, p. 92).

I have myself examined about a dozen of the modern reflexes of type 400, and none of them include the episode at the fountain or anything like the acts of prowess which Yvain must perform. Though this tale has been collected in great numbers in nearly every cultural region of the world, though it appears to have great antiquity, any claim that is is Chrétien's source cannot at this time, with the meager evidence in hand, be proven. The Aarne-Thompson composite is too close for one to think that *Yvain* and type 400 are unrelated, but until closer analogues can be found, in the field, the case remains open. The tale was available to Chrétien; Marie de France used some version of it as the bases of *Lanval* and *Graelent*, but that demonstrates only that its use for *Yvain* is possible.

In reduced form, then, Dorfman's narremic chain and the tale-type composite are more than roughly analogous, as shown in table 7.1. But the differences only seem trivial; they are surface manifestations of more profound discrepancies in the way the structure of this narrative is conceived. Dorfman believes the core of the story begins with the lovers' quarrel between Yvain and Laudine; the tale-type model interpretation begins the basic story when Yvain goes in search of the fountain, its protector, and the unknown land beyond: when he searches, in short, for adventure. Probably the major difficulty with the folktale

Table 7.1. Structural Analysis of Yvain

Narremic Chain	Tale-Type
Insult — against calogrenant	
Quest — Yvain seeks "revenge"	Prince on hunt (N 771)
Test — victory over Escalados	
Initial reward — marriage to Laudine	Marriage to enchanted girl (D 5)
Lovers' quarrel	
Insult: her doubt, his forgetfullness	Hero's visit home (taboo: D 1972)
	Loss of wife (C 932)
Acts of prowess	Search for lost wife (H 1385.3)
Reward: reunion	Recovery of wife (N 681)

analogue assumption and analysis is that *Yvain* can be described by the composite only but not by any of the tales examined so far. But Dorfman's reading has problems too. Does Yvain really seek "revenge" for the verbal insults inflicted on Calogrenant, or does the latter's story of exotic adventure in itself incite him to begin his own quest? (Do Arthur's knights require specific stimuli to move them to action in most of the romances?) Does Yvain really "quarrel" with Laudine? When Arthur and his court visit Yvain in his new surroundings, Gawain reminds him of his duty to remain proficient in arms, and not to deteriorate in uxorious bliss and complacency.

A folktale analogue interpretation would hold that Yvain's departure is a given of the narrative which Chrétien would have to deal with; that he makes Laudine somewhat dubious about the enterprise (of course she is unhappy at the prospect of losing her bridegroom of only a few days) is a further indication of Chrétien's sensitivity to human responses. Is Laudine's doubtfulness really an insult, to be typed with the exchange between Roland and Ganelon, or merely the insecure expression of a bride who hears from her groom that he wants to leave her in order to keep in shape? Lunete has already illuminated her mistress's insecurity in her argument that Yvain be accepted as lord of the realm; that insecurity, as in Chaucer's Criseyde, is a given of the story. And, why are the quarrel and the insult separate narremes? In Chrétien's narrative, if that is what the exchange between this couple is, quarrel and insult are simultaneous. One does lead with inevitable logic to the other.

The most important divergence of interpretations lies in an understanding of the total economy of this story. Dorfman believes — as has already been pointed out — that the core story begins with the lovers' quarrel. This seems to me too strenuous an effort to make *Yvain* conform to his established narremic pattern; by Dorfman's own definition, the hero's quest would be an antecedent narreme since it leads with organic logic to his discovery of and marriage to Laudine. The initial narreme, it seems to me, is Yvain's quest. The folktale analogue does not determine this evaluation — it must be stressed — but heuristically suggests the narrative's trajectory. Reason and sensitivity to the text must assume dominance at that stage.

Yvain does not seem to be a tale of lovers reunited after a quarrel but of a couple reunited after the man has matured, reestablished certain basic priorities, and demonstrated himself worthy of his wife's love. Dorfman has tried hard to make of Yvain's leaving a quarrel:

> The lover's quarrel results from the wife's admonition to return by a certain date. This is an incipient insult, expressing doubt in the strength of his love, possibly furnishing the motivation for his "forgetfulness." In overstaying his leave, Yvain offered his wife a more serious insult; she in turn compounded the first by driving him away altogether. (1969, p. 68)

The text does not seem to support such an interpretation. Yvain is moved to leave his bride by the arguments of his old and dear friend, Gawain:

> "What? will you be one of those," said my lord Gawain to him, "who degenerated after marriage? . . . Surely you too would have cause to regret her love if you grew soft, for a woman quickly withdraws her love, and rightly so, and despises him who degenerates in any way when he has become lord of the realm. Now ought your fame to be increased! . . . Inaction produces indifference. But, really, you must come, for I shall be in your company. . . . Don't misunderstand my words, my friend; if I had such a fair mistress as you have, I call God and His saints to witness, I should leave her most reluctantly; indeed, I should doubtless be infatuated." (Comfort 1914 rpt. 1975, pp. 212–13)

Yvain is quite timid about suggesting the idea to Laudine after he has accepted Gawain's logic. The "standard" interpretation of *Yvain* as a narrative balancing the chivalric ideals of *Frauendienst* and *Herrendienst* (or more precisely the maintenance of martial skills) seems reasonable. Yvain goes with Gawain to maintain those skills, and no quarrel develops:

> Then my lord Yvain at once asks her for permission to escort the king and to attend at tournaments, that no one may reproach his indolence. And she replies: "I grant you leave until a certain date; but be sure that my love will change to hate if you stay beyond the term that I shall fix." (Comfort, p. 213)

If Laudine doubts Yvain's love—despite her insistence that "if you have any regard for me, remember to come back again at the latest a year from the present date" (p. 213)—it does not seem to appear in these lines. The folktale similarity is almost irrelevant here; it may explain why Chrétien has Yvain return to Britain at all, but the author of this romance provides the motivation, the explanation, the justification. Yvain's motives are made clear; if Laudine imposes a taboo on him (to return within the year on pain of losing her love), Chrétien does not say that she is angry or doubtful of his affection. As copiously articulate on important points as he is in other instances, if Chrétien meant that, then one would expect him to say so.

Comort — in words that no doubt reverberate ceaselessly in the vasty halls of infamy of every Romance language department in the West — found Chrétien unconsciously prolix, somewhat indelicate, yet in comparison with other authors of his time, Chrétien's sentence must be "light"; more seriously (to us, not to Comfort), he lacked a "sense of proportion" and was careless in "the proper motivation of many episodes," for which no apology could be tendered. Comfort was especially discomfited because Chrétien was acquainted with some "first-class Latin poetry" and should have known better (p. xi). This idea, that even medieval poetry should conform to contemporary standards — in Comfort's case, the nineteenth-century psychological novel — is implicitly conceded by Jean Frappier's defense of what he calls Chrétien's "one serious improbability in his characterization," Yvain's departure with Gawain shortly after his marriage and his subsequent forgetfulness (Loomis 1959, p. 184). Is it really credible, Frappier wonders, that a devoted husband would leave his bride after a week or two of connubial bliss to stay away for a year and then forget the prescribed date for his return?

The situation is credible if Yvain is a folktale hero dressed in the sophisticated garb of a twelfth-century French court. Frappier thought that the lost *conte d'aventure* upon which *Yvain* is based contained "faery lore" from several sources, that its theme of the marvelous fountain and its defender had "traces of sympathetic magic and of sacred marriages" which had been noted among many peoples; other folklore elements, he noted, were the forest of Broceliande, the monstrous herdsman, the very love of the hero for a former "fountain fay." The motif of the grateful lion "undoubtedly" derived through a series of stages, from the "famous anecdote of Androcles" (Loomis 1959, p. 183). In such an admittedly "faery" world one should not expect to find convincing motivation. One might further add to Frappier's list the magic ring that renders Yvain invisible and the one that imparts invulnerability, the suggestions that Laudine's castle is in some way enchanted, the giants Yvain must overcome during his quest to be reunited with his wife (in addition to the monstrous herdsman near the tale's beginning), the sensitive and loyal lion whose commitments and sense of obligation one would only find in the noblest human conscience. If *Yvain* is to be treated as a psychologically believable narrative, what are we to make of the frequent, extraordinary coincidences (Yvain seems to run across Lunete at the most opportune moments), the failure of Gawain and Yvain to recognize each other in their combat though they have been close friends of long standing, and the uncanny ability of Laudine's maidservants to locate Yvain when they come to reclaim their mistress's ring? This list could, of course, be extended further.

In "faery lore," in a folktale, in a magical world, all of the above are possible and are to be accepted on the terms of the imaginative world from which they originate. I have suggested that *Yvain's* world is ultimately that of the folktale, a structural hypothesis supported by the narrative's atmosphere as well as the quality of its episodes. In this respect I am not in conflict with Dorfman, whose narremic substructure could certainly accommodate a folktale. We do disagree, however, on the tale's meaning, and that is in large measure determined by how it is decomposed structurally. In the final analysis, I cannot say with demonstrable certitude that one structuring scheme is correct and the other wrong; I have, in this chapter, tried to demonstrate that a structural breakdown of *Yvain* along lines suggested by "The Man on a Quest for His Lost Wife" is more compatible with evidence that is nonstrutural — the historical as well as the conventionally critical.

CHAPTER 8

ImPropper Usages

PROPP WAS HIMSELF AWARE THAT the system of morphological analysis he devised could be used to describe other kinds of narratives, specifically "certain novels of chivalry" (1968, p. 100). Presumably he was referring to the medieval romances; those of medieval England and Western Europe have been successfully analyzed with his system (Rosenberg 1986). To decompose other narratives meaningfully, some modification of the *Morphology* may be necessary, but it is a tribute to the power of Propp's method that this is even possible. Still, when analyzing narratives other than authentic folktales with his folktale morphology, one should be careful of the implications of the methodology and its conclusions. Structural analysis performed without a regard for historical and cultural considerations can lead to bizarre conclusions.

Beowulf has been analyzed using Propp's morphology, and perhaps this decomposition was inevitable. The researcher believes that our oldest English epic is a folktale, or at least something indistinguishable from it. We know that this poem was transmitted orally for two centuries or more and that it is closely related to the Aarne-Thompson paradigm for type 301. If *Beowulf* is a folktale, does that precisely describe the epic's life history?

The first important folktale study of *Beowulf* was that of Friedrich Panzer (1910), whose working assumptions seem to many medievalists somewhat paradoxical: the oral folktale can only exist in manuscript form from the early Middle Ages. Therefore, Panzer studied the modern oral reflexes of "The Bear's Son" tale-type, reconstructing the medieval model on the assumption that their form had remained stable for over ten centuries. As already discussed, this assumption makes the comparative method of folktale study possible. The very existence of the tale-type index is based on the assumption that the tale, almost independent of its teller, is a discrete, coherent, relatively consistent entity. That is not always the case, but it is true often enough. "The Bear's Son" appears to be one of the more stable oral narratives. Not only the Finns and Stith Thompson but Propp as well have insisted on the folktale's stability (1968, pp. 23–24), without which morphology would not be possible.

Panzer assumed that such oral tales must have been in circulation before *Beowulf* was written down. Yet *Beowulf* is very old even in terms of many Märchen (folktales). It is possible that the epic came first and that the folktales are reflexes of that.

If some version of "The Bear's Son" — or several versions which the *scop* may have heard — provided the origin of the Anglo-Saxon epic, then Unferth's role is an interesting one. Specifically, there is no such taunter or tester or court gadfly in the reconstructed tale-type, because no such actant is to be found in the tales. It is hard to believe, therefore, that such a character was ever an integral part of any sizable number of versions of type 301 since he would have had to be deleted from all of the collected versions. It seems much more reasonable that Unferth was never a part of the original folktale but was rather an addition by the *Beowulf scop* (or *scops*) when the *Märchen* was transformed into an epic. The Thompson paradigm is explicit on this point — no Unferth actant appears.

Nor do we find such a character when we examine the medieval literary analogues. The best known and most commonly cited of these stories, the *Grettis saga*, a life of the most notorious of Icelandic outlaws, Grettir the Strong, actually embodies several *Beowulf*-like episodes. In the most likely, the Sandhaugar episode, Grettir wrestles with a troll he meets in a deserted house in the woods, works off her arm, and then follows her as she disappears behind a waterfall. Steinn, a priest, has been enlisted to hold a rope for the hero while he descends into the lower world. In those depths Grettir overcomes a giant he finds squatting beside a fire, but when he shakes the rope (a prearranged signal to Steinn on the surface), there is no response; the priest, assuming Grettir slain, had returned to the house. Grettir has therefore to climb up the rope himself and, back on the surface, seeks out his erstwhile friend to rebuke him.

The *Grettis saga*, like nearly all of the modern folktale analogues, does not have an Unferth actant. Grimm #91 does have a donor figure, but one who bears no resemblance to the Old English challenger. The other Grimm analogue has no such actant. And the Grimms never concealed their rewriting of collected materials to make them more palatable; is the donor one of these casualties? There is no such actant in the fourteenth-century *Saga of Rolf Kraki*; in fact, as R. W. Chambers has pointed out, as we search further into Scandinavian antiquity, closer to the time of the composition of *Beowulf*, the figure of Unferth or of his counterparts disappears (1959, pp. 57–61). The importance of this observation is twofold: it suggests that the *Beowulf enfance* material, that portion of the narrative relating the adventures of the hero as a young man, which is present in most of the folktales and in the literary analogues, has been displaced by the *Beowulf* poet to what is now called the "Unferth digression" (Rosenberg, 1975a). But, more important for the present discussion of methodology, this displacement indicates that, for whatever purpose, Unferth and his *flyting* with Beowulf were inserted by the court poet, who was possibly literate, and apparently was not in any of the poet's folktale sources. If, as has been argued, Unferth is morphology's donor, we have the interesting and instructive phenomenon of a *scop* adding an oral folktale element to his narrative (as does a subsequent scribe to the manuscript), an element which is missing from the folktale source. Such a history is possible; it is even possible that Unferth did appear in the oral folk versions, but that the modern analogues (with a rare exception) deleted him. But the latter is not very likely.

The issue of the literacy of *Beowulf*'s creator is controversial; no doubt hundreds of *scops* sang this heroic song, but only a very few conspired to write it down. The latter were certainly literate, but how skilled were any or all of the former? If the poet of the form of the *Beowulf* known to us was literate, we have the unusual occurrence of an oral narrative element being added by a literate to his composition. If that poet was not literate — as the oral-fomulaic theorists suppose — there is still the interesting sign that a narrative, usually thought of as popular among the peasantry, has been integrated into the narratives of the ruling classes. In my own view, this is not surprising; and the movement of narratives among social strata is thus further demonstrated.

A comparison of the cardinal and integrative narrative units in both the *Beowulf* and versions of type 301 (which are consistent with the paradigm) has other hueristic possibilities. I have noted that Unferth appears to be the epic's addition to the inventory of characters received from oral tradition; but what function does Hrothgar's courtier perform? Why was he added to the epic? Several suggestions have been put forward over the years (for instance, Rosier 1962); and most are at least arguable. But the folktale analogues show us that the Unferth *flyting*, which relates the hero's youthful adventures, is in its natural position in the oral tales. Instead of beginning the story with an account of the strong man's youth — as do the folktales — the epic begins in medias res, but then, in the Unferth analepsis, doubles back to pick up that swimming match which establishes Beowulf's bona fides. The hero of the Geats has only just arrived at Hrothgar's court when he is challenged (Kennedy translation, p. 19):

> Are you the Beowulf that strove with Breca
> In a swimming match in the open sea,
> Both of you wantonly tempting the waves,
> Risking your lives on the lonely deep
> For a silly boast? No man could dissuade you,
> Nor friend nor foe, from the foolhardy venture
> Of ocean-swimming; with outstretched arms
> You clasped the sea-stream, measured her streets,
> With plowing shoulders parted the waves.
> The sea-flood boiled with its wintry surges,
> Seven nights you toiled in the tossing sea;
> His strength was the greater, his swimming the stronger!
> .... Beanstan's son
> Made good his boast to the full against you!

Having so informed the court of Beowulf's arrogance and his performance shortfall, Unferth predicts that a worse fate will befall the guest
when he seeks battle that night with Grendel. The hero replies, with
dignity, that Unferth has gotten his facts skewed, and that after out-
swimming Breca, he killed a savage sea-beast, (perhaps) implying that
the same will happen to Grendel (pp. 19–20):

> Beowulf spoke, the son of Ecgtheow:
> "My good friend Unferth, addled with beer
> Much have you made of the deeds of Breca!
> I count it true that I had more courage,
> More strength in swimming than any other man.
> In our youth we boasted — we were both of us boys —
> We would risk our lives in the raging sea.
> And we made it good! We gripped in our hands
> Naked swords, as we swam in the waves,
> Guarding us well from the whale's assault.
> In the breaking seas he could not outstrip me,
> Nor would I leave him. For five nights long
> Side by side we strove in the waters
> Till racing combers wrenched us apart,
> Freezing squalls, and the falling night,
> And a bitter north wind's icy blast.
> Rough were the waves; the wrath of the sea-fish

Was fiercely roused; but my firm-linked byrny,
The gold-adorned corselet that covered my breast,
Gave firm defense from the clutching foe.
Down to the bottom a savage sea-beast
Fiercely dragged me and held me fast
In a deadly grip; none the less it was granted me
To pierce the monster with point of steel.
Death swept it away with the swing of my sword."

With the sense of justice that only obtains in fiction, Beowulf's version of the swimming match is immediately accepted—and accepted completely—and he and his men are thereupon welcomed warmly by all the court.

Unferth will shortly afterwards give Beowulf a sword—a ceremonial gift—which will, in turn, fail him in the depths of the mere during his struggle with Grendel's mother. If Unferth has made this presentation with the expectation that the sword will fail its wielder, this act is distributional. If the gift establishes character, rather, and no treachery is intended, the giving takes on more of the character of an integrational element. The purpose of Unferth's gift does not seem to be determined by his evocation of the story of the swimming match—unless it is thought that, out of pique because he was bested in the *flyting*, the jealous courtier gives his antagonist a faulty weapon. When it fails Beowulf, so this reasoning must proceed, Unferth will have been vindicated in his initial judgment.

To point out that the Unferth contretemps is primarily a relocated *enfance* does not imply favoritism toward either of the above evaluations. Having shifted the episode of the swimming match from the narrative's beginning (where the folktales would have such an adventure) to its present site, the poet is then free to make whatever further use of it is his wont. The gift of the defective sword is, after all, not directly related to the Breca analepsis.

Why would the *scop* (or *scops*) want to make such a relocation? Perhaps some principle of Germanic epic composition dictated it; perhaps it was felt that Beowulff was already a young man when he landed on Hrothgar's shores, and that it would be distracting to precede the Grendel adventure with yet another one. Placing the swimming match in the context of the verbal duel with Unferth foregounds it somewhat: it is not merely the feat of a young man who has had several such notches in his belt. The dramatic tension of the confrontation with Hrothgar's courtier heightens our awareness of Beowulf's struggles in the North Sea, as it is a contest related within the context of an agon. Analepsis also makes the swimming match, with its almost incidental slaying of savage sea-beasts, an anticipatory unit which looks forward to the hero's successful struggle with the Grendel family — also underwater.

And Unferth forces Beowulf to establish his credentials to Hrothgar and the court. Word of his prowess appears to have been merely distant rumor before his arrival. Unferth's rhetoric implies that the court has barely heard of him, and so it is necessary to inform all of them that this bold stranger has an "unfortunate" history of physical contests. Beowulf's reply sets the record straight. He is accepted, and the action can continue; bring on the monster!

If the idea of such an actant — and of the personality of Unferth — was that of the creators of *Beowulf* in its present form, it was by no means unique. Several narrators have used quite similar devices — have created quite similar personalities — with which to challenge a newly arrived hero. The early Arthurian romances have the surly Sir Kay (Kei), who is rude to several different knights. In conversation with me, Francis Lee Utley remarked that the *Iliad*'s Thersites was a gadfly of the same ilk, as is Humbaba in the *Gilgamesh*, Dinadan in Malory's Arthurian stories, Falstaff in parts one and two of *Henry IV*, perhaps even Pandarus in the *Troilus*. Ulysses encounters some hostitlity at the court of Alkinoos and has to prove himself, as does Tristan at the court of Mark (or Horn in Westnesse).

The Unferth actant is quite serviceable in narratives of the hero's arrival at a distant court. He adds an element of verisimilitude as the jealous resident, who may feel that he is being taken for granted, and may resent the intrusion (in his psychological domain) of this (upstart) stranger. The pathology is not unlike the suspicion that greets new members of a country club. We may not like Unferth, but we can easily (probably too easily) understand his impulses; they are extensions of what we have experienced in our own lives at one time or other. And such an actant serves the additional function of contrasting with the hero, in order to enhance his character and our empathy with him. Unferth exists, in this perspective, to heighten our appreciation of Beowulf; without such an antagonist we might not learn about important events in the hero's earlier life — or we might not be told about them with such vigorous affect.

But this digression has taken me far from the morphological analysis of *Beowulf*, and now it is time to return. "Folktale Morphology and the Structure of *Beowulf*" (Barnes 1970) analyzes the epic using Propp's system and finds that all of the functional elements are present and, equally important, that they appear in the correct order. Although its author disclaims any intention of trying to prove that *Beowulf* is a folktale (p. 432), the poem is nevertheless examined as though it were a *Märchen*. Of particular interest to Professor Barnes is the role of Unferth (1970, pp. 421–24, 433), whose position in the poem seems more important to the critics than to the characters themselves. Unferth's morphological role, the argument goes, is that of donor, which Propp has defined as follows (1968, p. 69):

> Now a new character enters the tale: this personage might be termed the *donor*, or more precisely, the provider. Usually he is encountered accidentally — in the forest, along the roadway, etc. . . . It is from him that the hero (both the seeker hero and the victim hero) obtains some agent (usually magical) which permits the eventual liquidation of misfortune. But before receipt of the magical agent takes place, the hero is subjected to a number of quite diverse actions which, however, all lead to the result that a magical agent comes into his hands.

In this scheme Unferth "fulfills the functions of a *test* administered *in behalf of Hrothgar* and the Danes by Unferth" (Barnes 1970, pp. 422–23). Unferth's role as donor explains why Hrothgar does not chide him for insulting his guest or deflect his hostility and why Hrothgar then accepts Beowulf's offer of aid — subsequent to the revelation of the Breca episode. It follows that the proffering of the sword, Hrunting, should not be viewed with suspicion (as Rosier has proposed, 1962), but is the inevitable consequence of Beowulf's having passed the (verbal) test.

Should *Beowulf* be subjected to this kind of analysis at all? It seems to me that it should at least be attempted, if for no other reason than to see the results. But those results must be evaluated while keeping in mind that, whatever its origins, whatever its structure, whatever its primary mode of transmission, the *Beowulf* that has come down to us on Cotton Vitellius A XV is not a folktale. Some precursor of it may have been created for oral performance; earlier versions had been transmitted (and performed) orally for centuries; but the poem as we have it has been rerun through the mind and aesthetic faculties of a poet steeped in learned, aristocratic, pious traditions. Just because folktales get transcribed does not mean that they cease to be folktales; but the only evidence for the existence of *Beowulf* is on vellum, and while that certainly does not negate a rich and lengthy oral provenance, neither does it support such conjectures about a folktale status.

The clearest and most cogent warning about applying the morphological system of analysis to material other than folktales comes from Propp himself (1968, p. 100):

> The job [of decomposing tales into their constituent units] is complicated, however, by the fact that the uncorrupted tale construction is peculiar only to the peasantry-to a peasantry, moreover, little touched by civilization. All kinds of foreign influences alter and sometimes even corrupt a tale. Complications begin as soon as we leave the boundary of the absolutely authentic tale.

Therefore, we should be wary when we are told that "I have applied Propp's theory to *Beowulf* by testing the poem against the structural model presented in *Morphology of the Folktale.*" And we should proceed with alertness when an author asserts as a premise an

> examination of the poem in terms of a synthetic structural theory which attempts to describe the principles common to *all* folktales — *independent of content similarities* — [and which] offers, if not a less hypothetical means than the comparative method, at least a radically new approach to the question of the "folk-tale element" in *Beowulf.* (Barnes 1970, p. 418)

The argument is made that Hrothgar's geneaology "in the prologue to the poem" is Propp's "Initial Situation" with which folktales begin, and which frequently introduces the villian's victim and his family. Furthermore, we are told, "the members of a family are often enumerated in a manner similar to the *Beowulf*-poet's introduction of Hrothgar's lineage." (Barnes 1970, p. 419). The assumption behind this statement must be that folktales and literature derived from folktales — let me grant that *Beowulf* is one of the latter — develop in the same way. This is not always the case; and genealogies in narratives held to be "historical" hardly change at all, and then only when there is sufficient historical and political justification for such a change (see Goody 1968, p. 33). Even if genealogies are not in the contributing folktale, an epic poet might well add one. In such a case we have (again) the possibility that a literate poet has added a characteristically "oral" element to the manuscript. But we know that folktales and epics (or romances or lays) do not develop in the same ways. The Aarne-Thompson indexes are a tribute to the relative stability of most folktales; the frequent redactions of popular stories in the Middle Ages, the inclination to *amplificatio* as well as *abbreviatio,* and the individual (and occasionally eccentric) forms these narratives assume are convincing trestimony to the quite different development of manuscript traditions. The *Chanson de Roland* probably developed orally (from an actual event and grew to a narrative that hardly resembles that event at all), but *it* is not a folktale, nor did it develop like one.

Finally, we should consider the implied logic of the morphological analysis of *Beowulf.* Propp's system applied to this epic will account for all of the characters, and this leads Barnes to support the traditional view that, as one scholar once said, the folktale is "the germ pure and simple of the Beowulfian legend." Barnes's unstated syllogism (1970, pp. 432–34) may be summarized:

1. Morphology describes all folktales.
2. *Beowulf* is describable by Propp's morphology.
3. Therefore, *Beowulf* is a folktale.

The fallacy is in the undistributed middle term; reversing the order of its proposition reveals an invalid assumption: folktales are not the only narratives described by morphological analysis, as Propp himself noted: "On the other hand the very same structure is exhibited, for example, by certain novels of chivalry. This is a very likely realm which itself may be traced back to the tale" (1968, p. 100). As has been noted, if "certain novels of chivalry" are medieval romances and their reflexes, those works should not be included among the analyzable inventory.

Wrenched from history and its native culture, the narrative is defenseless against the assaults of the structuralist critic. One of Todorov's conclusions in *Grammaire du Décaméron* (1969) is that a disintegration of conventional morality in fourteenth-century Italy is signified. Many of the other findings are brilliant; but before we can accept Todorov's condemnation of Boccaccio's society, we will want to know what to make of Chaucer and his England, since *The Canterbury Tales* share five licentious narratives with the *Decameron*. What of the folktales that were the inspiration of Boccaccio or derived from his stories? Do they too indicate a dissolution of moral values? They are international, and are often found in Bulgaria and Russia, and are usually told for their entertainment value; based on the number of fabliaux popular in France, one would have to make harsh judgments about that society.

Structuralist analysis, then, particularly Barnes's morphological examination of *Beowulf,* is not by itself sufficient: although Barnes cites Propp's admonition about applying morphological analysis to other than "authentic tales," though he admits that *Beowulf* bears "obvious traces" of literary artistry, the poem is nevertheless decomposed as though it were a folktale. That in itself is not necessarily an error; but literary history is ignored to the detriment of the author's argument: because Unferth does not appear in the analogues, he becomes an even more interesting creation of the *Beowulf scops*. How valid is criticism of a literary text which is based on a structural analysis of a folktale, however similar?

We should be alert when Barnes writes that "Unferth's supposed 'treachery' is really irrelevant to his function in the poem" (1970, p. 433), because Unferth as a traitor would be critical to our understanding of his role in the poem—that is, to his aesthetic position and not necessarily to his ethnological ontology. We should also be cautious of the statement that "such an interpretation does . . . provide a satisfactory explanation for Hrothgar's failure to rebuke Unferth" (1970, p. 423). Such an interpretation does explain Hrothgar's silence, but only if the court's social dynamics are seen as a residue of an unassimilated folktale. However, we might well invoke Axel Olrik's "epic law" of "Two to a Scene" (*des Gesetz der scenischen Zweiheit*) which observes that only two characters ever speak in a scene—a tableau, as Olrik has it (in Dundes 1965, pp. 131–41)—and that if others are present they will remain silent until the two have finished and only then take their turns. (Olrik does not guess at the reasons for this—perhaps he felt that it was obvious—but a three-way conversation is, I believe, too intricate for an oral teller to manage, and perhaps too complicated for an aural audience to follow.) Barnes has provided one explanation for Hrothgar's silence; but there are others, and they seem to be at least equally cogent.

Finally decomposing *Beowulf* into three "moves" does not add anything to our knowledge or understanding of the structure that is not apparent upon a first reading. Such an idea had been suggested during the last century: the *Leidertheorie*. Such a decomposition or analysis does not confirm the view of those critics "(*contra* Tolkien)" who find in the poem an "integrally whole, *three*-part structure" (1970, p. 433). Such a structuralist reading implies that *Beowulf*'s three "moves" (or parts, or originally discrete songs) have been stitched together, but it does not now seem likely that the epic developed in that way. Integral wholeness is not demonstrated by this analysis any more than by a poorly told folktale which yokes together two or more tale-types.

And yet, despite the several arguable conclusions in "Folktale Morphology and the Structure of *Beowulf*," there is no doubt that structuralism as a method, and its critics, have made enormous contributions to our understanding and appreciation of literature and its composition; it has been and will continue to be a valuable method of literary (and folkloric) criticism. But, like any theory or methodology, it has to be rigorously implemented. Structural or morphological analyses of centuries-old literature should complement literary history rather than going it alone: certainly this is true when the work in question, though apparently orally derived, has descended to us in manuscript form; and most certainly this is true of *Beowulf*, no matter how much like a folk-tale it may seem to be. Propp himself deferred to literary historians on matters of origin, the connection between everyday life and religion, and the like (1968, pp. 106–7). Finally, one's skepticism is aroused on being told that the conclusion of a structural analysis could not have been possible without morphology. This assertion of exclusivity of approach does no good and lasting service to the substantial benefits Propp's system imparts to the analyst.

PART FOUR

The Oral Formula

AT THIS WRITING, ORALITY AND LITERACY are hot topics in American graduate schools. Academicians now realize that we have for too long taken literacy and its benefits for granted, and we have slighted nonliteracy. We have therefore taken a long, systematic look at the nature of literacy. This is no easy task, for hardly a society exists throughout the world that has not been touched in some influential way by literacy or writing. Pure orality is very hard to come by, and thus to study. And such study has not been easy because nearly all American academics, who are (obviously) literate, have a bias against illiteracy and nonliterates and are predisposed in their research toward literacy and writing. Further, they are inclined to the view that the only important narratives exist in writing or in print, and they are often baffled by the possibility of evaluating narratives that were orally performed and transmitted, particularly when those narratives survive in manuscripts. The irresistible inclination has been to treat such material as though it were literature, composed and performed (read privately by individuals) as in the literature of our day.

For literary scholars and critics, the research that first opened the vistas of the existence of the oral world was by Milman Parry and Albert Lord. Working initially to discover modern analogues to the composition of the Homeric epics, they developed a psycholinguistic theory of bardic performance. Hundreds, perhaps thousands, of scholars since have sought to apply the Parry-Lord theory to other bodies and other specific works of literature. The influence of the Parry-Lord ideas, particularly among medievalists and among scholars of many third-world countries where narratives are performed orally, has been inestimable.

Chapter 9 discusses the work of Parry and Lord and assesses their influence on literary scholarship. Chapter 10, tries to deal with the plight of contemporary scholarship treating texts that were at one time performed aloud. The focus here is almost necessarily on medieval narratives, which survive in writing but which were almost assuredly recited aloud to an audience. The final chapter of this section, 11, confronts one of the crucial lingering questions of putatively oral narrative in literate form, the literate author's inclination and ability to render oral poetry in print. William Faulkner's *The Sound and the Fury*, and not a medieval text, is used this time, since Faulkner's literacy is not a question.

CHAPTER 9

The Impact of Parry and Lord

WHILE ONLY A SMALL COVEN of literary historians might not entirely agree with Father Ong's handsome praise of Milman Parry—his "discovery was revolutionary in literary circles and [had] tremendous repercussions elsewhere in cultural and psychic history" (1982, p. 21)—there can be little quibble about the importance of the Parry-Lord formulaic theory to literary criticism as well as to folklore. Succinctly put, it has been epoch-making. Parry never published a book on his research and subsequent analysis; it remained for the magnum opus of his younger associate, Albert B. Lord, to sum up—in *The Singer of Tales* (1965)—decades of collection, analysis, and evaluation of Yugoslavian, Bulgarian, and Albanian singers of heroic songs. Parry's seminal ideas were that these orally performed Balkan songs—some of them several thousand lines in length—were created spontaneously by traditional singers, the *guslari* (guslars), who judiciously manipulated formulaic verbal constructs, and that the epics of Homer must have been created by the same techniques. Actually, the notion of the formulaic composition of the Homeric epics was already an old one, having first been suggested by J. Kail in an article published in 1889 (also see Ong 1982, p. 20, for other precursors); but it remained for Parry and Lord to field test this idea in the "living laboratory" of the Balkans, much as folklorists would, and to make the first enduring argument on its behalf to the scholarly community.

The original aim of those two Harvard scholars was to learn about the compositional process of what they considered literature, but the methods by which they amassed data were those of folklorists. They recorded and then analyzed performed narratives which they experienced during live performances, in natural habitats, in the field. Working by analogy, they concluded that, since many stylistic traits of the guslars were similar to those of Homer, he must have composed his epic in much the same way as the guslars did theirs.

Parry believed — as have thousands after him — that the Yugoslavian songs, whose narrative and lexico-syntactical constituents were certainly traditional, were composed at the moment of performance; performance was composition. Oral singers used compositional units that were variations of the oral formula, conceived by Parry as "a group of words which is regularly employed under the same metrical conditions to express a given essential idea" (Parry 1930, p. 80). Many of the formulas were found to be memorized, though far more were the products of (lexical and syntactical) creative variations on those memorizations. The theory has had its critics (e.g., Rogers 1966; Finnegan 1977), yet it has also inspired a major revision of our understanding of the process of composition and transmission of much of the world's poetry. In a single stroke (though it is a stroke that may have taken decades to be felt), Parry and Lord changed our focus of interest from the audience in a recital of epic poetry to the performer.

An essay by Lord's colleague Francis P. Magoun, "The Oral formulaic Character of Anglo-Saxon Narrative Poetry" (1955), was the first to apply oral-formulaic theory to a body of material other than Serbo-Croatian (but see Benson's rejoinder, 1966), and he was followed by hundreds of similar adaptations — in Old French, ancient Greek, biblical Hebrew, Middle High German, classical Arabic, among many others. The Haymes bibliography of works relating to the Parry-Lord theory (1973) — listing more than four hundred entries — is somewhat padded, at the urging of Parry's disciples, but balancing this bloat is the great number of its omissions. John Miles Foley's *Oral-Formulaic Research and Scholarship* (1984) includes nearly two thousand items in what Foley describes as more than ninety language areas. More of these materials are to be placed in the University of Missouri library collection for oral studies. On net, then, the amount of academic labor spent on defending, extending, and disputing Parry's given essential ideas has been enormous. And that is merely a quantitative appraisal; Parry's ideas and the fallout from them have been among the most exciting and important of the past half-century, rivaling in significance those of Propp. Perhaps even more important, the Russian did less for the promulgation of structuralist approaches than Parry did for an understanding of the way oral poetry was composed; we speak about "post-structuralist" criticism, but so far there is no such thing as a "post-Parry" approach. There have been only extensions and refinements.

Understandably, much of the writing in this area has been an attempt to demonstrate that various literatures were composed spontaneously, by the techniques described originally by Parry, though relatively little has been offered by way of modifying theory. Perhaps necessarily, nearly all of these demonstrations have been worked upon fixed texts, and not the transcriptions of oral performances. Authentic oral performances are hard to come by; they are not to be found in the scholar's study or the library carrel, a fact which folklorists learn in their first year of graduate school. Nevertheless, it does not seem to have discouraged most literary scholars. In analyzing such fixed texts — the *Chanson de Roland*, the *Nibelungenlied, Beowulf*, etc. — repetitive phrases, or in some cases single words, have been sought as a demonstration that they have been "regularly employed." In most instances the only available text is fixed — no one has yet been able to produce a sound recording of the *Chanson*, for instance. Repetitive phrasing, therefore, is said to be one of the keys to a determination of a narrative's formulicity, and by extension, its orality. The procedure assumes several important links in a logical chain — that repetitiveness signifies oral composition, that written narratives are not formulaic, that there is something quantifiable which we can recognize as an "oral style," etc. — but these assumptions make the entire enterprise controversial. The objections to the Parry-Lord theories have not maimed the essential ideas; rather, dialecticly, they have stimulated scholars to refine their ideas (and Parry's) further, to make it "work," to better describe their narratives.

One of the first applications of the oral-formulaic theory was in *The Art of the American Folk Preacher*. Its author had intended, in part, to dispute much of the Parry-Lord theory of oral composition. Because nearly all of Lord's work had been done in Yugoslavia and neighboring Balkan states, the resultant research was done in a language that few interested American scholars could read and even fewer could analyze. *Folk Preacher* was going to correct that problem by decomposing materials that were immediately available to English-speaking scholars. If the guslars used compositional techniques like those of Homer — thus making him accessible in ways that had not before been possible — then the sermons of the preachers, whose techniques were quite similar, could be analyzed to comment on both. Most folklorists, however, found that the sermons of certain American folk preachers only reinforced the Parry-Lord thesis.

The source for the inspiration and much of the language of the sermons is the New Testament; yet, though the American oral sermon is thus related to literature, it is also folkloric in that much of the New Testament has been modified through centuries of oral, folk transmission. The Bible has been thoroughly learned by the minister, who then preaches it from memory. But he/she has also been exposed to a great deal of nonscriptural lore during his/her life, and while the preacher intellectually recognizes that only the Bible contains the True Word, he/she nevertheless has usually deeply assimilated the unofficial traditions of the apposite culture.

Several psycholinguistic experiments whose conclusions have relevance for several aspects of folklore and oralatures are pertinent here. Sulin and Dooling (1974) found that their subjects stored data in memory according to their global perceptions of that information. Specifically, people were given information about famous and unknown personalities and later asked to recall what they had "learned." When recalling, the subjects tended to elaborate upon passages associated with familiar names; certain details of the lives of famous people were known, and new data was stored in such a way as to conform with what was known. For example, subjects claimed they had learned that their "famous person" was blind — it was Helen Keller; actually, no such data had been presented. In a related experiment, Bransford, Barclay, and Franks (1972) found that their subjects were storing presented sentences based on the content of the statements and the relations presented in them. The subjects were asked to identify control sentences — the content of which had only been implied in the presented passages — and they later thought that these had actually been stated in the original. Again, the evidence suggests that in the data-storing process we file information away in memory very much under the influence of what we already know about the subject — our global perceptions of the way things are or should be — and that in recall there is distortion, so that we are not able to recognize the creative functions of our own memories.

This explains why many oral preachers believe they are preaching from Scripture when their lexicon is closer to popular traditions. For example, when the late Reverend Rubin Lacy was preaching on the appearance of Jesus at the end of the world, he described Him "dressed in raiment / White as driven as the snow" with a "rainbow 'round His shoulder." Revelation 10: 1 reads (in part): "and a rainbow was upon his head." Lacy's primary inspiration was a line from a popular song: "there's a rainbow 'round his shoulder, and a sky of blue above," not even a spiritual one. So, in this most scripturally influenced of traditions, the popular song and the secularized spiritual have made their influence felt. Ostensibly and officially deriving exclusively from the written, learned Word, American folk preaching is in fact heavily influenced and tinted by folkloric oral traditions.

Some of the preachers have also shown how the oral performer is affected by literacy, specifically when preaching a sermon that he or she has written out. Albert Lord thought that literacy and the acceptance of the idea of a fixed text lost the singer to the oral traditional process (1965, p. 137). The "disease" of literacy implied accepting the principle of the "correct" text, and, Lord complained, nearly all of the younger singers had become so infected (p. 137).

In those rare instances in which a preacher has prepared a manuscript, the text is written out as though in prose, but once behind the pulpit during a holy service, oral preachers (of the kind described here) will break away from their own prepared text toward a delivery using their own rhythm and melodies. The following is an excerpt of a sermon (retaining original spelling) written by the Reverend J. H. Lockett of Charlottesville, Virginia:

> Shadrach, Meshach, and Abednego were three fellows from Jerusalem. They were three Hebrew boys whitch had been caught in a crisis away from home. The men of the text can justly be styled as fellows, because they were pardners, and comrades, in every secse of the word.
>
> They were from the same country, held the same religious convictions, and had been appointed to the same position there in Babylon, by the same King for the same purpose. These three men had reached the same conclusion as to what to do about their religious conclusion.

The Reverend Lockett's sermon ("Three Strong Men from Jerusalem") began with these two paragraphs; by the time he had reached the last sentence, he had begun chanting. The division of his utterances into sentences – and of those units into paragraphs – deteriorated. The basic unit of Lockett's performance became the phrase, its length determined by the length of time required to articulate his utterance. However, the structure he intended when he wrote out the sermon remained, in large part, because he always had his notes to remind him of the sequence of events he wished to relate. (In this sermon that sequence was simplified because they followed the chronology of the Old Testament account.) After the narrative had been delivered, Lockett interpreted the moral values to be derived from his story.

Although the original idea of studying the folk sermon was to learn about the compositional technique of the guslars – and by analogous extension, of all oral singers everywhere – the folk sermon differs from other traditional narrative forms in idiosyncratic ways. Sermon formulas are somewhat different from those of Homer, of the guslars, of the central Asian *akyn* (native singers). The Homeric unit, for instance, is metrically rigid and does not allow variation. Anglo-Saxon verse alliterates, and its metrics are more flexible. The Yugoslavian meter is bound neither to formal metrical patterning nor to alliteration. Nevertheless, the methods of composition are similar enough to allow meaningful comparisons. In several ways what is said about the oral (folk) sermon may be tentatively extended to other singers of tales.

Lord explained (1965, pp. 65–66) the compositional process of oral narrative:

> From the point of view of usefulness in composition, the formula means the essential idea. . . . But this is only from the point of view of the singer composing, of the craftsman in lines.
>
> And I am sure that the essential idea of the formula is what is in the mind of the singer, almost as a reflex action in rapid composition, as he makes his song. Hence it could, I believe, be truly stated that the formula not only is stripped of its essential idea in the mind of the composing singer, but also is denied some of the possibilities of aesthetic reference in context.

Psycholinguists long ago demonstrated that people can retain only (about) seven bits of information in a random string (Miller 1967, pp. 12, 25), but several dozen in a sentence. We, like the oral performer, are not limited so much by the amount of information we can process as by the number of symbols we may try to assimilate. An essential compositional device, then, in successful oral performance is for the performer to find ways of organizing his or her material. Repetition of episodes within the narrative, specifically of certain stories or exempla (for the sermon) within the frame of the entire narrative, greatly helps. In repetition, the smaller units, whether sentences or formulas, tend to be grouped in the performer's mind into larger groups, bringing about a patterned string such as the episode, the event: the rider mounts his horse, the warrior is dressed for combat, David sees and is enamored of Bathsheba, the hero and his men arrive on a foreign shore, etc. Literary scholars come to call such sequences "themes" and "type scenes," the former focusing on the passage's formulaic structure, the latter on the subject described (Fry 1968). If the oral performer can retain with reasonable accuracy—enough to be communicative in different narratives—a few themes, his or her job has been made much easier than if trying to manipulate and create anew several hundred formulas.

The tradition-oriented audience brings to each performance a knowledge of narrative tradition, of language (not only lexicon but formal considerations such as ritualized openings, closings, the means of advancing the story, etc.), and, if the performance is live, of aural style.

The audience enjoys the narrative because they know what is coming next and approximately how it will be expressed. Too much has been made of the comfort the audience allegedly derives from hearing familiar material; being able to anticipate the performer allows audience members to participate actively in the performance, to contribute to it (though probably silently), to help in the creative process of what is at the moment being made.

Literary critics used to attribute the simplicity of oral narrative diction to the performer's concern for the audience. This understanding held that, if the language was too complex, or the metaphors too recondite, the listener would lose the thread of the story. While trying to interpret what a particular line (and its image) meant, dozens of following lines would have been recited — and not apprehended. That is why, this theory went, the style of the oral epic was deliberate and repetitive. Now, however, in the wake of the Parry-Lord research, we know that the simplicity of oral syntax comes about because it is easier for the oral performer to recite that way. While there is no evidence that simple active sentences have linguistic priority, they may have some kind of psychological priority. This would be demonstrated if we interpreted complex sentences by first reducing them to their basic propositions in simple ones. But the evidence for this is not at all decisive (Deese 1970, pp. 42–44).

Traditional art — to reinvoke a truism — has no surprise and little suspense, if these qualities are dependent upon the revelation of new information. The listener is satisfied aesthetically because of a sense of the logic and justness of the procedure, the inherent dignity of it, because of the gratifying fulfillment of traditional expectations. Those expectations can be satisfied on the level of the narrative, as when the master returns and casts out the lazy servant who has merely buried his talents. In learned art this can be accomplished, as Wagner did in *Tristan und Isolde*, by the retardation and diversion of the foregrounded melody until the final scene when that melody is presented fully at the moment of the lovers' death. A sermon by the late Reverend C. L. Franklin — to name just one exemplar — has many such retardations, as does *Beowulf*. When Beowulf wants to come ashore, he is first challenged by the coast warden, to whom he must state his purpose. He is brought to the court, but before he can be received he must establish his bona fides with Hrothgar. Before he can gain the confidence of the court and prepare for battle with the monster, he must counter Unferth's charge of physical inadequacy. And so on.

One of the most important leitmotivs of this chapter — of this book — has been the insistence that oral performances will never be adequately understood when represented solely on the printed page, that oral performance is everything that does not get copied down in the transcription of that performance. "You've got to have been there." And yet, in an important way, (nearly) all of us have "been there." (Nearly) everyone remembers hearing, or has heard of, or seen videotapes of the Reverend Martin Luther King, Jr.'s "I Have a Dream" speech. On the morning of August 28, 1963, King preached this memorable sermon, though it was received by the more than 200,000 in the audience as a civil rights "speech" — which it also was. The Reverend King knew how to deliver a speech when he wanted to (he knew the rules of rhetoric and logic and the principles of public speaking), and he knew how to preach. His address to the Fellowship of the Concerned, delivered on November 16, 1961 is a model of a well-reasoned, precisely organized statement on behalf of "Love, Law, and Civil Disobedience," and has been anthologized for these qualities (Hill 1964, pp. 345–56).

And he could preach. At the Washington Monument in late August 1963 the teacher in him was subordinated to the preacher, demonstrating, among many other things (contra Lord), that oral-formulaic performance did not necessitate illiteracy (Rosenberg 1970). The Washington Monument speech called for rousing oratory, not for finely reasoned philosophy. The subject was basically religious, though heavily freighted with patriotic cargoes. Situation and subject called for just such a sermon; the formulas, the repetitive syntax and phrases, were produced by a literate and sophisticated man, whose speech to the Fellowship of the Concerned was appropriate to his audience. And his message showed that he could adjust his style of address according to the needs of the situation, and do it with great effect. His speeches stand up as literature; his oral performances, particularly in the formulaic style of the preacher of spontaneously composed sermons, were deeply moving, as anyone who heard the Washington Monument speech will know. In such artists as the Reverend Martin Luther King, Jr. (and the Reverend Jesse Jackson), the talent to create blends the folkloric and literate modes.

While it may not take any specialized, erudite knowledge to appreciate the talents of King and Jackson, an appreciation of their oral compositional skills is one of the ramifications of the Parry-Lord research. Those scholars might not have been able to teach us how to be moved, but they did show us the skills required of oral performances. And these skills are not trivial. Parry and Lord elevated the stature of the oral, folk performer as no scholar since Child had done—even more than Child, since his "informants" (he did not interview or record them himself) were bearers of a tradition, and not innovators to the degree that the guslars were shown to be. Indirectly, probably unintentionally, Parry and Lord enhanced our knowledge and appreciation of written expressions.

CHAPTER 10

Evaluating the Performed Text

PARRY AND LORD MADE THE DISTINCTION, crucial in their research, between the processes of creation and performance. For the oral singer, creation was performance (Lord 1965, pp. 13 ff.). For the literate poet and his or her fixed-text artwork, these processes are distinct in time as well as in function. The artist thinks, makes notes, writes drafts, edits and reedits, revises, and then submits to the editorial process (probably) of several more revisions. The oral poet composes for performance; the composition comes into being at that moment. If we imagine that the oral singer is like the improvising jazz musician, we will have a clearer notion of the singer's "spontaneity." The singer will have heard many songs sung in his or her native tradition long before beginning a performing career. The singer will have learned his or her tradition's narratives, the melody to which they may be sung, the allowable rhythms, the effective intonations and expressions and gestures, learning to accompany himself or herself on an instrument — in Yugoslavia, the *gusle*.

Barbara Herrnstein Smith rephrases this distinction: the literary artwork, a representation of an inscribed discourse, is constituted by its own text; other narratives are representations of spoken discourse, related to their own texts as a musical score is related to its live performance (Smith 1978, pp. 3–9). Oral-formulaic theorists, analyzing for example *Beowulf*, the *Chanson de Roland*, or the Homeric epics, assume that their poem is the representation of spoken discourse, possibly even the actual record of an oral performance. These distinctions have only recently been understood; for a long time narratives, which are the representations of spoken discourse, have been evaluated as though they were fixed-text products, the representations of inscribed discourses. The results have been uncomfortably anomalous, wrenching these narratives out of their performative contexts, and consequently inducing us to misjudge them.

Even though *Beowulf* is known to us in written form, even though we know very little about the aural performance of narratives in the Middle Ages, and nothing about the recitation of this poem, nevertheless the manuscript has carried with it many of the features of the oral performance-as-text. As an artwork representation it is liminal, no longer alive in the flux of the minstrel's performance but solidified on parchment, yet it was not originally composed to be performed in a fixed state. The degree to which the manuscript accurately reflects the features of live performance is unknown; enough can be deduced, however, from what is known of live performances and what is understood of fixed-text renderings, to outline criteria for an aesthetic of orally derived narrative available to us now only in print. Defining that aesthetic will be the intention of this chapter.

In a literate society we assume that poets and fabulators of prose narratives will compose in writing with written performance (publication) in mind. The oral poet composes at the moment of performance. In a third compositional mode, the poet writes out the text to be used before an audience in a live, oral presentation. Thomas Cooke (1978, p. 65) feels that "all the evidence that we have indicates" that the Old French fabliaux were first written out by hand and later recited to an audience. That recitation could be either from the prepared manuscript or from the minstrel's memory. They were not intended "primarily" for a private reading audience. Albert Baugh, writing about the presentation of the Middle English romances to fourteenth-century audiences, notes that since there was no reading audience, poets and minstrels "wrote with oral presentation in mind, adopting a style, so far as they were capable of it, natural to live presentation" (1967, p. 10). Susan Wittig (1978, p. 15) assumes that nearly all of the poetry of the Middle Ages was "published" by oral delivery: "Chaucer's poems were certainly written for oral presentation," or so "we are told." The Middle English romances, she asserts, "were produced, orally or in writing, for a listening audience" (p. 20).

The "proof" is not irrefutable. Cooke cites the opening line of one of the fabliaux: "now I shall tell you a very courtly tale about a bourgeois wife" (translation his, p. 65). But the opening words, "Call me Ishmael," also imply direct discourse between narrator and audience, as does the opening line of Thomas Berger's *Little Big Man*, "I am a WHITE MAN and never forget it, but I was brought up by the Cheyenne Indians from the age of ten" (1964, p. 25).

Part of the reason Cooke wanted to insist that the jongleurs of medieval France first wrote out the texts of the rhymed narratives they

would later perform before a live audience was his claim that the fabliaux showed no instances "of a meaningful contrast between the voice
of the narrator and the author of the poem." Professor Cooke's intui-
tions about these poems may well be the right ones, but they do not
of themselves constitute demonstrable proof. Little is known about the
authors of these poems to begin with. And then, they abound in irony.
Deciding which code, which "level of meaning," belongs to which persona — or to insist that they all belong to the same "voice" — is an intricate matter demanding many proofs and demonstrations. Cooke provides none.

I, however, feel — though my feelings may not always be firmly based —
that the narratives of the Old French jongleurs were recited aloud. And
further, since many of the "same" stories exist in somewhat different
tellings in various manuscripts, each is likely to have been in the repertoire of different performers (on folk communities, see Lindahl 1987).
If they were recited aloud — and we know texts vary even when relating
the "same" narrative — then individual performances would certainly
vary even more. That is, each jongleur would invest a performance with
his or her own personality and understanding of how that particular
narrative should be enacted:

> they could be recited in a different manner by the same poet on different
> occasions as circumstances changed (such as variations in audience response,
> the amount of wine consumed, or the amount of money expected), and they
> [the narratives] surely must have been told differently by all the individual
> jongleurs who recited them. (1978, pp. 65–66

We see in this interpretation just how deep Parry's influence has been.
Unknown to Cooke are the observations of Russian folklorist P. Rybnikov (in Jason 1977) about one of his informants: "make him repeat
[the tale], he will render much [of it] in different words."

Cooke proceeds, correctly I think: "it is inconceivable that a jongleur would stand up in front of an audience and read these tales in a
monotone or with an expressionless face. Entertainers do not survive
that way" (1978, p. 66). That was Parry's (and Lord's) understanding
exactly. And on the assumption that the situation in medieval France
was analogous in certain particulars — jongleurs sang for their night's
pay, and the more effective the performance the more coin was forth-
coming — what was observed first-hand in Serbia and Croatia may be
extended, implicitly, to the courts of medieval France. "A good jongleur," Cooke concludes, "could have used myriad facial expressions,
variations in the tone, volume, quality of the voice, and even have

gestured and posed as much as he could" (1978, p. 66). The jongleur was, in short, an actor as much as a storyteller, as are all oral performers, especially those whose livelihood depends directly upon their entertainment skills.

These assumptions about the performance of the fabliaux, the romances, and Chaucer's poems are supported by a recent (and innovative) book by Betsy Bowden, *Chaucer Aloud* (1987). Using techniques which fall vaguely under the rubric of "performance analysis," Bowden asked more than thirty Chaucerians to read specified Chaucerian passages aloud (from *The Prioress's Tale, The Pardoner's Tale*, and *The Merchant's Tale*) for a cassette recording, which she later analyzed. Were Chaucer's poems read aloud? This chapter argues that they were, and that moot point is germane to Bowden's findings, one of which is that the results of her subject's readings were at least as varied as are conventional literary criticisms of the textual Chaucer.

Her conclusions provided "audible evidence" that performance of Chaucerian narratives sustains widely divergent interpretations, even by qualified readers — scholars whose specialty is Chaucer. Such findings were to be expected. Why would the interpretations derived from reading aloud be more homogeneous than those derived from reading a printed text? And then there are the further complicating factors of the readers' abilities — they were university professors, after all, not trained actors — and the varied degree to which they could precisely communicate their interpretations. A reader might hold one interpretation but not have the ability to communicate that feeling, that emotion, that evaluation, that nuance, that understanding, with precision.

Bowden's interesting approach, using modern audio equipment to address a critical problem hundreds of years old, does not unify Chaucerian criticism — if that was ever her hope. It does show that, if Chaucer's narrative poems were read aloud, the audience would form as many different interpretations of it as readers do today. Some scholar — perhaps Bowden herself — may one day want to use this technique to evaluate some aspect of the performance of his poems. But for now we are cautioned by Bowden's observation that in one experiment several of her subject listeners agreed fairly uniformly on the interpretion implied by one reading, a reading which the reader himself felt was "the wrong" one.

Professor Cooke would have found support here for some of his beliefs about the performative situation of his Old French narratives, that for example the written texts of the fabliaux were unaffected by their mode of delivery, except in those few instances where the writer —

thinking ahead to live performance—addresses the audience directly. Other observers of oral performances believe that only rarely can a poet shift styles radically; that is, if the poet is used to composing in the style demanded by the exigencies of oral performances, he or she will write that way as well. The exceptions are rare, and they are contemporary—the Reverend Martin Luther King, Jr., and the Reverend Jesse Jackson, for instance. Alternatively, perhaps the jongleurs did not perform within a context of a flourishing oral tradition of poetry that would have been spontaneously composed during performance; if so, that would explain why their narratives appear to have been written. If Cooke is right, then the surviving manuscripts of the fabliaux are working texts, used by the jongleurs as a theatrical script would be used today to rehearse a performance allowing improvisation and a cadenza.

Albert Lord, by contrast, could, because he was there, evaluate the performances of the guslars he recorded. The live performance was primary; Lord could hear the singer's voice, see the gestures and expressions, see and hear how the audience reacted to each performer and each performance; and, using their appreciation or condemnation of each, Lord could arrive at a sound evaluation. From many of those he could construct principles of performative excellence. The text that he and Parry recorded (on wire recorders, not tape) and later transcribed were decidedly secondary; it was a representation, as Smith has it, of spoken discourse. Much was deduced from those texts alone, as we all know, but not evaluations of the performer's excellence. That judgment had to be made by someone who experienced the totality of the performance: sight and sound, not merely words printed on a page. The oral performance is what gets left out of the transcription.

At present, in the absence of the sight and sound of the life of the oral performance, we are left with the fossilized remains, the printed transcription. Understandably, the written/printed text is approached as though the composition has been prepared in writing (as the fabliaux probably were) for a (silent, private) reading audience. *Beowulf,* for example, is usually given high critical marks because of its originality of phrasing and expression. This judgment is based on contemporary standards; *Beowulf* does not seem to have new and innovative diction and phrases, nor to have novel descriptions, unless these were vehicled in traditional ways that would make it possible for an audience, hearing them for the first time, to interpret them almost instantly (Stewart 1976). Witting finds in the Middle English romances a stateliness and dignity which give them a "very real beauty" (1978, pp. 43–44). But the prevailing opinion holds that the simple and unsophisticated tastes of "primitive peoples"—as Sir C. M. Bowra has it—do not allow innovation on any substantial scale; such peoples like to be comforted by the traditionally familiar (in Wittig 1978, p. 44).

How can we say that *Beowulf* is a great poem? If it is the oral record of an authentic live performance, or to put it less controversially, if the poem existed for centuries in a living tradition, then as the Parry-Lord people have pointed out, each performance would have been different, some quite a bit different from others. What we have, then, is the unique record of one performance. Other *scops* would have performed it differently; even the same *scop* who gave us the known version would have performed it differently each time.

Professor Robert Creed for a time experimented with the performance of *Beowulf*, reciting it aloud (to audiences of interested academics) while a guitarist (the modern counterpart of the Anglo-Saxon harp?) accompanied him. This was an important step in understanding the poem as performed art, though that major factor in authentic performances, the traditional audience, was lacking. Creed's interpretation of the poem's metrical scheme has not been universally received, but his personalized rendering does not seem to have ruined the audience's enjoyment. The aesthetic direction was right; but it may have gone as far as possible in an age more than a millennium removed from the moment of the original tradition, to an audience that could never approach the receptive attitudes of the original listeners. One wonders, finally, given the rapid pace of Creed's delivery (as rapid as oral performance is known to proceed), whether a poem so rhetorically polished, so free of the frequent repetitions that mark known authentic oral narratives, could have developed as claimed.

The Middle English metrical romances were recited to live audiences—untitled or aristocratic depending on whether one believes Sands (1966) or Ramsey (1983)—yet were probably composed in writing, in a process analogous to the composition of the jongleurs described by Cooke. Here, as with *Beowulf*, there is disagreement among contemporary critics; the language of the romances is far too repetitive and unimaginative for modern tastes. Wittig states the present situation when she notes that "the stylistic characteristics of the romance have been considered only slightingly at the very best, and they have always suffered in comparison in one way or another to other literary kinds" (1978, p. 11). Laura Hibbard blamed the situation on the audience, newly literate and literarily unsophisticated, for whom the romance writers pieced together their compositions in secular scriptoria (1960). A. C. Gibbs thought the poets were professional commercial writers (1966).

Critics have also been displeased with the genre's stereotyped imagery, conventional rhythmic patterns, redundancy of constituent narrative elements and motifs—the episodes, the distributional and integrational units. For example, the following analysis of *Sir Eglamour of Artois* (taken from the "definitive" *Manual of the Writings in Middle English*) relates several episodes in the narrative but sees no coherent connection between them (1967, pp. 124–25):

> The second part—the adventures of the cast-out Christabelle—is a patchwork' of equally well-worn incidents: the calumniated wife (see Chaucer, *Man of Law's Tale*; *Emare* [87]; *William of Palerne* [Guillaume d' Angleterre] [11], the loss of children (see Eustace legend, above) by robber animals (see *Isumbras, Torrent, Octavian, Valentine and Orson* [103], *Bevis* [6], the griffin as robber beast (*Octavian, Torrent*), the recovery of treasure (*Isumbras*), the recognition (*Torrent*). *Sir Degaré* . . . may have given the hint for the Oedipus-like episode; and a popular theme (Sohrab and Rustum) inspired the combat of father and son.

When this romance is analyzed at though it were a patchwork, it becomes one. The critic's assumption controls his/her perceptions, and the conclusion will comform to those a priori assumptions. But is this the way that minstrels, rather than scholars of medieval literature, construct narratives? To use just one of the fragments from the above patchwork, the "popular theme" of the combat of father and son also occurs in *Sir Degaré*, which, we are told, may have provided "the hint" for the Oedipus-like episode. But what is gained by fragmenting *Sir Eglamour* when one source will account for more than one episode? This is list-making with a vengeance. If the second part of this romance does derive, coherently, from a single narrative, that provenance would certainly be obscured by such an analysis.

More unsettling still is the condemnation of a number of the romances as "in great part artificial composites of elements derived from sophisticated courtly romances" (Severs, ed. *Manual* 1967, p. 147). We know that medieval authors usually did not "sign" their works because they felt that they were perpetuators of a tradition, not innovators of new ones. And this has led contemporary critics to assume a literary tradition in medieval narrative; when that assumed tradition cannot be identified, when we come across a work that has no antecedent (no earlier narrative composed of an analogous set of distributional elements), the work is denigrated as an artificial composite. Curiously, these works without exact antecedents may not be "composites" at all so much as genuinely innovative attempts to create new narratives out of the traditional language and motifs of the old. These "composites," then, would not be inept narrators' failures to construct coherent stories out of some tradition but the first signs of a genuine attempt at originality in the late Middle Ages — and all of the so-called "composites" are late. So fixed have we become with the idea of a tradition — which we assume the poet would necessarily borrow from — that, when no tradition can be found, we are confused about evaluating these "free-floating" narratives. Genuine innovation, and the praise that is owing to such originality, have not been considered. Several of the Middle English romances are denigrated as "composites" in our critical canon because they cannot be placed in a tradition; it seems likely, however, that for that reason they are most deserving of our study and our critical generosity.

Characterization is also so much a part of the contemporary critical canon that we have assumed that is a criterion by which medieval narratives are to be judged. Henry James's often-quoted dictum seems impossible to circumvent: "What is character but the determination of incident? What is incident but the illustration of character?" Yet James's own aesthetic practice did not strictly observe that balance between action and character — the latter having by far the greater weight in his writing — and neither does ours; characterization in fiction has been, for a century, dominent. So embedded in our critical assumptions has the primacy of characterization become that we insist on it everywhere, even in such unlikely places as the Middle English romance which, akin as it so often is to the folktale — that genre which Barthes correctly places at the extremity of doing as opposed to being, action versus description (1982 p. 265) — and when we don't find it in those popular works, we relegate them to second-class status, guilty by generic identity.

In *Generides*, for instance, "the incidents are well-told, although there is no attempt at characterization" (Severs, p. 149). Elsewhere in the same volume *Sir Degaré* has been termed "interesting," yet "its interest is not his character so much as the situation involved in the search for his mother and father" (p. 141).

Nor is there agreement or understanding about such important stylistic phenomena as brevity and amplification. The English author of *Floris and Blaunchflur* is praised for "condensing or omitting details and descriptive matter (e.g. the accounts of the emir's garden, the flowers)" (Severs, p. 146), thus securing "greater unity." But the *Sguyr of*

Lowe Degre "has often been noted for its decorative and pictorial description of armor, birds, plants, diversions — a glamorized view of fifteenth century life" (p. 157). "Pictorial and terse," one critic praised *Eger and Grime*, "the poem has variety and great charm" (p. 152), while the Anglo-French *Ipomedon* "is an elaborate, humorous, leisurely composite of effective and striking elements" (p. 154). But, "the couplet *Lyfe of Ipomedon* . . . cuts down sentiment, introspection, and conversation. . . . the couplet version is admirable for its rapidity and vigor" (p. 155).

Finally, though Parry and Lord have shown how the performer's diction is determined by the exigencies of oral composition, we have not been able to construct an aesthetic appropriate to this discovery. Repetition is denounced in modern writing, and we are not able to acknowledge that medieval authors may not have valued stylistic innovation. An audience in a traditional society expects, appreciates, even demands traditional diction and rhetoric. Still, a modernist bias persists in recent criticism: in *Sir Isumbras*, "characteristic incidents and well-worn phrases link the poem with a great body of folklore, romance, and saint's legends" (p. 123). *Sir Torrent* "abounds in trite phrases, repetitive incidents, trivial details . . . all bespeaking the work of a crude hack-writer" (p. 127). The diction of *The King of Tars*, we are told, "abounds with conventional pietistic expressions. . . . despite pedestrian diction and exaggerated feelings, the early portions are dramatic and pathetic. The last section on the battles is anti-climactic and dull" (p. 131).

This patchwork composite of evaluations does not take into account the derivation of the romances from narratives which had been in oral circulation for many years, their performance at a time when oral performance was the usual transmission mode (the romances themselves were performed aloud to a listening audience, or their reflection of the aesthetics of oral transmission. Oral composition is a less likely possibility since nearly all of the Middle English romances (except the composites) have written antecedents, and it is not likely that any of the manuscripts are written records of authentic oral performances.

It is not reasonable, therefore, to judge the romances as we would recent fiction. Certainly we should not look for elegant phrasing, the kind of well-turned diction that was to be found on the Elizabethan stage. When a medieval aesthetic still governs, we will not find much originality either in style or in plot. We remember both T. S. Eliot's dictum about good authors borrowing and great authors stealing and C. S. Lewis's imaginary interview with Chaucer describing the medieval attitude toward originality: why didn't Chaucer bother to think up his own plots? The Chaucer of Lewis's imagined parable replies, "surely we are not yet reduced to that" (1964, p. 211).

Characterization in narrative was not a feature of the Middle Ages, and though we commonly ascribe psychological insights to Chaucer — in most cases too enthusiastically — he was for his time rare. Roland Barthes correctly characterizes the folktale as a genre of action, of things happening, of the predominance of linked events (1982, p. 265); the romance, the traditional epic, are at the same end of that spectrum. Characterization and its subsumed feature, psychological motivation, are to be found neither in most oral narratives nor in the romances. Are these works inferior because of that? Folktales too have scant descriptions of the inner life of their characters but convey that life nonetheless. Instead of saying that the parents were unhappy to see their son go out into the world, a story will note the external evidences: "the parents wept day and night until their eyes were dimmed and they could no longer see." Considering the state of knowledge of the human psyche during the Middle Ages, little besides the judicious use of proverbs and aphorisms which imparted insight into externally observed human behavior can be expected from medieval authors. Folk narratives today, like many narratives a millennium ago, rely heavily on active events — and repetition — for their effects.

Instead, in evaluating romances and modern oral narratives, a sense of the intricacy and effectiveless of plotting should be examined. In such a regime the characters lose much of their credibility as "real," but realism is also a culturally and historically defined and determined criterion. We have for too long sought realism where none was intended; the semioticians have reminded us that all re-creations are fictions, and that no fiction can be profoundly "real."

In 1938 Ruth Crosby made several observations about the performance and transmission of literature which seem fundamental to us now: "in the Middle Ages the mass of the people obtained their knowledge of literature through hearing others read or recite rather than through reading to themselves." Medieval writers realized this situation and addressed their hearers as well as their readers (Crosby 1936, p. 100). One should press the issue even further: to say that they "realized this condition" implies that the condition — oral delivery — was novel or unusual in some way, and that narrators had to make an adjustment to this unconventional communicative mode, when in fact oral transmission was the prevalent mode, and had been for centuries. If there was any condition to which adjustment was required, it was writing. So with Chaucer's poetry, as with the other narratives of the day; *The*

Canterbury Tales were known to many more people orally than in the silent reading of manuscripts. Why should we think otherwise? Was Chaucer different in this respect from every other poet of his day? The percentage of literate people in the fourteenth century, and the level of literacy (matters which Crosby did not develop) argue for the frequency of oral performance of much of Chaucer's poetry.

Chanting and the vocal recitation of narratives were "the almost inevitable accompaniment of feasting"; stories were also told during nobles' leisure time and while on journeys; and minstrels frequently sang for commoners on the streets of villages and towns (1936, pp. 92–93). Froissart read aloud to small courtly audiences; Petrarch had his works read publicly by others while he was in the audience so that he could share the audience's critical perceptions; and Chaucer's friend, Gower, "seems to imply" that he knows his Ballades will be read aloud (1936, pp. 95–96). In the *Confessio Amantis*, book IV, lines 2794–95, he wrote,

> Or elles that her list comaunde
> To rede and here of Troilus. . . .

In the *Bruce*, book III, lines 435–37, Barbour describes oral/aural transmission within the narrative:

> The king, the quhilis, meryly,
> Red to thaim, that was him by,
> Romanys off worthi ferambrace.

The romances again and again indicate that their creators meant them to be recited: *Athelston* begins with "lystnes, lordyings that ben hende"; and *Le Morte Arthur* opens with the injunction, "lordings that ar leff and dere, / lystenyth and shall you tell." The narrator in *Piers Plowman* laments that, since the introduction of fireplaces in what are now called decentralized rooms, people no longer huddle around the central hearth and tell stories to each other.

More controversially, the illustration from the Corpus Christi manuscript (MS 61) depicts Chaucer "reading" to a courtly audience. "Reciting" to a courtly audience better describes this conventional, highly stylized illustration, since there is no manuscript on the lectern in front of him. This has led one medievalist to remark to me that the illustration supports a theory of memorial recitation. Perhaps so. The stylized, mannered aspects of this illustration demand that we approach generalizations about the reader and his audience with some care. On the other hand, its stylization does not a priori invalidate any observations one might make about modes of verbal transmission in the Middle

Ages; even stylized pictures may have considerable bases in observed behavior. Several members of the audience are shown in a conventionalized garden; a castle is in the background. But, taking the stylization into account, we can nevertheless deduce something of the nature of Chaucer's pictured performance and something of his interaction with his listeners.

Professor Edmunc Reiss has argued (in a paper given to the MLA's Chaucer Division on "Chaucer and Late Medieval 'Hearing and Reading' ") that authors during the late Middle Ages prepared the narratives with both modes of presentation in mind (December 28, 1979, San Francisco). Chaucer's miller cautions his audience (his readers?) that he will tell his tale exactly as it happened, offensive though that may be:

> And therefore, whose list it nat hyeere
> Turne over the leef and chese another tale. . . . (*Canterbury Tales*, Book I, lines 3176–77)

Many scholars take the metaphor of the book literally. But even if this is so, and "turne over the leef" is not a metaphor, about sixty lines earlier the narrator has observed of *The Knight's Tale* that no one among the pilgrims

> . . . he ne seyde it was a noble storie
> And worthy for to drawen to memorie. . . . (I, 3111–12)

Chaucer the pilgrim has oral delivery in mind when he begins to tell his *Tale of Melibee*:

> Therefore, lordynges alle, I yow biseche,
> If that yow thynke I varie as in my speche,
> As thus, though that I telle somwhat moore
> Of proverbes than ye han herd bifoore
> . . . . . .
> And therefore herkneth what that I shal seye
> And let me tellen al my tale I preye. (VII, 953–56, 965–66)

The *Troilus* has it both ways; the narrator wishes well for the story's "litel boke" (V, 1786), but he has earlier declared that "the double sorwe of Troylus To tellen" (I, 1) was his intent.

After Chaucer the narrator has described his fellow pilgrims, he begins a lengthy preamble to the *Tales* which is laced with the verbs to "telle" and to "seye":

Now have I toold you shortly, in a clause,
Th'estaat, th'array, the nombre, and eek the cause
Why that assembled was this compaigny
In Southwerk at this gentil hostelrye
The highte the Tabard, fast by the Belle.
But now is tyme to yow for to telle,
How that we baren us that ilke nyght,
Whan we were in that hostelrie alryght.
And after wol I telle of oure viage
And al the remenaunt of oure pilgrimage.
But first I pray yow, of youre courteisye,
That ye n'arette it nat my vileynye
Thogh that I pleynly speke in this mateere,
To telle yow hir wordes and hir cheere,
Ne thogh I speke hir wordes proprely.
For this ye knowen al so wel as I,
Whoso shal telle a tale after a man,
He moot reherce as ny as evere he kan
Everich a word, if it be in his charge
Al speke he never so rudeliche and large,
Or ellis he moot telle his tale untrewe,
Or feyne thyng, or fynde wordes newe.
He may nat spare, althogh he were his brother;
He moot as wel seye o word an another.
Christ spak hymself ful brode in hooly writ,
And wel ye woot no vileynye is it. . . . (I, 715–40)

If Chaucer's poetry was recited aloud, our assumptions about *The Canterbury Tales* as fixed texts are called into question. Were they, in Chaucer's time, on-stage guidelines for transactional reading between speaker and audience? It doesn't matter whether the reciter was Chaucer himself or someone else. The question must be asked despite Chaucer's "Wordes Unto Adam" to be true to the poet's intent and word. If writing were the only transmission mode for narrative, we would be able to be more definite about the implications of this poem; but since it is questionable whether the text of the *Tales*, when recited aloud before an audience, was fixed, the Adam injunction would seem to apply to one mode only. Did Chaucer feel one way about the fixity of his verse when he had written it for Adam, and another when he was reciting it? We can understand that he would not want his scribe to alter a single letter, while he would have no compunction about a few modest ad libs in a reading. He was, after all, the poems' maker, and as such he reserved the rights to such modifications.

When Chaucerians have theorized about the performance of the master's verse, they inevitably scrutinize the text—the product. This is a natural inclination of scholars habituated to narrative in print. But there is more to performance, as Parry and Lord demonstrated, and as folklorists have long appreciated. Chaucer, or whoever read his poetry aloud, must have interacted with the audience, and this immediate situation would have affected the performance. Chaucer or another reciter addressed responding listeners—perhaps calling out or merely changing facial expression, as our experience with every audience at other times suggests—thus changing the communication medium in ways that book readers usually do not consider.

No doubt Chaucer's precise relationship with his immediate audience varied, even with each performance, as the members and their moods varied, as the setting varied, as the reciter's temperament differed from reading to reading—or recitation to recitation. Nevertheless, several invariables may be inferred: the tastes, status, and attitudes (religious, political, historical, epistemological) of the courtly audiences were likely constants, as was their attitude toward the poet, determined in part by his status vis-à-vis theirs and his performing for their amusement and, if possible, their edification.

Chaucer's status as reader of narrative poetry to a courtly audience was determined long before he stepped up to the rostrum. I assume that some sort of interaction took place—unless his audiences were radically different from all others in all other places at all other times. This interaction—the lack of any would be equally important—would have an impact on the performed text. But the details of that interaction are not known to us. Was there conversation before Chaucer began reading? Did it continue during his recitation and, if so, to what extent and in what key? That is, was their conversation loud (as at a twentieth-century nightclub) or interruptive (many stand-up comics developed their reputations for ad-libbing by having to squelch hecklers); were interruptions made at all, even to ask questions of the reciter? I will conjecture that the poet—Chaucer or anyone—is not likely to have performed to a hushed, attentive audience, such as would attend a concert today (but see Lindahl, 1987, p. 161).

All of the medieval illustrations of recitations to audiences show casual listeners busy with other diversions at the same time that the performer is trying to entertain them. We have all been to concerts of medieval and Renaissance music: we sit without movement or noise (perhaps having to suppress a cough) during the performance by musicians who are accustomed to, who may even demand, rapt attention.

At the appropriate time we applaud; the musicians relax until the applause ends, and will even, prescribed by custom, acknowledge this acclaim. When the audience signals its openness to the concert's resumption, the music may recommence. Medieval and Renaissance painting does not show such a formal, highly structured, framed procedure at musical performances; it does not seem likely that performances of narratives (and lyrics) enjoyed a different status. Several of the Canterbury pilgrims — the Monk, the Wife of Bath, the Squire, Chaucer the pilgrim — are interrupted during their tale-telling; only the Monk's social status merits delicacy at the time, and then the Knight is the person to venture it. Chaucer (the narrator) was not interested in describing the storytelling event exactly as it happened; if such events were frequently punctuated by interruptions, he does reproduce it in his fiction. And for good cause: what would be the effect on his character's narratives if they were continually interrupted? What writer has ever ventured to describe such a situation?

The Corpus Christi illustration, like all other medieval depictions of the storytelling event depicts the audience in various postures, engaging in various social interactions, but hardly any of them are listening to the reader. While no conclusions may be drawn from this with photographic certainty, we should never conclude that Chaucer's entire audience sat before him enthralled. No doubt some did; others may have been distracted from time to time (the Corpus Christi scene is outdoors); others may not have been interested at all. However, since Chaucer was a court poet — and, judging from his reputation among the so-called Scottish Chaucerians, he was respected — the suggestion is that most of his audience did pay attention. If they didn't, there might be little interaction (unless they continually heckled); perhaps his performances were dull, with Chaucer plodding through his text hoping only for its end; or perhaps he would have histrionically pulled out several stops to enliven his performance, as Parry and Lord observed among the guslars in Yugoslavia.

Did Chaucer's actual audience, as the one depicted in the Corpus Christi manuscript does, talk during the reading? And what did they talk about? The story being read to them, or some gossip at court, or the high price of ground wheat? From what we know of similar situations in the late Middle Ages, conversation went on during the reading, and a few in the audience may even have called out comments, possibly expecting the poet's reply. Even more likely is the discussion that might have followed either each tale's recitation or each subdivision in such narratives as *The Knight's Tale, The Squire's Tale,* or *The Canon's*

Yeoman's Tale. During these pauses, we can speculate, Chaucer would have elaborated on some point or other, clarified others, and debated still others with his listeners — for instance, "whose deed was the noblest"; it was a contentious age.

What was the role, then, of interaction in performance? We can only adumbrate, of course, but it has to have been much greater than, say, in a reading in a college auditorium by W. D. Snodgrass or Gary Snyder. The audience felt free to call out, ad libitum. Chaucer would have to have been a flexible enough performer to withstand interruption without flustering. But is that all? Did he ad lib replies to his interactants, or was he too dull-witted for that? And to what extent did he improvise remarks, comments, ripostes? To what extent has Chaucer's voice been blended into that of his characters? For instance, the lines of the franklin (V, 1017-18):

> For th'orisonte hath reft the sonne his lyght, —
> This is as muche to seye as it was nyght.

If Chaucer was writing exclusively for a literate audience, these lines would be those of the ironically self-deprecating Franklin. But if Chaucer, or another performer, were reciting them, as though in an apostrophe, who becomes the speaker? And what then of the Franklin and his self-deprecation?

Who, also, becomes the speaker of the line, "He knew nat Catoun, for his wit was rude: (I, 3227)? A reader getting this line from the printed page is inclined to understand this evaluation as coming from the Miller, though only after some very willing suspensions of disbelief. But how must this line have been recited in the Middle Ages? The Miller did not know Cato, for *his* wit was rude; but not Chaucer's, and not those of his audience.

I have implied at several points that matters of interpretation are often involved if we consider that most of Chaucer's audience heard his poetry and did not acquire it through private, silent reading. Even to suggest that we might read Chaucer in another way is a very controversial matter; and I do not want other points in this book (and in this chapter) to get lost in such a controversy. On the other hand, I do want to suggest, however tentatively, that certain critical assumptions about his poetry might well be reexamined. For instance, if we are told that Chaucer repeats words or entire lines — allegedly those words and lines are keys to remembrance when they appear the second time — as a signal to the audience (the reader?), and these echoic lines are several hundred verses apart — many minutes apart — we should be suspicious.

Did the medieval reader train himself/herself to retain syntactical and
lexical structures for several minutes and then refer to the context and
ideology of the earlier usage?

To begin with, Chaucer's intentions are usually clear enough: Nicholas is "hende," Alisoun had "a likerous ye," John's "wit is rude" and
he must endure his "care"; joly and gay Absolon goes "fetisly," singing
in "a loud quinible," and is "somdeel squaymous / Of farting," "of
speche daungerous." We are really not left in the dark about what the
narrator, and we, think or should think about the Prioress, the Parson,
the Pardoner, or the Clerk. In very recent years the moral stature of the
Knight has been questioned (perhaps he was another butt of Chaucer's
satire, slaughtering as he did in the name of Christianity), but without
pausing to defend his honor, I think that such interpretations are more
in the satiric imaginations of the readers, and do not seem to have been
Chaucer's intent. Nearly all of Chaucer's narratives were traditional
stories (that is, the sequence of distributional elements was traditional).
The audience knew the "basic plots" nearly as well as he and so would
not need subtle echoic forewarnings, certainly not after they had heard
the narrative once. If a sentence or a clause is uttered fifteen minutes
after its twin, there is no assurance that its initial usage and context
would be remembered. With a fixed text in front of the reader, leafing
back to reexamine a particular line in any poem is a simple and frequently performed procedure. An oral audience has no such recourse
to this instant replay. Would they remember the syntax and precise diction of a line recited several minutes earlier? Such a case might be made
for some of the language used to describe the clerk in the *General Prologue* and Nicholas in *The Miller's Tale*. Of the former scholar we learn
that:

> For hym was levere have at his beddes heed
> Twenty bookes, clad in blak or reed,
> Of Aristotle and his philosophie
> Than robes riche, or fithele, or gay sautrie. (I, 293–96)

While of Nicholas we are told that:

> His Almageste and bookes grete and smale
> His astrelabie longynge for his art,
> His augrym stones layen faire apart,
> On shelves couched at his beddes heed. . . . (I, 3208–11)

Chaucer does seem to be playing the character of one clerk off against
that of the other, the one devoted to the love of learning, the other to

the love of worldly things. When we read about the books at the head of Nicholas's bed, we are meant to think of those in the same position near the clerk from Oxford. But the relationship between these two is contrastive. Of Nicholas we also learn that:

> His presse ycovered with a faldyng reed;
> And al above ther lay a gay sautrie. . . . (I, 3212–13)

A contemporary enough device which the New Critics would find to their liking. But are Chaucer's intentions so very opaque here? Is it possible that similar dramatic/narrative contexts have evoked from him similar means of description? He depicts two scholars, one frivolous, one quite serious, yet each has been receiving a formal education. Why not describe this one quality, erudition (though in one instance serious and in the other frivolous), in conventional ways, using codes (the books by the bed's head) which the audience would easily interpret?

If it is to be argued that Chaucer intended his audience to think of the clerk when (nearly 3,000 lines) later he described Nicholas with similar lexical cues, such an association must have been based on the contrastive nature of their personalities. But in other cases this argument is not so easily made; for instance, in the *General Prologue*'s description of the Squire, we are told that "Curteis he was, lowely, and servysable" (I, 99); 151 lines later we read of the Friar that "Curteis he was and lowely of servyse" (I, 250). What is the connection? In the instance of this pair it might be more convincingly argued that Chaucer would expect his reader to remember the former when he read the latter; but are the Squire and the Friar a contrasting pair? What do they have in common; how are they similar enough for Chaucer to set off their differences effectively? Isn't the creative context rather that he is, again, describing a situation, or idea, or trait in conventional codes that his contemporaries will instantly interpret?

Conventional phrases occur often enough: bifil that . . . on a day," "whilom," "lief and deere," etc. It seems unlikely that an aural audience would recall those phrases, uttered as they are several minutes apart (most especially if the audience was only listening casually), and quite unlikely that a silent reader would remember the Clerk when he read of Nicholas's books at his bed's head. How closely did Chaucer's contemporaries listen to and carefully criticize the narratives they heard? When the same linguistic features appear in other fourteenth-century manuscripts, such intentions are never considered. For instance, in the romance, *The Earl of Toulouse*, the following lines appear:

The erl answeryd wyth wordys hende (I, 229)
The marchand seyd wordys hende (I, 955)
He was a fayre man and an hye (I, 994)

Isumbras approximates this last line:

He was bothe fayre man and heghe (I, 616)

The composers of these romances are not privileged; they would never be thought to have the sophistication to play one phrase off against the other for an augmented effect. Yet they appear to be doing what Chaucer has been praised for. In the fourteenth century there were no concordances and no New Criticism.

Psycholinguistic research has not been conducted on the retention of poetic lines within the context of performance and cannot therefore offer precise solutions. One experiment (Sachs 1967) has shown that subjects have good recall of identical sentences after short periods (several seconds to a minute or so), but after that, their retentive capabilities deteriorate. The participants in this experiment were asked to identify a sentence which, compared with an original, was either identical in form, altered in form but with an "identical" meaning, or changed in meaning. Sachs found that identical sentences were usually recognized after both long and short intervals. He also found that, while his subjects were able to differentiate sentences different in form but not in meaning at short intervals (following the presentation of the original, "control" sentence), they were less accurate after the longer intervals.

Chaucer's sentences particularizing the Clerks' books are identical in meaning but not in form; hearing them recited many minutes apart, his audience was not likely to have identified these two sentences as being semantically associated. If the *Canterbury Tales* were closely read, however, by meticulous readers who carefully leafed back though the manuscript when they came to lines (or longer passages) which they recognized, the identification of similar sentences presented on the parchment many leaves apart would have been possible. Is that the way manuscripts were perused in the Middle Ages? By close reading? We cannot know with certainty; Chaucer's contemporaries do not appear to have composed their narratives with the reflective reader in mind (religious writing excepted; and that does not make the kind of demands on the reader that has been discussed above). Did Chaucer compose this way? Was he a century ahead of his time? Perhaps; but then he was composing for an audience that was still used to the old modes of narrative communication. Considering all that a close reading of Chaucer implies—his innovative "New Critical" use of language and an attentive readership whose creative reading was equal to his experimental poetics — we might wish to rethink the relationship between poet and audience in the fourteenth century in Britain.

Literates inevitably think of narrative in terms of fixed print. Subtlety in this mode is of an entirely different sort than in dramatic performances. Allusiveness is also different, and I think that by its nature it would be of less use and potency aloud, particularly in a tradition that fosters repetitiveness. Are memories of narratives and sections of narratives recited long ago really to be cued when we read or hear that "pity renneth soone in gentil herte" (*Canterbury Tales*, IV, 1986)? Our conjectures on the interaction during performance will be somewhat clarified by taking account of the social rules under which this entertainment was played, and those in turn are largely a function of the maker's role vis-à-vis his audience, a situation about which we are not ignorant; the highly structured status roles of fourteenth-century English society help here. This relationship is a major factor in determining the degree of negotiability concerning the types of stories to be told, their length, the teller's tone, etc. Can we assume something, generally, about the interest of Chaucer's audience — certainly broadly eclectic — from the "God's plenty" range of the Canterbury materials?

To entertain the idea that Chaucer's poetry was recited aloud to an aural audience at least as often as it was silently and privately read is very difficult, especially for those scholars who have for all of their adult lives read his words fixed on a printed page. All great authors write, this argument goes, and since Chaucer lived in an age when writing was common enough among his circle, he must have written his narratives knowing that they would be read by his friends, fellow courtiers, and patrons in London. Just as Shakespeare, Milton, Wordsworth, Keats, and Yeats have done. If Chaucer composed his poetry knowing that it would be recited aloud, he probably did not compose with the same mind-set as did Milton or as does Graham Greene. And that idea seems to imply that a great deal of the close reading we have been doing, especially in the United States, is misleading, particularly when it involves those subtleties of language and meaning that only a carefully trained and thoughtful literate audience could grasp. And, of course, even without considerations of oral delivery, we would all agree that a lot of this close reading is wrongheaded. Now, to argue for the oral delivery of Chaucer's poetry suggests that a great deal more of those "subtleties" exist only in the mind of the critic, because we consistently fail to take this performative situation into account. Many people writing today on Chaucer's poetry may, regrettably, be threatened.

But if it can be demonstrated convincingly that Chaucer's poetry, like that of so many of his colleagues, was read aloud, close reading (if we must have that!) is not proscribed; but it must be recast. Oral poets do not lack subtlety and sophistication; theirs is merely of another kind. Learning those other ways involves mental work, of course, and people tend to go with the flow of least resistance. Chaucer as poet whose poems are read aloud is Chaucer still, full of complexity and intricacy and genius; we have not yet fully appreciated those qualities because, as D. W. Robertson has written (about Chaucerian criticism in another context), we still think that our poet was a nineteenth-century novelist.

This chapter has throughout argued negatively: we have no agreed-upon standards; we have no understanding of the mode of presentation or of what that means for the text; we judge the wrong qualities in the fixed texts of the literature that does survive. These criteria need to be stated positively, however, so that they can stand as an evaluative program that can be applied to literature we know to derive from oral performances. The Middle English romances are the most suitable models here, since their oral currency is not seriously denied. The language of such narratives is not polished, it is paltry in metaphor and imagery. To a great extent that is a reflection of their authors, but even in Chaucer we do not find the rhetorical richness that characterizes the work of, say, Elizabethan playwrights. Chaucer is capable of the "high style," as we know, but on the few occasions when he does use such flourishes he does so defensively, having one of the other characters comment negatively on it. Metrical sophistication is usually also lacking: witness the heroic songs of the guslars collected by Parry and Lord; the metrical refinement of the Homeric epics and of *Beowulf* are arguments for their chirographic composition. So too with intricate plotting; whether of *entrelacement* or of contemporary spy novel, this is a mark of written composition, a preparation for an audience that has the reflexive capability to return to passages read earlier, to check up on what has already transpired.

When narratives (or lyrics) are presented aloud, the manuscript which we now take to be canonical would have been at the time considered a working text. It was not sacred, and could be varied at the performer's discretion without the sense of hopelessly "corrupting" the performance. Repetition is common in oralatures, e.g., the Homeric epics and *Beowulf* (to stay with well-tried examples). Not only language but entire episodes are repeated, and often with much the same lexicon and syntax.

Oral narratives are characterized by a fluidity rather than a fixity of plot. Originality as we conceive of it does not exist — it is not valued — as every writer on the subject has noticed, but originality exists (as recorded in *Sir Degaré*) in plot combinations of subsumed, previously discrete narratives. Narrative strands interlock, often end-to-end, rather than interweave. And the plots (the stories) of oralatures are usually well designed and leanly sparse, acquiring that hardness through constant retellings to audiences free to comment on what they consider unacceptable variations.

CHAPTER II

The Literate Rendering of Orality

NEARLY ALL FORMULAIC ANALYSES are of older literatures available to us only in chirographs. This is unavoidable, given the age of such material. But just because poetry is rhetorically formulaic, it does not necessarily follow that such poetry was composed or performed orally. There are no simple tests or criteria to determine the nature of the composition, transmission, and performance of literary works. The evidence is always cumulative and almost always tentative. Even if we were to possess documents referring to the oral performance of a specific text, we could not be certain that the text ever had an independent life in an oral tradition. Suppose that some material should come to light referring to the recitation of *The Fight at Finnsburg* at some court or other; we would still be faced with the problem of deciding whether the manuscript fragment known to us was one of the records of an authentic oral performance or merely an "imitation," written down by some anonymous poet composing in the traditional style of the day.

Faulkner could imitate oral performances superbly (see below); and Benson has shown (1966) that Anglo-Saxon literates also composed in the formulaic mode. Formulicity of style is not sufficient evidence in itself to demonstrate the oral life of a narrative; there must be corroboration, difficult as that may be to acquire. Such supporting evidence may be contained in external documents or may reside in an intimate knowledge of either the culture that generated the poetry in question or the compositional mode of the poet during the performance being examined.

If a text, however densely formulaic, is said to be an oral record of its performance, we will want to know how it came to be transcribed. This is one of the problems in any consideration of *Beowulf*, which is available only in the Cotton Vitellius A xv imanuscript. If that unique version had been taken down from an actual performance, how accurate is that transcription? Albert Lord long ago noted that, when an oral poet dictates verse, the meter is thrown off and the poem's quality suffers accordingly (1965, pp. 126 ff.). If, as sometimes has been suggested, the oral poet — illiterate, as Lord as first insisted — dictated compositions to a scribe, the metrical system also disintegrates. How then did we come by the finely crafted manuscript rendering of this (putatively) oral poem? If the *Odyssey*, for instance, was taken down from a live performance, would its intricate metrical system be as we know it today?

The first application of oral-formulaic theory to an English-speaking tradition was in the American South (Rosenberg 1970). The subjects were "folk" preachers whose sermons were also (like other singers of narrative) composed and transmitted orally. Most folklorists view this work as a demonstration of the existence of Parry-Lord compositional principles in the United States. For the immediate focus of the present book we should note that Milman Parry's original intention had been the elucidation of Homer's creative techniques. To accomplish this, he and Albert Lord became folklorists, recording the songs and interviewing live singers in the singers' native milieus. All of these recorded performances (that I know of) were done for a microphone in the house of an intermediary, and not in concert; but this procedural irregularity has not led potential critics to challenge their findings. The Parry-Lord research methodologies were folkloristic, though their final aims were literary. Much later, Lord and his followers studied folk composition, occasionally for its own sake. So too with Rosenberg (1970 and 1988): while the last sentence of my 1970 book offers the hope that "one day" the analysis of the Reverend Rubin Lacy's preaching will be able to "tell us something important about the composition of *Beowulf*" (p. 120), in fact it has revealed a great deal more about the art of the American folk preacher.

Oral-formulaic studies of literature have usually analyzed works from classical and medieval times, poetry which survives only (and necessarily) in manuscripts. Almost nothing has been written about the oral formula in modern fiction, the chief reason being, no doubt, our knowledge that poetry is no longer composed and performed formulaicly, and would therefore not be elucidated by oral-formulaic analysis. But, if recently created formulaic fixed-text narrative could be found, an analysis of it would be instructive: we would know for certain that writers can compose in the old repetitive style; we could develop a precise methodology for appraising the writer's skill; and we would have the means to examine the claim that the so-called "formulaic style" results only from oral composition. In the case of the Reverend Shegog's sermon in Faulkner's *The Sound and the Fury*, we can evaluate the imaginative writer's ability to imitate the oral style of a genre—the oral, "folk" sermon—on which considerable analysis has already been performed. Much is known about folk sermon style: Faulkner's imitation of it can thus be rigorously evaluated.

The intention of this chapter, consequently, is to evaluate Shegog's sermon as an example of an imitation "oral" sermon within a conventional literary context. The grammar with which such performances—the real ones—must be structured was formulated during the late 1960s and early 1970s when nearly one hundred such sermons were recorded and analyzed in the wake of theories first developed by Milman Parry and Albert Lord. However, the implications of Faulkner's use of oral genres reach beyond the scope of his novel, even of Faulkner studies, as some of the conclusions presented here concern the nature of orally composed narratives.

To comprehend more richly what Faulkner was trying to do in his *The Sound and the Fury* sermon, a description of the authentic oral sermon as it is commonly chanted by many African-American preachers (sometimes called "old-time country preachers") will be essential. Most important to our analysis are diction, syntax, and a few larger architectural elements; content is decidedly secondary. Characteristically, the preacher begins the sermon rather prosaically in the meter and intonation of an ordinary public speaker; more specifically, in the style of the conventional "manuscript" preacher. Martin Joos would probably classify the sermon's opening moments as "formal" in style (1967, p. 38), though it becomes in a very short time "consultative" (1967, pp. 33 ff.). The talented performer, having an acute sense both of dramatic performance and of the dignity of his or her station, addresses the congregation with stateliness. As the sermon develops, the intensity of delivery (as measured by changes in voice timbre, rapidity of delivery, the introduction of chanting and the shortening of uttered lines, etc.) increases, though the curve of this delivery may be modified by local rises and falls. The preacher soon moves from a prose style to a rhythmical delivery during which lines are punctuated into regularized time periods by a distinctly audible sound that resembles a gasp or grunt. Gasp or grunt it may be, for as the preacher feels more and more "in the spirit," he or she must gasp more deeply for the breath that will sustain the enervating ecstasy; and this increased intake of air also serves to hyperoxygenate the preaching, in turn reinforcing his or her religious ecstasy. As preaching style slides into chanting, the preacher again increases the rhythm and intensifies the pitch, usually with a recognizable tonic. At a dramatic climax the preacher will break off suddenly and resume speech in prose, though a dignified prose appropriate to a recitation of the Word of God.

For formulaic analysis, the most important element in the preacher's style is his or her chanting which breaks up the language into rhythmical and (more or less) metrically regular lines. These utterances closely approximate the formulas of which Parry and Lord spoke (Lord 1965), and they occur in oral sermons only when the preacher has broken into the meters of a chant. Actually, many ministers who preach spontaneously (without a manuscript) — those who refer to themselves as "spiritual preachers" — do not chant, probably because their musical abilities are meager, and consequently their speech patterns are more like those of conventional manuscript preachers, closer even to a formalized register of certain conversations than to oral poetry. Faulkner had his St. Louis preacher speak metrically, and it is the chanted sermon which will be described.

The flow of the sermon is regularly broken up, as already noted, by a grunt/gasp which seems to have a physiological as well as an ecclesiastical basis. Preaching of this kind is hard work: the preacher struts back and forth before the congregation, motions and gesticulates as would an actor in a melodrama, and works himself or herself into a near-emotional (i.e., spiritual) frenzy. The preacher loudly gasps for sustaining oxygen; and so conditioned is this gasp, so obviously useful a punctuating device is it, that many preachers who seem not to need the brisk intake of air will still make some audible sound to regularize their speech rhythms.

Not only the preacher but the congregation punctuates the rhythm throughout the performance by joining in almost invariably at the end of each "line." They may shout such exclamations as "yes" and "Yes, Jesus," "that's right," and "you tell it," "come on now," and "pray with me, church." These services are more unified than the word *antiphonal* suggests, implying as that does two discrete entities, preacher and congregation, separate yet responding to each other alternatively. The success of the sermon depends on how well the preacher can induce the congregation to identify with — become one with — the Spirit, and not with the preacher — which makes the relationship not one of leader and chorus but one in which both entities are responding to the Spirit intuitively, spontaneously, rhythmically, ecstatically unified however different their verbal expressions.

The oral sermon, like most orally composed genres, is textually characterized by the frequent repetition of syntax and of diction (Finnegan

1977, p. 90; Ong 1982, p. 22; Lord 1965, pp. 30 ff.). By way of illustration, I have reprinted below a transcription of several lines from a sermon by the Reverend Rubin Lacy, late of Bakersfield, California (recorded on June 6, 1967, at the Union Baptist Church); my transcription numbers each line, usually comprising one "formula," as is the practice with fixed-text poetry:

```
        And God
        Made a year
        With fifty-two weeks in the year
        Mister Hoyle
5       Made a deck of cards
        With fifty-two
        Cards in the deck
        Ain't God all right
        And . . . God
10      Said there's two ways to go
        Heaven
        Or either hell
        Mister Hoyle
        Made a two-spot
15      He called it a deuce
        God from Zion
        And put it in the deck
        And God
        Made the Father
20      Son and the Holy Ghost
        Ain't God all right?
        And Mister Hoyle
        Made a three-spot
        And called it a trey
25      God from Zion. . . .
```

The repetitive — formulaic — quality of this passage is visually obvious; if the lines were to be underlined, as is done by the students of oral literature to designate repeated formulas, with broken underscoring to designate syntactically similar formulas, each of the twenty-five lines in the above excerpt from Lacy's sermon would be so marked.

The preachers themselves recognize that many of their phrases are repeated during their sermons; for them the purpose of verbatim repetitions is to "stall for time," to allow them a moment during which they can think of what to say next; the "stall," being "automatic," requires no thought to utter — or so they would have it. However, most preachers do not like to concede that they repeat themselves and will admit to repetition only (in my experience as an interviewer) when confronted by the tape recorder's irrefutable evidence. The Reverend Elihue Brown (also of Bakersfield) metaphorized his stall formulas as "rests on the highway" where he could stop for a moment and marshall his thoughts for the next leg of the journey. His metaphorical description of this technique shows that he had thought about it. However, not all formulas are stalls; not, for instance, the "God from Zion" and "Ain't God all right?" of Lacy's, above. These may stimulate the congregation (such as the Reverend C. L. Franklin's "I don't think you know what I'm talkin' about"—see Titon 1989); some introduce embedded narratives ("I want to call your attention to the fact that . . ."); and others advance narratives ("every now and then"); and still others introduce dialogue ("I heard Saint Peter/Moses/Jesus/God/Ezekiel, etc., say the other day").

Much of the spiritual preacher's performative language is memorized, as has just been shown. And much of it, probably much more, is repeated though not memorized, because it is re-created anew at the instant of performance. And not only single lines are repeated; many spiritual preachers retain whole passages which they can use at the appropriate time in any given sermon. Usually such passages are neither semantically restricted nor highly contextualized and are therefore usable in any of several sermons. They are the sermon's counterparts of the Parry-Lord themes (Lord *Singer* 1965, pp. 68–98). The following examples were extracted from two sermons of the Reverend Elihue Brown: the first, "God is Mindful of Man," was performed on June 11, 1967; the other, "Thou Shalt Have No Other Gods before Me," was preached eleven months later.

> Jesus was so concerned about man
> Until He left His richness and glad glory
> Came down here in this old sin-cussed world
> Stepped on the train of nature with a virgin woman
> 5   And brought Himself out an infant baby
> On the train of nature nine months
> Stepped off the train at a little old station called Bethlehem
> Wrapped over there in swaddlin' clothes
> Stayed right there
> . . . .
>
> Same Jesus this evenin'
> Was concerned about us so much so
> Until he left glad glory
> Came out of glory to this old sinful world

5   Got on the train of nature
     Stayed there nine months
     Stepped off at the station one mornin'
     Early one mornin'
     Stepped off the station at Bethlehem
10   Wrapped up in swaddlin' clothes. . . .

The many similarities and analogies of diction, syntax, and image do not need explication; this "theme" — these passages — have not been memorized, obviously (unless the Reverend Brown has a poor memory), yet just as obviously both passages emerge from the same lexico-syntactical mold. Or, more probably, no mold, no Platonic ideal of Jesus stepping off the train of nature into this sinful old world at Bethlehem exists. Probably just the imprecisely conceived notion, the same given essential idea, exists. The Reverend Brown's themes are not faulty renderings of a fixed mold; they are variants of each other, existing for the nonce in a galaxy of similarly rendered lexico-syntactical clusters. Brown has dozens of such themes; so too did Lacy. And so too did nearly all of the other spiritual preachers recorded for this field research. Their compositions, their sermons, are structured largely by the judicious employment of traditional themes.

The preachers of oral sermons are fond of groups of utterances which maintain a single syntactic pattern while repeating the initial word (or words). In this respect also are the preachers stylistically similar to other performers of oral narrative throughout the world. In classical rhetoric such developments were termed *anaphoric*. The following sequence may serve as an illustration; the preacher is the late Reverend C. L. Franklin, and the sermon is on "Moses at the Red Sea":

     What are ya cryin' about Moses
     What are ya lookin' for
     What do ya think that ya want
     Why, the rod of your deliverance is in your own hands
5   Stretch out the rod that's in your hands
     I don't have a new rod to give ya
     I don't have a new instrument to give ya
     I don't have a new suggestion for ya
     I do not have a new plan
10   Your course has already been charted by destiny
     Stretch out the rod that's in your own hand. . . .

Two clusters of oral parallelism occur in the above passage. The Reverend Franklin asks his rhetorical Moses a question in line 1 ("What are ya cryin' about Moses"), which he follows with another question retaining the syntactic pattern as well as the first three words. This pattern is altered slightly in line 3, with the insertion of an intransitive verb; only the first word, "what," is retained. An answer to the questions posed in the first three lines follows. Line 6 justifies the earlier assertion (lines 4 and 5) that Moses's means of salvation is through self-help and that no aid can be expected from outside: "I don't have a new rod/instrument/suggestion for ya." "Rod" is a transition between the answer of line 5 and the justification of line 6. Lines 7 and 8 preserve the same syntactical pattern as line 6 (the first in this triad); they are amplifications of it. This second triad begins to drift in line 9, and by the next utterance/formula (line 10) Franklin has begun another pattern (though line 11, "Stretch out the rod that's in your own hand," essentially repeating line 5, may be a stall here while he thinks of what exactly to say next). This parallelism emerges because the preacher cannot control all of the elements of the utterance—syntax, lexicon, idea—quickly enough. Consequently, he relies on repetition to enable him to gather his thoughts and to make a statement in a structurally different form. If the preacher wants to advance his thoughts somewhat from the line (the utterance) of the moment to the imminent line, he may retain the syntax of the immediate line simply because it is easier for him: it is one less aspect to worry about. So too with Lord's singers of tales, who have little enough time to think about what to say next, even when they are singing a well-known narrative; any of the stalling devices described above are welcome, and the singer employs them frequently, on whatever level of awareness.

The architecture of oral sermons is not as lawful as conventional narratives. To use a commonplace example from oral literature, Beowulf must first cross the Baltic in order to meet Hrothgar, after which he can engage Grendel, after which he may struggle with Grendel's mother, after which a celebratory banquet is held, and so forth. If any of these distributional elements were to be scrambled, narrative chaos would result. Such structural inevitablility is not necessary for the oral sermon. Very few preaching performances are based on a causally specified sequence of events; it is true that many sermons do embed narrative episodes, but almost always as exempla whose placement within the sermon is variable. In about a score of sermons recorded between 1968 and 1971, this kind of flexibility was always found: the oral sermon is thus flexible structurally (as regards its narrative and hortative constituents) as well as verbally, though the best preachers devise their structures so as to most cogently convey their messages. Techniques, of course, vary: Lacy habitually used four episodes from the life of David when preaching on the Twenty-third Psalm (two sermons on this psalm recorded a year apart showed these episodes occurring in the same order), while the Rev. D. J. MacDowell (also of Bakersfield, California), for instance, will use several descriptive themes in variant order within the same sermon.

To make comparison with authentic performances, possible, Faulkner's sermon in *The Sound and the Fury* must be transcribed as though it had been recorded in the field. This involves, mainly, the deletion of all narrative material used as descriptive support. For the most part Faulkner's punctuation has been unaltered: where he put a period in the novel, a new line is begun in the rendering below; the same procedure has been used in the instances of his semi- and full colons. In a few instances a comma in the original has been interpreted to indicate a break in the speaker's meter; lines 11–13, for instance, are transcribed as

> Wus a rich man
> Whar he now
> O breddren?

while in the original it was rendered thus: "Wus a rich man: whar he now, O bredden?" Presumably Faulkner's comma signifies a pause, as does my sectioning of the line. Formulaic analysis does not depend upon such typographic divisions, since the sole criterion must be the language's metrical units. Performance overrides typographic conventions. The Reverend Shegog's sermon, thus based, is as follows:

> Brethren and sisteren
> I got the recollection and the blood of the Lamb
> Brethren
> Brethren en sistuhn!
> 5   I got de ricklickshun en de blood of de Lamb
> When de long, cold
> Oh, I tells you, breddren, when de long, cold
> I sees de light en I sees de word, po sinner
> Dey passed away in Egypt, de swingin chariots
> 10   De generations passed away
> Wus a rich man
> Whar he now
> O breddren?
> Was a po man
> 15   Whar he now
> O sistuhn?
> Oh I tells you

Ef you ain't got de milk en de dew of de old salvation when de long, cold
    years rolls away!
I tells you, breddren, en I tells you, sistuhn, dye'll come a time
20 Po sinner saying Let me lay down wid de Lawd
Lemme lay down my load
Den what Jesus gwine say, O breddren?
O sistuhn?
Is you got de ricklickshun en de blood of de Lamb?
25 Case I ain't gwine load down heaven!
Breddren!
Look at dem little chillen settin dar
Jesus wus like dat once
He mammy suffered de glory en de pangs
30 Sometime maybe she helt him at de nightfall
Whilst de angels singin him to sleep
Maybe she look out de do' en see de Roman police passin
Listen, breddren!
I sees de day
35 Ma'y settin in de do' wid Jesus on her lap
De little Jesus
Like dem chillen dar
De little Jesus
I hears de angels singin de peaceful songs en de glory
40 I sees de closin eyes
Sees Mary jump up
Sees de sojer face
We gwine to kill
We gwine to kill
45 We gwine to kill yo little Jesus!
I hears de weepin en de lamentation of de po mammy widout de salvation
    en de word of God!
I sees hit, breddren!
I sees hit!
Sees de blastin, blindin sight!
50 I sees Calvary, wid de sacred trees
Sees de thief en de murderer en de least of dese
I hears de boastin en de braggin
Ef you be Jesus, lif up yo tree en walk!
I hears de wailin of women en de evenin lamentations
55 I hears de weepin en de cryin en de turnt-away face of God
Dey done kilt Jesus
Dey done kilt my Son!
O blind sinner!
Breddren, I tells you

60   Sistuhn, I says to you
    When de lawd did turn His might face, say,
    Ain't gwine overload heaven
    I can see de widowed God shet His do'
    I sees de whelmin flood roll between
65   I sees de darkness en de death everlastin upon de generations
    Den, lo! Breddren!
    Yes, breddren!
    Whut I see?
    Whut I see, O sinner?
70   I sees de resurrection en de light
    Sees de meek Jesus saying Dey kilt Me dat ye shall live again
    I died day dem whut sees en believes shall never die
    Breddren
    O breddren!
75   I sees de doom crack en hears de golden horns shoutin down de glory
    En de arisen dead whut got de blood en de ricklickshun of de Lamb!

As text, Faulkner's (Shegog's) sermon has the unmistakable marks of an oral performance. Though only one of Shegog's formulas was collected in the field (for the research for *The Art of the American Folk Preacher*), "Lemme lay down my load", line 21, the style is heavily formulaic. Ten lines begin with the pronoun/verb, I sees . . ." (8, 34, 40, 47, 48, 50, 64, 65, 70, and 75; line 63 begins with "I can see. . . ." Five lines begin with "I hears . . .": 39, 46, 52, 54, and 55. So, fifteen of the seventy-six lines in the sermon begin with one or the other of these formulas, or nearly 20 percent. As in authentic oral performances, the "sees . . ." lines are only minimal adjustments of those beginning with "I sees . . ."; "I hears . . ." belongs to the same formulaic system, as does the "I tells you . . ." (7, 17, 19, and 59, where it closes the formula). All told, these formulas comprise about one-third of the sentences — the metrical utterances — in Faulkner's/Shegog's sermon. More convincing is this literary imitation's use of traditional themes, phrases, and exclamations. Laying down one's burden is a commonplace of black American Protestantism, and it is especially popular among African Americans who were either themselves slaves or the immediate descendants of slaves. Many gospel songs and sermons "lay down the burden" — enter paradise. Faulkner uses it twice (lines 21 and 25), and echoes it in line 20 ("Po sinner saying Let me lay down wid de Lawd") and line 62 ("Aint gwine overload heaven").

Scattered throughout Shegog's performance is the traditional litany, "I got the recollection and blood of the Lamb," the closest this literary

rendering comes to a stall formula. It is a realistic detail; stalls are obviously not needed in a printed rendering, though Faulkner's ear knows
that authentic performances "use" such phrases frequently, and that
the preacher can use them to stall as the writer uses them as unifiers.
This phrase occurs twice near the beginning (lines 2 and 5), once medi-
ally (line 24), and terminates with it (76). The many "I sees . . ." and
"I hears . . ." marshal the congregation's emotions, though these words
are not emotional in themselves. "I got the recollection and the blood
of the Lamb" is potently charged, emotionally and spiritually, would
not be forgotten during performance, and so is well suited as a unifier.
Having been used near the beginning to declare a theme, its subsequent
use unites the sermon while capping subsumed climaxes.

Oral parallelism, exemplified by the Reverend C. L. Franklin's "Moses
at the Red Sea" sermon, is a keynote of the Reverend Shegog's performance as well. The brutality of the threatened act is foregrounded by
the repetitions:

> We gwine to kill
> We gwine to kill
> We gwine to kill yo little Jesus! (43–45

Elsewhere (lines 63–65) syntactical repetition (and not verbatim restate-
ment) incrementally elaborate the preacher's vision, each utterance ac-
cumulating emotional weight:

> I can see de widowed God shet His do'
> I sees de whelmin flood roll between
> I sees de darkness en de death everlastin upon de generations (63–65)

The most illustrative development of formulas from a syntactic/
semantic formulaic system occurs in the several lines following 34. This
subset begins with "I sees the day," now focusing on Mary. "De little
Jesus" of line 36 is recalled by "dem chillen dar" (37), then repeated
in line 38: "De little Jesus." The focus of Shegog's vision rises skyward:
"I hears de angels singin de peaceful songs en de glory (39), the syntax
of which is replicated in line 40: "I sees de closin eyes." The "sees . . ."
formula is repeated: "Sees Mary jump up / Sees de sojer face," amidst
a crescendo, then switching to the "gwine to kill" sequence. As an oral
performance, as oralature, this is an excellent example of parallelism and
a demonstration of the creation of new formulas out of the moments-
old system. It is also, superfluous to say, quite moving.

A common pattern of oral performance is the repetition, sometimes

with slight variations, of groups of lines. For instance, the Reverend
Lacy used to describe the appearance of each of the four horsemen of
the Apocalypse — and the consequent response to their observers — with
quite similar rhetoric:

> They tell me
> In the mornin'
> When the horses
> Begin to come out
> 5   And the riders on the horses
> Want 'em to come out
> God from Zion
> Riding a red horse
> There's somebody gonna say
> 10 Is that the general
> That I was fighting for
> And I heard another cry
> Saying no-oo
> That's not the one
> 15 That you been fightin' for
> Another one rode out
> Riding a black horse
> Is that the man
> That I been fighting for
> 20 I heard another voice say
> No, no-oo
> That's not the general
> That you been fighting for
> Another one rode out
> 25 Riding a pale horse
> Is that the general
> That we been fighting for
> A voice said no
> That's not the one
> 30 That you been fighting for
> Another one came out
> God from Zion
> Riding a white horse
> Rainbow round his shoulder
> 35 Hark Hallelujah
> Dressed in raiment
> White as driven as the snow
> From his head down to his feet
> God from Zion

```
40  In his—from out of his mouth
    Come a two-edged sword
    Cuttin' sin
    Both right and left
    I heard a cry
45  Is that the man
    That we been fightin' for
    They said yes.
```

The subsets devoted to the red, black, and pale horses are described nearly identically. "Man" is interchangeable with "general" here, and the whole scene owes at least as much to popular songs and folk religion as to Revelation. In each riding out, "somebody" asks if this is the awaited rider, and someone else responds in the first three cases that it is not. This phenomenon, which simplifies the oral performer's compositional burdens, is common to a wide range of oralatures. Conjoined, as by Lacy, the aggregate has body, fullness, and greater emotional impact than if merely stated in outline. Faulkner gives Shegog a similar sequence: "Wus a rich man: whar he now, O Breddren? Was a po man: whar he now, O Sistuhn?" (lines 11–16 of my transcription).

Shegog's sermon is necessarily short, Faulkner giving him only 76 lines, about as much as fiction readers would want in a narrative. Sermons recorded in the field usually run to 350 lines when transcribed. One is reluctant, therefore, to denigrate the structure to the literary rendition; too little of it exists. Nevertheless, Shegog's performance is not inconsistent with what is known about oral preaching products. The oral sermon is quite flexible in its structure; the preacher does not have a Platonic ideal in mind, a perfect model towards which he or she strides, but rather a generalized "outline." Each performance seems to have been formulated in large structural blocks or themes. A few favorite metaphors (or groups of them) may be kept in storage for particular sermons, but the details, the improvisations, emerge during performance. The situation of that performance as well as the preacher's memory—and creative powers—at the particular moment of execution gives the sermon its detail.

As with all spontaneously composed performances, the speaker/singer/preacher is relatively free to adjust his or her song/sermon to the conditions of the moment. There is little, for instance, in the oral sermon that demands a necessary progression of ideas or of narrative elements. The most popular format among spiritual preachers is the traditional "text and context" order of presentation: the sermon begins with an announcement of the scriptural text for the day, elaborates on the biblical context in which the passage appears, and then applies Scripture to contemporary morals. After the declaration of the context, most oral sermons are rather free-ranging, being held together mainly by the preacher's associational train. The better sermons, those of the Reverend C. L. Franklin, for instance, have discernable organization. The Reverend Shegog's sermon is in fact well-structured, a feature we would expect from a big-city preacher — and a sophisticated novelist — who had great self-possession and thorough control of the material. Lines 1–26 are hortative; the next thirty-one lines narrate the envisioned story of Mary and the infant Jesus; and the last nineteen lines (58–76) are again hortative. This circular structure is common in oral performances; narrative elements in sermons are the most stable (over time), and in *The Sound and the Fury* one could easily imagine that the narrative of Mary and the threatened Jesus was the preacher's stable core around which he wove the day's messages. The core could be used with any of a great number of other messages and then worked back toward exposition and hortative urgings in the conclusion.

If one came to this sermon apart from Faulkner's novel, therefore, one could hardly identify it as a literary creation. The language is densely formulaic, and formulas of the same system are clustered together. The "I sees . . ." subset, for instance, occurs most frequently between lines 40 and 75, and is used only twice before that grouping. Traditional phrasing, from Scripture and gospel songs as well, occur in Shegog's lexicon. Several lines develop parallel syntax; the diction is simple, as in authentic performances. Faulkner's diction is also authentic, or authentic seeming. Nothing in this literary imitation of an oral sermon marks it as literary, and there is much evidence to commend it as an oral composition.

This is one more piece of evidence of Faulkner's great ear for dialect and speech. He must have gone to services in black churches; the details of his descriptions are too precise, have too much verisimilitude, for it to be otherwise. The women and children enter the church first while the men linger outside talking in groups until the bell stops; the congregation fans itself constantly although it is not especially hot, the women seat themselves on "their" side of the room; the small boys and girls are playing; and the posturing of the visiting preacher — all these details are too real, too precise, for Faulkner to have invented the scene.

Shegog's sermon is a literary tour de force: virtually indistinguishable from its authentic oral models, it is also one of the most moving sermons in American letters, surpassing those of Melville's Father

Maple and Ralph Ellison's *Invisible Man.* The literary artist's skill is the deciding factor in such comparisons, of course. But, more than a model of Faulkner's sensitivity to speech, this sermon testifies to the emotive power of the spoken word, even when emasculated for dissection on the printed page.

Yet Faulkner's ear for phonology and rhythms, his sense of phrasing and syntax and lexicon, and his ability to imitate all of them and to build his own, ersatz, sermon is only part of his accomplishment. This imitation folk-form evokes the reader's responses, engages the reader, with great power. The "original" sermons are performed aloud; they are moving — if they are moving at all — when they are heard and seen and experienced, not merely read. Part of the aesthetic of the folk sermon is the swishing of the mortuary fans, along with the restless squeals of infants, the exclamations of the congregation. Normally the transcription of such orations is as tepid as dishwater; witness the sermons printed in the appendix of *The Art of the American Folk Preacher.* But in Faulkner's printed text, the Reverend Shegog's performance lives. In this "naive," "elemental," and psychologically direct form, the reader sees — as did Faulkner and as he contrived for his reader to understand — a vital expression of feeling. The reader is compelled, activated, to participate in its performance, just as the live performance is antiphonal. In this respect, too, literature is much like folklore; they are both performances which engage the audience (see Abrahams 1972). Here Faulkner uses a folk form which is intense, compellingly transposing it to a fixed form, retaining its power to enthrall and to induce passion. In this evocative sense, Faulkner has "used" folklore to the glory of his literature.

PART FIVE

The Literary Context of Folklore

WE ALL KNOW, OR SHOULD KNOW, that a great deal of folklore occurs in literature, and that the more an author mimetically describes human life, the more lore is likely to appear. Folklore is an inevitable and ubiquitous expression of existence. The identification of folklore in literature, therefore, is hardly startling. The two chapters comprising this section are not as startling or as theoretically important as the contributions of folklore to literary study — structuralism and oral-formulaic theory. But they do show how literature provides a (fictional) lifeworld which highlights lore and yet provides a natural context for its existence. No ethnographic study, no matter how great or eloquent the elaboration, can equal the vivid context of good fiction.

Chapter 12 supplies only three examples of folklore in literature, by way of introduction. The number of possible examples is infinite, nearly as great as the number of fictions ever written. Chapter 13 examines one novel in detail and demonstrates how its author, William Golding, has made a folk belief (in the magical properties of fire) the central symbol of this book. This belief has greater antiquity than the Old Testament; in Golding's fiction, fire is not merely a biblical allusion and symbol, it is used as a frame around which the novel is structured.

CHAPTER 12

Folklore in Literature

FOLKLORISTS ENJOY LITERATURE as much as anyone does. But when they read for professional reasons, their purposes are often narrow. Richard Dorson's often-cited essay on the verification of folklore in literature (1957) had as its purpose the gleaning of literary texts to locate ethnographic data. The inevitable qualitative leveling inherent in Dorson's analytic suggestions have already been discussed: William Gilmore Simms, for instance, becomes more valuable than John Barth because there is much more authentic lore in the former. Such a methodology, therefore, may be inexplicable to those who evaluate literature for its artistic merits.

Professor Mary Ellen Brown (1976) points out that folklorists have a lot more to gain from reading literature (pleasure aside) than Dorson had suggested—that in addition to items of folklore, literature often contains vivid and accurate descriptions of folklore and its context. This happens, Brown says, because "authors [are] often endowed with a sensitivity far exceeding the powers of the social scientists" (1976 p. 51) and are thus able to reveal vividly "the complexity of . . . culture" (p. 51).

Brown's demonstration was upon Chinua Achebe's *Arrow of God*, more of which later. In this chapter I want not only to follow through on this insight but to illustrate how the literature of eras before folklore was systematically and knowledgably collected reflects the storytelling event itself. People told stories to each other a thousand years ago (and millennia before that); what was the situation like? On their own, folklorists can only surmise; it remains for literature to provide this description about communicative events that took place centuries ago.

What was storytelling like in the Middle Ages? Chaucer gives us some clues, but the best evidence is to be found in Boccaccio's *Decameron* (VI, i). A gentleman has offered to take Mistress Oretta on horseback—their company is traveling through the country—and to entertain her with a story. But he tells it so badly that, with great delicacy, she requests to be allowed to proceed on foot, thus interrupting his delivery. Details of the ways in which the story is judged to be poorly told are not lacking. Filomena comments that it was "a beautiful tale" but that its telling was faulty (1955, p. 357). The bumbler was repetitious, using the same word three and four times over; his choice of words was poor, and "entirely out of keeping" with the circumstances and the quality of his characters; he could not relate his tale smoothly, continually correcting himself with such statements as "No, no, that's not right"; and he made a "dreadful mess" of things by continually confusing the names of the characters.

Chaucer is less explicit. Several of the characters in the *Canterbury Tales* comment on the tales of others, usually by cutting short their narrations. The Knight "stynteth . . . the Monk of his tale" after the cleric has gone on at some (unreasonable) length with examples of great men who fell from fortune, but we do not know how the Knight "stynteth" that other pilgrim. The Franklin graciously terminates the distended tale of the squire (*Canterbury Tales* V, lines 673–708) with gentle praise: "I preise wel thy wit," / Quod the Frankeleyn, "considerynge thy yowthe, / So feelyngly thou spekest, sire, I allow the" (V, 674–76). And though he goes on to declare that "ther is noon that is heere / Of eloquence that shal be thy peere" (V, 677–78), he interrupts the Squire nevertheless. Why? Probably because the young man is too rhetorical, too bombastic, too digressive — but that is our surmise. Too discursive also is the introduction of the tale of the Wife of Bath; laughing, the Friar exclaims that "so have I joye or blis, / This is a long preamble of a tale" (III, 830–31).

With much less grace and sensitivity, the host "stynteth Chaucer of his Tale of Thopas." He is more detailed than the other pilgrims, but since his critical mode is the ad hominem screed, he is not explicitly helpful in understanding why Chaucer's *Tale of Sir Thopas* has been a failure. Host Harry Baily complains that *Thopas* and its teller "makest me / So wery of thy verray lewednesse / That . . . / Myne eres aken of thy drasty speche" (VII, 920–23). Harry's objections seem to be stylistic: "This may wel be rym dogerel. . . . Thy drasty tymyng is nat worth a toord" (VII, 925, 930). What he wants, he says (V, 935) is "som murthe of som doctryne."

For the most part, the storytelling faults of Chaucer's characters are not those of Boccaccio's (in Filomena's anecdote); the English are boring because they are too lengthy or their rhymes are insultingly unsophisticated. Boccaccio is more specific; the "doughty knight" of Filomena's is repetitive, but equally important is that he get the details of his story wrong, continually has to correct himself, and constantly scrambles the names of his characters. Finally, Mistress Oretta, seeing him "hopelessly entangled in a maze of his own making" (p. 357), asks to be set back on the ground. The Franklin, meanwhile, intruded to save all of that company from further pain just the squire was about to embark on yet other digressions; "First wol I telle yow of Cambyuskan, / That in his tyme many a citee wan; / And after wol I speke of Algarsif, / How that he wan Theodora to his wif, / For whom ful ofte in greet peril he was, / Ne hadde he been holpen by the steede of bras; / And after wol I speke of Cambalo, . . ." (V, 661–67).

The standards of good storytelling then differed little from those in force today, but that in itself is interesting to know. The teller had to tell as direct a tale as possible, without distracting digressions, without stumbling over his or her own words, getting details and characters' names right without confusing the order of the plot or the nature of the episodes. Too many distracting rhetorical flourishes bored the listeners, as did too many examples, however ennobling and edifying the subject. Everything in moderation.

The courtesy with which the Franklin interrupts and the brusqueness of the host's termination of Chaucer's tale tell a lot about the protocols of interruption in the late Middle Ages. Mistress Oretta also does not want to offend the "doughty knight," and so most gently hints that his narration falls short of the mark: she asks to be put down from the horse where she is a captive listener. We have an idea of who may safely interrupt whom, and how that may be done. We see the fourteenth century's concept of politeness (not very different than ours), and we know how nonaristocratic social equals may deal with one another. (For a close examination of the pilgrims' manners, see Lindahl 1987, pp. 73 –123). Still, these are outlines, not full elaborations. Interactions are between two characters, and we are left to guess how the others in the audience felt. The interrupter in all of these examples faces no opposition from other audience members. The interruption is always successful and seems to be unanimous. The suggestion, then, is that the disruption is justified socially, and that everyone would agree with the interrupter's judgment.

Professor Brown saw in *Arrow of Gold* the characters' use of folklore in ways that revealed its contextual usage in the lifeworld. Chief Priest Ezeulu's return to his village rekindles a rivalry between his two wives, Ugoye and Matefi. One night the junior wife (Ugoye) is besought by her children to tell a story, and the narrative she chooses is of the jealousy of the senior wife for the junior, and the consequences of this feeling for the world: a version of "the Kind and Unkind Girls." The nature of the tale-within-a-tale is not all we are told. Sensitively described also are the interactions of Ugoye and her children, the setting (haunted farmland), and suggestions of the narrator's vocal intonations and gestures. While this embedded (folk)tale entertains the children listeners, it also cautions them against the evils of envy; at the same time Ugoye eases her own feelings of tension about her conflict with Matefi, she simultaneously soothes her children, who have become nervous about the recent change in their family structure.

At the same time, this storytelling event has a literary/symbolic function—a message from author to reader. One critic finds that the folktale is a paradigm for the story of the entire novel; Professor Brown sees it as a microcosm for the ongoing rivalry between the two wives and, at the next level of abstraction, the conflict between "the largely negative power of the dominant, intrusive culture on the delicate, yet strong fabric of the traditional pattern of life" (1976, p. 51). Perhaps unintentionally, Achebe nevertheless successfully describes, in all of its implications and subtleties, the contextual meaning of a folktale and the significance of the act of its telling.

We do not have to go such a great distance to see how a folktale-within-a-novel can, in the imagination of a perceptive literary artist, richly depict the contextual implications of the tale-telling event. My own demonstration is from *My Antonia* by the somewhat neglected Willa Cather. Before the story is far under way, one of the minor characters, Pavel, has been taken to his bed, deathly ill. He is attended by a close friend, Peter, who has immigrated to Nebraska with him from Russia. Antonia, her father (Mr. Shimerda), and her friend (the novel's narrator) Jim Burden are in the cabin also, to comfort their sick neighbor. Pavel had strained himself lifting timbers while working on a new barn, gushing blood from his lungs so violently that the other workmen thought he would die on the spot (Cather 1954, p. 51). "Misfortune seemed to settle like an evil bird on the roof of the log house, and to flap its wings there, warning human beings away. The Russians had such bad luck that people were afraid of them and liked to put them out of mind" (p. 51).

Gusts of wind rattle against the windowpanes and whistle through the cracks in them. Each gust calls to the narrator's mind thoughts of "defeated armies, retreating; or of ghosts who were trying desperately to get in for shelter, and then went moaning on" (p. 53). Outside, coyotes are yapping and whining, as if warning them all that winter was coming. In response to the coyotes, Pavel let forth a "long complaining cry," as if he "were waking to some old misery" (p. 53). And, leaning on an elbow, in tones barely above a whisper, he tells Mr. Shimerda a troubled tale. Antonia, who understands Pavel's language, will only tell Jim that "it's wolves. . . . It's awful what he says" (p. 54). Later, when Jim and Antonia are riding home in the back of a hay wagon, she relates Pavel's tale (pp. 56–60).

Years before, when Pavel and Peter were young, they were asked to be groomsmen for a friend who was marrying a young woman in another village. After the ceremony, the company was invited to the bridal dinner, and then a supper, and then an evening of drinking and feasting. When it was finally time to go, Pavel got into his sledge, the bride and groom in the back seat, Peter beside him. The wolves were said to be bad that winter, but their first cries (while the six sledges slid back to their home village) were ignored, lulled as everyone was by alcohol. Then, in open country, a black drove swarmed up over a hill behind the wedding party. Shortly, something happened to the last sledge: the driver, probably drunk, lost control, and the vehicle swerved off the road and into some trees, where it overturned. The screams of the occupants sobered everyone, and the drivers whipped their teams on to their greatest speed. But nothing stayed the wolves; they gained on the hindmost sledges, panicking the horses and occupants further. According to Pavel (in Antonia's retelling / in Cather's narrative), the wolves "ran like streaks of shadow; they looked no bigger than dogs, but there were hundreds of them" (p. 57).

Minutes later, topping a slight hill, Peter looked back, and to his horror saw that there were only three of the original sledges left. How many wolves? "Enough for all of us. . . . Twenty, thirty, – enough" (pp. 58, 59). Then, the middle horse of the troika began to give out, and the others were nearly carrying him as well as pulling the sledge. Terror-stricken, Pavel called to the groom that they must lighten the load still further (they were already the lightest of the sledges), and he motioned that they must throw the bride over.

> The young man cursed and held her tighter. Pavel tried to draw her away. In the struggle, the groom rose. Pavel knocked him over the side of the sledge and threw the girl after him. He said he never remembered how he did it, or what happened afterward. (p. 59)

This narrative – told as a memorate (personal-experience story) in the novel – is not listed in *The Types of the Folktale*, but is a folktale nevertheless. I have myself heard it more than once, and not as an excerpt from Cather's fiction. It has an unlikely quality common to so many oral narratives, that just the closest scrutiny reveals. Experts are divided about whether wolves attack humans, some saying that it has happened (when the animals are hungry or diseased or maimed), others insisting that such attacks are extremely rare. But in any case, wolf packs usually number less than a dozen, so that Cather's/Pavel's "there were hundreds of them" and at the final kill "twenty, thirty—enough" is not to be believed. Also suspect is the central act of this narrative— throwing the bride to the attacking beasts. Is this the act, however desperate, of peasants when they as well as their friends are threat- ened—even though their culture expresses such fierce prohibitions against such barbaric cowardice? Such infamy is humanly possibly, of course, but it does sound more dramatic than mimetic. The wolves are not satisfied with the flesh of the occupants of the first five sledges they are able to overturn; they must have Pavel and Peter and their newlywed passengers in the last vehicle and so relentlessly, demoniacally continue their murderous pursuit.

The tale has an epilogue. Peter and Pavel were soon run out of their village; Pavel's mother would not look at him. The brothers traveled from town to town, but the story followed them, as insatiable as a starving wolf. They saved enough money to emigrate, and worked in Chicago, Des Moines, and Fort Wayne, but now bad luck and ill health dogged their footsteps. When Pavel's health all but failed, they tried farming. A few days after the moment of this memorate of the wolves, Pavel died. Peter sold what few belongings and farm implements they had (at a fraction of their cost and worth) and went to work with a railroad construction crew that had hired a number of Russians. With the farm sold, Peter sat despairingly on the floor of his cabin eating melon rinds that he and Pavel had put away for winter. When they came to take him to his train, "they found him with a dripping beard, surrounded by heaps of melon rinds" (p. 61).

The impact of the story—which Jim heard but did not understand until later—"was never at an end" (p. 61). Yet they never told anyone of Pavel's shameful night, as if it had all happened to "give us a painful and peculiar pleasure" (p. 61). Before the story had begun, Antonia had whispered that "he's scared of the wolves. . . . in his country there are very many, and they eat men and women" (p. 54). The coyotes have been howling outside on the prairie, and Pavel has begun to talk of "his" wolves. The gusting wind, the imminence of autumn, the dying man, all prepare the youngsters, and us, for the tragedy to come. Jim and Antonia "slid closer together along the bench" (p. 54).

This is not a major event in the novel, yet Cather lavished all of her insights and sensitivity on it. Because of the bride and their wolves, bad luck (we are made to feel) plagues Peter and Pavel. Driven from town to town, and then to another continent, Pavel is driven to death; guilt over the episode, we are made to understand, has contributed to his death. The strain from lifting timbers is only the immediate agency; guilt has done the rest. The Russians who hear of the catastrophe will not tolerate their presence. And the story's haunting resonance will not leave Antonia or Jim, who often has dreams in which he is himself in a troika-drawn sledge dashing through a country that looked something like Nebraska, and something like Virginia (his birth state).

Cather has given as much context for this legend (memorat) as would any social scientist. We know the background of the Russians' unhappy wandering, the scary setting of the relation of the tale, its consequences — for Pavel, for Peter, and the haunting repercussions of the narration for Jim. And Cather adds a writerly quality that is not likely to occur in an authentic folk telling of this narrative. The episode is related immediately after Jim has killed an old rattler which had crawled through their cornfield for years, becoming a legend in its own right. Though it is old and relatively sluggish, the snake is slain by young Jim, who is reckoned a hero in Antonia's eyes for the deed. Jim slays a lethal creature as a sign of his maturation; then we learn that Pavel had committed one of the most infamous acts of cowardice in modern fiction. The contrast is obvious, and the placement intentional; Cather's communications with the reader are simultaneous with her description of the interdynamics of the characters within the novel who are witnesses to Pavel's tale. She proves herself yet again a master of fiction.

More penetrating than either of the above demonstrations are the results of the intensive research presented in Carl Lindahl's recent *Earnest Games* (1987). Lindahl does not concern himself with the narrative forms in *The Canterbury Tales* and analogous folktales; rather, he applies contemporary folklore to a literature in which the characters tell each other stories. Chaucer's *Tales* are analyzed within the context of the poet's storytelling community, which Lindahl points out was also the author's everyday, work-world community. By deeply penetrating the social history of the time in order to learn something about the subject poetry as well as closely scrutinizing the poetry to learn somethings about the social history of the era, this research may well stand as a model for subsequent folkloric analyses of medieval literature.

Earnest Games is a study of Chaucer as storyteller, an appraisal of the poet as a verbal artist. Necessarily, Lindahl argues that Chaucer's poems were commonly recited aloud to an aural audience. Lindahl further observes that Chaucer was strongly influenced by the speech-act rules of folk oral performance and that the fictional setting of *The Canterbury Tales* contains a realistic depiction of medieval storytelling. Relying on current findings about memory and audience response in oral communities, he observes that fourteenth-century listeners would have been able to follow a poem more easily if read aloud to them than if they had read the narrative privately. One of Lindahl's observations equates Chaucer's poetic community — those who heard his poems recited and who recited theirs to him, a group who talked about the arts and about their poems communally — with the interpersonal dynamics of a contemporary folk community; thus, what we know about the latter can be meaningfully applied to the former.

Lindahl's perception explains why the verbal and narrative structures of some Chaucerian narratives were similar to those of others in the poet's circle. We need not assume that Chaucer copied their poems; when members of the group read to each other, discussed their poems among themselves, and listened critically to one another, certain similarities were bound to occur. Ideas, phrases, even generic manipulations and mutations were "in the air," the common property of the community, free for any member to pick up and use.

CHAPTER 13

Folk Beliefs in Fire
in *The Lord of the Flies*

WILLIAM GOLDING WROTE *The Lord of the Flies* in such a way that nearly every critic of the novel has been concerned with its philosophical and theological structure. It is the allegorist's and the exegete's dream. Employed with critical minuteness mainly by academics, such approaches seem ideally tailored for people who like to solve puzzles, and academics are among the most avid of those. The book is easily taught as an exercise in ideology, and "allegorical levels" are almost always the easiest to discuss in a classroom. Golding's work, by its nature, challenges analytic minds to decipher its cryptic parallels and meanings. After all the discussion to date about the book's philosophy, we can now weave our way through it with considerable profit; but our understanding of its symbolism — and the architecture built upon that symbolism — is somewhat less rich. By this title, Golding has induced us to think of the pig's head as the central symbol; but fire plays at least as important a symbolic / structural role in the novel. This chapter examines Golding's use of fire as a literary symbol that derives from centuries of folk belief, at least as old as the Bible.

The boys in Ralph's camp found themselves in an impoverished condition after the defection of so many of their original number, especially of the "biguns," to Jack's tribe; only Piggy and Sam-neric were left to carry out the tedious though necessary chores of their daily life. What worried Ralph most, even more than the "beast" he believed he had seen on the mountain, was the fire. The fire frightened him: "I'm scared," he confessed to the disconsolate Piggy, "not of the beast. I mean I'm scared of that too. But nobody else understands about the fire. If someone threw you a rope when you were drowning. If a doctor said that this because if you don't take it you'll die — you would, wouldn't you? I mean?" (1959, p. 129). His fear was not groundless, for without the fire and the folklore of fire — on their mountain, or on the altars of most Western religions — neither rescue nor salvation would be possible, and without fire *The Lord of the Flies* would be without not only its most pervasive and powerful symbol but its structural skeleton.

Ralph's and Piggy's solemn meditation was disintegrated by the shrieking assault of Jack's painted raiders breaking from the cover of the nearby forest. Ralph was prepared to defend himself where he stood; Piggy, in one of the few mistakes he made on the island, ran directly for the conch which had been left on the platform. Jack had never had any use for the conch: it "doesn't count" at his end of the island, and Roger will soon demolish it anyway. What Jack wants, frantically needs, is fire, and, grabbing up some half-burned sticks, he and his boys raced away to their Castle Rock.

The element of fire has not burned out; it is an essential part of this novel which we have always acknowledged was executed with broad strokes of theological pigment and vivid folkloric tints. Not by mistake or coincidence are all the boys under thirteen—the traditional age of candidacy into the adult community—nor is it by accident that they are placed by Golding's omniscient hand virtually naked on an isolated, seemingly uninhabited, seemingly paradisaical island which Ralph recognizes as "good" (p. 30), an Edenic isle that has known no evil until the "snake-like" beastie of fear and frustration inspires savagery and lawless violence. From this coral den the boys at first seek salvation from ships at sea which they hope will rescue them; the means that Ralph chooses to contact this desired agent of rescue/salvation, realistically enough, is fire.

Most pantheons have fire-gods, and in the rituals of nearly every Western religion (and many of the East as well) fire occupies a central place. The death and resurrection of Jesus, for instance, is symbolized by the extinguishing and rekindling of a liturgical candle. The burnt offerings of the Old Testamental Hebrews were made suitable for Yahweh by purification in flame. The Lord often appeared as flame, a column of fire that led the Israelites out of Egypt (Exodus 13: 21-22); He spoke to Moses from a burning bush, and appeared as fire to lead the way (as in Deuteronomy 1: 33).

To the Istaelites, He looked like a "a consuming fire"(Exodus 24: 17 and such instances could be extended by more than a dozen. Moses labored up to the top of his mountain the better to be nearer his God, just as Jesus would later ascend His in order to commune with the Holy Spirit. A mountain's height brings the climber nearer to God dwelling in the heavens just above its highest peaks; the majesty, the sense of awe that a mountain produces in the man or woman who views its im-

mense mass from a distance, signifies a power and an order of life
redolent of the divine.

When Ralph lights his first fire on the mountaintop at "his" end of
the island, it is ostensibly for the function of signaling ships that might
chance to be in the area. By this same action, Golding signals to us
that, though unknown to Ralph, this fire has a religious purpose as
well, a purpose understood by author and reader. For the reader the
mountain is Ralph's altar on which he tries to keep alight his patheti-
cally less-than-eternal flame. Again, the lore is very old. The Lord told
Moses that fire was to be kept burning continually upon the altar —
originally as a sacrifice (Leviticus 1: 7) but later as a signal of uninter-
rupted worship. The altar light is never to be extinguished. The Easter
light in the Catholic Church is to remind us of the presence of Christ,
and its flame, struck from rock, is like Christ risen from His tomb of
stone.

Common sense was used in Ralph's location of his fire, the highest
ground being the most likely spot on the island to light a signal fire.
At the same time that Golding instructs his character to kindle this
blaze and makes the boy innocent enough to think nothing more about
it, he is speaking to us in another, though simultaneous, code. Having
decided that they should start a fire, Ralph and Jack are suddenly confronted with the realization that they lack the equipment to do so: "The
shameful knowledge grew in them and they did not know how to begin
confession" (p. 35). That theologically freighted word is repeated a moment later when Jack glances at Ralph, "who blurted out the last confession of incompetence." But the quick-thinking Jack is not at a loss
for very long; seeing Piggy's specs, he immediately knows how to start
the fire. This fire is crucial to their salvation, or so the boys feel at the
moment, and though it is Jack who snatches the glasses from Piggy's
nose, Ralph finally takes them when the fire is to be kindled.

This detail is in keeping with Ralph's character as the purveyor of
order, reason, and lawful purpose. Universally, sacred fires are created
anew, either by rubbing sticks together or by focusing a glass or prism
on kindling, as Golding's boys do. The Catholic Easter flame is usually
set with a cigarette lighter so that the flame will be struck from stone —
the flint. Profane fires, on the other hand — those used for warmth, in
the preparation of food, or whatever nonreligious purpose — are never
created anew but are always taken from existing flame. Thus Jack's fire,
which is certainly profane, the blaze with which he rouses the blacker
passions of his tribe, is not created afresh but is stolen, first by stealing

Ralph's smoldering logs, later by assaulting Piggy and appropriating his specs. In exasperation Ralph cries out:

"No use."
Eric looked down at him through a mask of dried blood. Piggy peered in the general direction of Ralph.
"Course it's no use, Ralph. Now we got no fire."

It takes a few moments for Ralph to reply:

"They've got our fire."
Rage shrilled his voice.
"They stole it." (p. 156)

The boys decide to launch a peace mission over to Jack's camp, and when they arrive Ralph at once points out to the apostates, in another line freighted with at least two codes, the difference between the two fires:

"Look at that! Call that a signal fire? That's a cooking fire" (p. 164).

Simon's character as prophet in the novel is also related to the galaxy of folkloric meanings signified by fires. Golding has himself said that he intended Simon to suggest Jesus, and on this point, dangerous as it often is to accept an author's word about his/her fictional meaning, we can profitably accept what he says. Simon's care of the "littluns" (his flock) is overtly Christlike, as is his temptation by the pig's head simply to forget the whole thing, as is, finally, his death at the hands of the hysterical mob to whom he brings good news – about the nature of evil. Simon, in his role as carpenter, helps in building the huts on the beach while the others are either away hunting or resting near "home." But when Simon comes down from the mountaintop, having seen what the beast really is, and finds Jack's tribe in a frenzied dance around their (profane) fire, he is less like Jesus (although he becomes a sacrificial victim) than he is like Jesus's type, Moses.

Golding would seem to be coining his own anti-maxim, "never trust the tale, trust the teller," yet the situation he has created more closely parallels that of Moses descending from the mountain where he received the commandments than it does any event in the life of Christ. When the Hebrew prophet descended from the mountain, carrying the tablets on which God had inscribed the law with His own finger, he found Aaron and the other Israelites dancing around a fire. They had taken off their golden rings and had melted them down, molding a golden calf which they worshiped as the god of Israel. Golding's Jack Merridew worships the demons of fear, undisciplined passion, and torment. He is able to control his society only when the boys become fearful, and he maintains his mastery of them with threats, beatings, and torture.

When Simon enters the swaying ring of frightened, hypnotically dancing boys, he is no longer like Moses, though the contrast between him and the Hebrew prophet is significant for us. The leader of the Jews smashed his tablets in anger and, grabbing the golden calf which Aaron and the others had cast, heated it and ground it to powder and cast the remains over the waters. Standing at the gates of the unruly camp, Moses demanded of the Israelites whether they were for or against the Lord. The Levites joined him and together they slew "about three thousand" of the idolators (Exodus 32: 2–29). Simon, being no great prophet, is all too tame a prey for the savage young idolators, and it is his remains that they toss into the water.

In the preface to *The Spoils of Poynton*, Henry James discussed the uses of contrasting parallels in literature:

> We may strike lights by opposing order to order, one sort to another sort; for in that case we get the correspondences and equivalents that make differences means something; we get the interest and the tension of disparity where a certain parity may have been in question.

The Old Testament is a "good book" where the good — at least in this narrative from Exodus — survives; *Lord of the Flies* chronicles the progress and eventual triumph of evil. Moses slays the apostate Jews; Simon, very Christlike in his meekness, is himself slain by those who are full of passionate intensity, while the best, Ralph and Piggy, lack the conviction to save him.

Simon, then, is a prophet whose actions are reminiscent of Moses, at times of Jesus and of others. His epilepsy is another sign of his holy character. Jack sneers that "he's always throwing a faint" (p. 17) when his fragile classmate passes out at the first assembly, and later, when confronting the Lord of the Flies, he falls into what seems to be another epileptic faint:

> Simon's head wobbled. His eyes were half closed as though he were imitating the obscene thing on the stick. He knew that one of his times was coming on. The Lord of the Flies was expanding like a balloon . . . Simon's body was arched and stiff. (p. 133)

In former times epilepsy was a much-cherished visitation. Shamans, priests, and oracles were often chosen from among those who suffered from this "falling sickness," and in many societies some sort of nervous instability is demanded of religious leaders. Few ethnologists now believe entirely in Paul Radin's theory that all shamans were (are?) epileptoid despite the large number of examples assembled in *Primitive Religion* (1957) arguing that such is the case. Radin collected several accounts of initiations into various priesthoods—African, Amerind, Eskimo, and others—in which the candidate is starved, drugged, or deprived of sleep, and even infected with such diseases as malaria so that, if he were not epileptoid originally, he might well experience the hallucinations symptomatic of epilepsy during the novitiate. Simon, far from simple, has been drawn from the template of Arunta, Winnebago, Malekula as well as Christian and Jewish models. His epilepsy in another society would be regarded as an actual seizure by some supernatural agent, as in fact the Greek origin of the word implies. Only through the medium of a trance or seizure can the shaman pass into the spirit world from whence to reemerge reborn, with his divine message. Simon's fainting is an infallible sign of his divine, prophetic character.

And Simon is received as are most other prophets: his classmates, his fellow island dwellers, never profit from his insights. His inspirations are actually disdainfully ignored. He tells his fellows that the "beastie, maybe it's only us" (p. 82), and is jeered for his wisdom; he tells Ralph that "you'll get back to where you came from" and in return gets told that "you're batty" (p. 103). Such has been the traditional destiny of prophets.

If fire is a universal purifier and (on certain occasions) the visible manifestation of God, it is also the agent of His righteous indignation and wrath—witness the annihilations of Sodom and Gomorrah and that of Babylon in Revelation. "For the Lord your God is a consuming fire, a jealous God" (Deuteronomy 4: 24). This evil, destructive fire in the novel is Jack's, as the holy fire is Ralph's—both as folk symbol and structural framework. The obvious connection between Jack and the profane fire is that he ignited it; but it has many of his personal attributes as well, especially that it excites the boys to overcome the restraints of their humane responses. When Ralph lit the fire on the mountain, they danced, but they danced themselves out harmlessly and finally "flung themselves down in the shadows that lay among the shattered rocks" (pp. 36–37). Later, when another signal fire was set—on the beach—the littluns became "wildly excited" but as "the fire died down so did the excitement. The littluns stopped singing and dancing and drifted away toward the sea or the fruit trees or the shelters" (p. 121).

It was not in Jack's plan to let the boys' energy expend itself harmlessly, because he sensed that the exciting fire and the frenzied dancing that it induced and the ritualized chant, "kill the beast, cut his throat, spill his blood," could be channeled to his own uses. When the tribe began to panic during a thunderstorm while gathered at Castle Rock, he seized the moment by jumping up in front of them and shouting, "Do our dance! Come on! Dance" (p. 140).

The luttluns, who had been running about screaming while the lightning and thunder reached a crescendo, joined with the other boys in a wild dance around Roger, who, for the moment, was a surrogate pig. Here was a mock fear they could strike at and beat. Ralph would have let them dance themselves to exhaustion or else would have tried to reason with them, but Jack is by far the greater perceptor of mob psychology: he kept the boys going and channeled their aggressions to accomplish his personal vision of the way society should behave. Into this seething, roiling swarm of frightened boys, Simon appears—with his word from on high—and the response of his people is murder.

Jack's followers readily recognized the fire's potency to ritualize savagery. They danced around the pig-surrogate, Robert, jabbing at him while they chanted.

> "We ought to have a drum," said Maurice, "then we could do it properly."
> Ralph looked at him.
> "How properly?"
> "I dunno. You want a fire, I think, and a drum, and you keep time on the drum."
> "You want a pig," said Roger, "like in a real hunt."
> "Or someone to pretend," said Jack, "you could get someone to dress up as a pig and then he could act—you know, pretend to knock me over and all that." (pp. 106-7)

And so they conceive their dance of death, their demoniac ritual of the worship of darkness, while the fire on the mountain grows faint.

Ralph has discipline and purpose, and his fire is intended to be controlled and purposeful. His first attempt, however, quickly becomes uncontrolled, and much of the surrounding forest is burned because, as Piggy is quick to notice, they got careless and made the blaze too big. This seems to parallel the Bible's improper fire which Nadab and Abihu offered to the Lord, Who later killed them for their presumption (Numbers 3:4). No one knows with certainty why this fire was "improper." Golding's fire lacks control, and this is sufficient reason for its condemnation as evil in the novel; the littluns see creepers flailing about in the blaze, rising and falling, and they scream, with more significance for us than for themselves, "Snakes! Snakes! Look at the snakes!" (p. 41) We later learn that the littlun with the birthmark on his cheek has perished in this unholy conflagration.

When Ralph is elected chief by the boys in the novel's opening scenes, one of his first commands is to organize a fire-watch:

> Now we come to the most important thing. I've been thinking. I was think-ing while we were climbing the mountain. . . . And on the beach just now. This is what I thought. We want to have fun. And we want to be rescued . . . . So we must make smoke on top of the mountain. We must make a fire. (pp. 32–33)

The fire is so important to Ralph that he relentlessly harps on it, con-tinually nagging the others so that they soon begin to resent him for it; Ralph is so persistent that Jack at one point snaps in exasperation, "You're nuts on the signal." Ralph's answer is, "That's all we've got" (p. 99), and he is right even though he has failed to make those who elected him realize the fire's significance. His is a failure of leadership communication. Nevertheless, in the beginning when Ralph is undis-puted chief and the island society is running smoothly, the signal fire is kept blazing constantly on the mountaintop.

The fire is left unattended for the first time when Jack and his choir desert it in order to go hunting. This is more than coincidence, for if the fire is a symbol (amongst other functions) of Ralph's benign order, or any order, then we should expect such order to be violated by the chaotic Jack—the id's representative—as he indulges his savage im-pulses. Just as in giving in to his need to kill he breaks the restraining walls of humane reason, so he neglects the signal in order to kill pigs. And it is more than coincidence that, when Ralph arrives on the moun-taintop, panting, only to find the deserted fire extinguished and grown cold, he cries out, "Oh God, Oh God!" The balance of the first line of the Twenty-second Psalm is, "Why hast thou forsaken me?" Or that when the hunters finally do return to the smoldering twigs they are chanting, "kill the pig, cut her throat, spill her blood," the same savage ritual they will later sing around another fire as they slay Simon. Jack has let the fire go out and, though he gathers more branches to begin another blaze, again Ralph is the one who uses Piggy's specs to light it (p. 67).

During the next few chapters, Ralph's power and control over the boys wane, as the fire on the mountain grows weaker and smaller. Sev-eral times it is left to die. Finally, when Jack bolts the community and takes Roger and Maurice with him, not enough biguns remain to keep the signal going, and the fire is moved down to the beach. The lowering (though ostensibly only of location) is as revealing of Ralph's loss of potency—and the potency of what he stands for—as it is a loss of altitude. A turning point in the action occurs when Jack seizes the balance of power; when he has enough followers, they raid their old camp, not, as Piggy feared at first, for the conch, but for fire. When Jack takes Ralph's burning branches, he takes not only the balance of power — he has shown his strength in a successful aggressive act — but the emphasis of the novel back (with him) to his camp on the rock. The action in the remainder of the book centers increasingly on Jack and the fire he builds for his tribe: Ralph and Piggy come to him for meat and are witness to Simon's murder; later, when they come to ask for, not demand, the return of Piggy's specs, Roger lets fly the lethal boulder, and Ralph is driven from the camp amid a hail of spears. And, as we sadly know, the novel ends in fire.

Golding's fires, then, are both sacred and profane, sometimes at the same time. They indicate the political, social, and moral shifts within the novel; knowing the traditional associations and uses of fire is thus very important for a fundamental understanding of this novel. For a more sophisicated understanding, the reader should know the history of these traditions. We have recalled how Ralph's original signal fire burned out of control, how it was in some way an "improper" fire created more with zeal than with restraint, even though lit with "good" intent. Golding seems to have manipulated this event to reinforce the polarity, present throughout the book, of order and chaos. Yet he is ironic, for if Ralph's well-intended fire can kill if improperly executed, Jack's fire — lit to roast its prey or at least to drive him out of cover where he may be speared — ultimately seems to save: "We saw your smoke," the naval officer explains to Ralph; "What have you been doing? Having a war or something" (p. 185)? Ironically, Jack lights the fire which is meant to kill, but it is also lit anew — like the other fires which are meant to save. And it is lit with a certain calm, reason, and purpose, however demoniac. Clearly, Golding is twisting the meanings of the symbols around, but if he is going to have the boys rescued at all, the signal fire lit by the wrong boy for the wrong purpose but in the right way is as good a method as any. What this says about the arbitrary and unreasoning nature of humanity's attainment of salvation and the irrelevance of its striving is not in keeping with Golding's Catholicism, though once more we must "trust the tale"; getting the boys rescued was necessary to the author's "theme," and the deus ex cruiser was not so much a gimmick as a device to force the reader both to reconsider the entire story and to look out at the world of humanity to see the parallel.

Thus, the eventual fire of salvation must be taken as dramatic irony, for only the boys think themselves rescued. We know better. Like Northrup Frye's "mythic" fire which destroys all, this one destroys Ralph — the last remnant of goodness — and he weeps for his loss of innocence. This momentary and superficial "rescue" is more akin to the plot than to Golding's "theme"; anyone who finds a "happy" ending has let the story overshadow the author's concern with plot.

The most striking aspect of Golding's use of fire in *Lord of the Flies* is that it is an organic symbol: without the fire the book could not exist in its present form. Golding could get by without the conch and not alter the structure substantially: something else could be found to substitute for it, either a reed of a hollow tube fashioned from some dead branch or trunk. Even the pig's head, the "lord of the flies" itself, is not the central symbol many have claimed for it; here too, Golding might have used any of several surrogates, and little more than the novel's title would have to have been changed. For neither the conch nor the pig's head function as an element of structure; neither gives this story unity, nor does either serve as a constant reminder of the shifts in character, social dynamics, and plot. The fires do. Without them *Lord of the Flies* would be a very different story with no folklore resonance, an important symbol would be lost, and the action might well become blurred without the signal fire to illuminate its shifting headings.

PART SIX

Contemporary Literature and Folklore

THOUGH THE INTERESTS AND METHODOLOGIES of recent American folklorists are largely anthropological, literature still figures importantly in folkloric studies. This final section surveys some of the notable examples. Traditional narratives, some of considerable antiquity, are still performed and transmitted today, though usually without an awareness of the narrative's history or of it even being traditional.

The "classic" folktale, the kind told around the world for centuries, collected by the Grimms, analyzed by the Finns and then the structuralists, is being supplanted in many industrialized societies by a kind of tale that often masquerades as a personal-experience narrative. Folklorists have called this new kind of folktale the urban — or contemporary — legend. And as literary authors once found something of value in the classic folktale, contemporary writers have constructed some of their fictions around these new narratives.

Meanwhile folklorists have expanded the concept of their discipline to include narratives that are not traditional in nature, that may not have a history. In America, professional interest in folk-narrative traditions seem to be fading; simultaneously, scholars have become increasingly interested in the communicative act and in the item transmitted, though that item may be individual in character. How do we recapitulate our experiences? Sociolinguist William Labov thought there was a "natural" way of doing so, presumably inherent in human behavior. Chapter 17 discusses that possibility.

Finally, folklore has become important again in certain aspects of literary study. Not, as in former times, because of the content or structure of folk narratives. Now the interest of literary theorists is on the folktale as simple, somehow elemental narrative; if we can learn about the folktale, this rationale goes, we will be in a stronger position to learn something about more complex (and sophisticated) narratives. Today the folktale is not thought of by literary scholars as merely a primitive tale told within cultures that have not developed literature; it has become a model of the narrative seed out of which fully developed narratives grow.

CHAPTER 14

Traditional Narratives Today

ARE THE STORIES THAT PEOPLE TELL TODAY of interest to folklorists? William Labov (1967) first drew attention to personal-experience
narratives, and they were almost always original, not traditional. Thus
they could not be indexed or otherwise classified in the usual ways,
making analyses based on assumptions of genetic relations impossible.
Further, Labov is a sociolinguist, and while one of his stated aims was
to come to terms with simple narratives, the real drive of his research
was linguistic, not folkloric. Nevertheless, several folklorists became
interested in personal-experience narratives qua orally transmitted stories and have found much of value about simple narratives.

However, since few personal-experience narratives are embedded in
literature, they lie outside the scope of this book. Other current narratives, some of great interest to folklorists, must for the same reasons
be neglected. Some rumors circulate as narrative and enter our cultural
consciousness in a consistent form and may be subsequently classified
as legends. But for the most part rumors, however rich their narrative-
ness, have merely a slight impact on literature, and only occasionally
appear in fixed texts: Mark Twain's *Roughing It* includes several stories current in his day in the trans-Mississippi West — such as those about
the character and deeds of Slade of Colorado — but their relation to
literature ends at their inclusion in Twain's book. Indiana University's
Linda Dégh has studied the way certain folklore — for instance the rumor
that some Halloween "trick-or-treat" candy has been laced with paper
clips, razor blades, thumb tacks, etc., actually influenced people's
behavior (they copied the idea, having heard about it or read about
it in the media, just as the Chicago "Tylenol" poisonings were copied
elsewhere in the country once the "news" was out).

For closely related reasons, the great number of orally transmitted
local legends will not be examined here either. The contemporary versions of legends — local and migratory — are the urban legends, and are

discussed elsewhere. Local legends of the traditional type, such as "Lovers' Leaps," ghost stories, tales of haunted houses and of "kissing trees," also appear in literature from time to time, particularly in nineteenth-century American literature (Washington Irving's "The Legend of Sleepy Hollow" is perhaps the most famous example); they deserve the care and time that scholarly observation affords, but not in an essay on traditional narrative today.

Finally, another category this chapter is not going to consider is of those traditional stories so well known as to have already been indexed. Aarne-Thompson tales are occasionally found in twentieth-century literature, e.g., Eudora Welty's *The Robber Bridegroom*. In the late 1960s I recorded a sermon which assigned to each playing card in a standard deck a religious significance: the two designated heaven and hell; the three symbolized the Father, Son, and Holy Ghost; the four gospel writers were indicated by that number card, as were the five wise virgins by the next one, and so on. D. K. Wilgus had been collecting data on modern country-and-western versions of this tale-type (#1613), and we collaborated. "The Deck of Cards" tale-type can be traced to the late Middle Ages, though its appearance in literature is rare. In any event, chapter 5 reviews the relationship of folktales and literary tales, and so they too will not be included here.

What is left? Many genres, of course, though this chapter will concentrate on recent re-creations of historical and local legends whose sequences of distributional elements parallel traditional narratives — for one reason or another. Those reasons, and others, make them important and interesting enough to devote a chapter to.

Shortly after John F. Kennedy was assassinated, in November 1963, several stories sprang up that he was still alive, though seriously wounded. These stories — rumors of a traditional nature — specified his residence as well as the treacherous nature of his death and reported his anticipated return at some later day (Rosenberg 1976). Most college students (and of course many others) had heard these stories when they were interviewed during the early 1970s; many believed that they were true.

One version had it that JFK was being kept alive at Bethesda Naval Hospital in Washington. One of my (Penn State) students had heard the story from a fraternity brother who had, in turn, heard it from a candy-striper at Bethesda. The hospital staff was said to have been circulating a story that Kennedy had not really died in Dallas but was being kept alive in "a vegetable-like state" on the hospital's top floor. That whole area had been sealed off from the public, and entrances to it were guarded by armed men at the elevators and staircases. Admission to the top floor was strictly prohibited. That JFK was still alive was "known" by the staff who one day saw Jacqueline Kennedy taken to the top floor, where she stayed for several hours.

Analogues to this tale noted that, since the Kennedy coffin had never been opened after it left Parkland Memorial Hospital in Dallas, only a select few had actually seen the former president's body; and they, for reasons of national security, weren't talking about it. Another of my informants (who asked not to be identified) had been one of the president's Marine guards and knew Bethesda Naval well enough to know that Kennedy, in whatever condition, was not there. The version he had heard — one he did not entirely disbelieve — had it that Kennedy had been taken to Camp David. This story was widely accepted by the other Marine guards, in Washington and at Quantico. They cited Kennedy's widow's many visits to Camp David at a time when no one (according to this informant), not even cabinet officials, had been allowed entrance. Not even the wives of former presidents were normally allowed on the grounds.

A third version gave Parkland Memorial Hospital as the place of the president's confinement. This account was given nationwide prominence when the Milwaukee *Metro-News* attributed to Truman Capote the story that Kennedy was still alive. Capote had for years been known to have been a friend and confidant of the Kennedys, and attributing his name to this story gave it credibility. The Milwaukee story was immediately repeated in a number of other newspapers nationwide, and was aired by disc jockeys in New York City and Chicago. Supporting evidence for the Parkland Memorial version had it that Mrs. Kennedy had visited the (empty) grave of her husband only 5 times in the four-and-one-half years since his publicized "death," but since November 1963 she had called at Parkland Memorial more than 340 times. The scenario was, in the mid-1970s, an old one at Parkland, where an official spokesman said that, while they had heard reports about the president's "survival," these were of course "utter nonsense."

A great many public heroes — even a few of the more notorious villains — are the subjects of such stories; the one version of the "hero's alleged death" that most closely draws a parallel between that of JFK and King Arthur (Kennedy's most famous legendary and literary antecedent) places the former president on Aristotle Onassis's island off the coast of Greece. According to the rationale for this version, the Kennedy family is said to have made a "deal" with the Greek magnate to provide John with a remote and secluded island where he could enjoy the tranquillity necessary for his recovery. The "deal" included a mock wedding, with Jackie playing the female lead, which, we are told, no outsider actually saw. Those informants who believed this account cite the opposition of the Catholic Church to remarriages, even those following the death of a spouse (!). Furthermore, the match was an unlikely one, to many, yoking the beautiful and sophisticated young widow with a much older man. Other informants could not understand how she could want him to be the father of her and John's children.

When a public leader of Kennedy's stature is killed (his youth and his personal charisma also had a lot to do with it), we can almost expect such stories to appear. Analogous tales have been told about Charlemagne, James Dean, FDR, Che Guevera, Frederick Barbarossa, Nero, Thomas Paine, Lincoln — who walks at midnight — even Hitler, "alive and well in Argentina." King Arthur is probably the most familiar of the heroic survivors, though the Kennedy legend was almost assuredly created spontaneously and not in conscious imitation of the Matter of Britain; nevertheless, we now frequently hear metaphors of JFK's years in office as "Camelot." Arthur was killed by the traitor, Mordred. So were a great many of the other "alive-and-well" heroes dispatched by villains: Siegfried was stabbed in the back by "friends" while hunting; Custer was betrayed by his (allegedly) cowardly subordinates; Jesse James was shot in the back by that "dirty little coward"; Roland and all of his command were betrayed by Ganelon; Sam Bass was sold out to the Texas Rangers by one of his gang members (much as were the movie personae of "Bonnie" and "Clyde"); Zapata was lured into an ambush by a pretended ally, and so on.

To date the traitors alleged to have shot Kennedy include the FBI, the CIA, Cubans working for the CIA, and private American citizens — including Clay Shaw, who has been acquitted by a jury in New Orleans. Delillo's *Libra* dramatizes the conspiracy theory. This notion is remarkably resilient, and among those agencies and individuals at one time or another thought by various segments of the public to be guilty, the CIA is the culprit of choice. The nature of the Central Intelligence Agency's work makes it suspect: its necessarily clandestine activities make denials difficult and dubious. When the agency is publicized, it is always for some blunder or controversial project. Right or wrong, the idea of covert operations arouses the suspicion of Americans, whose paranoid tendencies increase in times of stress. In 1975 UPI reported "a spreading of suspicion that John F. Kennedy might have been the victim of a plot involving the Central Intelligence Agency," a report so plausible that it is said to have "aroused" (then) President Ford. Trial lawyer Bernard J. Fensterwald was quoted by UPI as betting that "the full story will be known within a year." A Washington University philosophy professor was quoted in the same article as predicting that the truth would be out in six months, and that the nation's press had recently published an increasing number of embarrassing disclosures about the agency's activities. The CIA was at that moment being reviewed by the Rockefeller commission, whose executive director felt obliged to say publicly that "thus far we have not found any credible evidence that the CIA was involved in the assassination." Still, the rumors/legends persist.

That this legend was created in imitation of Arthur, (barely) alive on the isle of Avalon, across the sea, as Onassis's island is across another sea, is not believable. Such stories about Kennedy would be kept current mainly by believers, and they in turn are likely to be Kennedy admirers, however naive. Ardent worshippers are not likely to create stories about their hero in imitation of another one long dead. Such legends are perpetuated because people want them to be true so badly that they repeat stories as though they were true. In addition, those less emotionally involved know a tellable story when they hear it, knowing also that it is all the more tellable if it is true. A number of my informants were not sure whether Kennedy was alive; they hedged by prefacing what they had heard with a personal disclaimer that they were not sure whether they believed it or not. They were not believers, but neither were they active bearers of this material; they had heard the stories, but they did not repeat them — unless asked to by this folklorist.

Truman Capote vehemently denied any involvement in the "Kennedy Is Alive" story. On the April 15, 1969, "Tonight" show he denounced the *Metro-News* story as a "very vicious hoax. It's a nasty, cruel and disgusting thing. When I first saw it I thought it so stupid that nobody in the world would ever believe anything about it for one instant." Yet even Capote nods; a *hoax* implies intent to deceive, and that does not seem to be the case in this legend's creation or transmission. Then, however preposterous the story now seems, it appealed to millions of Americans who, for not very obscure reasons, wanted to believe that Kennedy was still alive. To his "total amazement" Capote was receiving "sixty to seventy letters a day." The truth of this legend, implicit in these letters, eluded him. An "extraordinary number" of them, as he put it, were from young women who said they hoped that the story was true because, no matter in what condition the president survived, it was very important to them.

Many of the young president's admirers, with visions of that perfect past that never was, thought that his three years in office were like that perfect reign of Arthur's, and they called those thousand days "Camelot." In the noblest American sense, it was naive yet touching — and certainly revealing. Yet another Camelot had ended with the wanton betrayal of the leader; Americans wished that it wasn't so, and their desires lived as long as their ideals. No king has been harder to put to rest. The mystery enshrouding the king's death implies that he is not really dead. Amid howling and lamentation, the grievously wounded Arthur was borne to sea. For years the English have expected his return, but the time was never right. When will his time come at last? When will our situation grow so grave that our king can stay away no longer? These nasty and vicious stories have elevated Kennedy, among his people, to that pantheon where few Americans besides Lincoln dwell, to that imposing chamber where sit in perpetual council Charlemagne, Siegfried, Odin, El Cid, and Arthur.

Yet if America is the country where ennobling desires can be brought to life, it is also the home of stories that express the basest racism. Los Angeles *Times* reporter Paul Coates wrote (April 20, 1965) that "there was rumor spreading all across Southern California that a little white boy had been assaulted and multilated in a public restroom by a band of adult Negroes" (cited in Ridley 1963, p. 156). Unimportant details (from the standpoint of narrative) varied: the assault's location, the age of the victim, and the ethnic origin of the assailants, depending upon the teller and the ethnic prejudice of the neighborhood. Also cited was a similar "incident," alleged to have occurred in Washington, D.C. In the eastern versions the locales were Oxen Hill, Maryland, and Prince George County.

The narrative is the one used by Chaucer's prioress; it is known as the "Ritual Murder" (motif V 361) from the assertion that assailants required the victim's blood for their religious observances. Julius Streicher's *Der Stuermer* regularly warned its readers about the sanguine needs of Jews at Passover, cautioning them to watch after their children closely. Another writer for the Los Angeles *Times* remembered that during his attendance at Hitler Youth meetings, he had heard of a German youth mutilated by the Jews (cited in Ridley 1963, p. 155). The Nazis were not unique in the dissemination of this legend; it has been found as early as the fifth century in Syria and was current in Chaucer's England.

In *The Prioress's Tale*, set long ago in a kingdom whose ruler tolerated the Jews because he needed their money, a young boy walks to school each day through the Jewish quarter, singing the *Alma Redemp-*

toris mater. This hymn of praise is offensive to the Jews who hire an assassin to cut the boy's throat and to cast him into a cesspool. His mother becomes frantic with worry for him, and the townspeople launch a search. Mary's love for her worshipper brings about a miracle; though his throat has been severed, he is given the power to continue his song, and his voice of faith leads the searchers to his body. The guilty Jews are punished, while the little boy ascends to heaven, there to sing his hymn perpetually.

Sources and Analogues of Chaucer's Canterbury Tales (Bryan and Dempster 1941) mentions twenty-seven analogues of *The Prioress's Tale*, plus more than a score that told of the martyrdom of Hugh of Lincoln and William of Norwich, the former murdered in 1255, the latter in 1144. William's biographer, Thomas of Monmouth, reported that the innocent and devout William was put to death by Jews "in scorn of the Lord's passion" (in Ridley 1963 p. 153). William was tortured, stabbed, and then crucified, his body finally hidden away in the woods. On finding his corpse — again thanks to a miraculous revelation — the townspeople, horrified, set about fervently to kill all the Jews they could find.

In recent years critics have attempted to rescue Chaucer's reputation by arguing that the tale's anti-Semitism is the Prioress's, not the author's. Others have replied by pointing out that such hostility was widespread during the Middle Ages, and that Chaucer could not be expected to feel in deep ways contrary to such a powerful ethos of his day. The intention of this chapter is not to add anything to that argument, but to point out that this narrative, which has great longevity as an oral legend and saint's life, has been the basis of reputable literature, and is once again an active legend. Believed in, its power is such as to induce violence in its hearers. When the legend migrates to the United States it retains the elements of the ritual murder and the youth (and innocence) of its victim. Only the ethnic origins of the villains are changed, the better to conform with local American hatreds: now blacks and Chicanos instead of medieval Europe's Jews.

That this legend would have been intentionally made up in the pattern of its older analogues again seems unlikely; the Germans had revived it in the 1930s, so it was available in print, to be reprinted in anonymous pamphlets circulated in the United States at about the same time. As an expression of hate, this motif (V 361) lends itself easily to a condemnation of a local minority and is an incitement to violence against them. It is around, "in the air," whence it may have been given concrete and specific form, intuitively, because it is no less than "one would expect" from such people — whoever those people happen to be, the victims of the haters.

Bernard Malamud's novel *The Fixer* is based on this legend. The hero of the title (Yakov Bok) is a Jewish handyman in czarist Russia who doesn't know his place. He goes out into the Christian world in search of a decent living, which he expects to earn with honest work. But his world won't let him; almost at once he arouses the suspicion of those around him, and finally he is accused by a poor widow of killing her son; at the initial investigation the suggested motive for the boy's repeated stabbing and extended bleeding is "possibly for religious purposes" (1966, rpt. 1986, p. 59).

The rabbi he had once entertained is accused of being the inspiration of Bok's murderous behavior; and, on learning that the fixer is a Jew, all those who have had contact with him rush to denounce him. Bok is thrown into prison where he is brutally treated for his "heinous crime"; he is not permitted visitors, and only after years of systematic degradation is he even allowed an attorney. A trial is vaguely alluded to, but always seems to be far away in the future.

This is the ritual sacrifice motif told from the perspective of the accused killer, and in Malamud's fiction the accusation is false. But in an anti-Semitic society this legendary lie is believed; the widow is not the wronged grieving mother, she is aggressively malign (possibly even having murdered her son herself); and the outraged society of Chaucer's tale is, in this modern novel, indifferent to the truth and desirous only of satisfying its hatred. In such a world, Yakov Bok's triumph can only be a moral one.

Another popular legend, recreated anew in the United States in (probably unconscious) imitation of European analogues, describes the last days and the heroic death of that notorious Indian-fighter, George A. Custer. As his story emerged in a variety of sources — newspapers, popular novels, biographies, personal letters, poems, movies, etc. — he was depicted as the great hero whose consummate martial skills were of no avail against the inundating hordes of his Indian foes. In this legend cluster, the hero and his small band are surrounded and eventually overwhelmed by a much larger force of ethnic or other traditional aliens. Only the hero's pride or rash courage has induced him to fight in the first place; though the fight is at first successful, treason or cowardice on the part of one or more of his men turns the tide against him. Pressed to the point where defeat is inevitable, many of the enemy are killed, usually on or near a mountaintop. A last-minute call for help is made, too late. The hero is offered a chance to escape, but declines, choosing to die with his men. With his magical sword — or an extraordinary one which he has used triumphantly in the past — the hero fights to the last and is himself among the very last to succumb. A lone survivor, usually an insignificant actor in this great drama, carries the news to the awaiting world outside. The hero is eulogized, often by his slayer; and the villain's countrymen are punished by the hero's vengeful comrades who have been inspired by his ennobling fall (Rosenberg 1974).

A few newspapers at the time called "Custer's Last Stand" the "Thermopylae of the plains" (the scenario, above, does describe the account of Leonidas and his Spartans at Thermopylae: Rosenberg 1974, pp. 165-74). But those news accounts never pressed the comparison beyond a most superficial level, and after the initial burst of stunned patriotism inspired by the battle had faded, the comparison died. A great many of the above details were at least dubious, and some were simply wrong. For instance, not only did Custer not have a special sword, he had no sword at all. There is little evidence about how the battle went for Custer's five companies (seven of the regiment's companies survived, more or less); but those who wanted to believe that Custer was heroic and that white soldiers were qualitatively superior to Indians would naturally want to believe that the battle had gone well at first. That detail establishes the superiority of the losers, defeated only by the far greater numbers of the victors. That Custer had an opportunity to escape, offered by his Crow scout, Curley, or anyone, seems extremely unlikely (Rosenberg 1974). No eulogy was uttered over Custer's corpse, certainly not by Sitting Bull as was once reported; Captain Benteen's comments are said to have been truly denigratory.

Such is the legend as it developed, largely orally, in the United States in the late nineteenth century. Yet this scenario must not be thought of as merely the wild fantasy of the great unwashed; it appears in literature as well — the scenario is similar although the battle described is not the Little Big Horn — in Flaubert's *La Salammbô*. There is no evidence that Flaubert modeled his last stand of his hero, Mathô, on Herodotus or the *Chanson de Roland*. So similar in outline — in the sequencing of distributional narrative elements — are the literary accounts and the folkloric that one is once again forced to realize the similarities between high and folk art, and of course at the same time to understand the real differences.

We happen to know Flaubert's sources for this, his first novel after *Bovary*; it is the account of Polybius's "Inexpiable War." There are no hills in the Greek account of the battle, though Flaubert invents a hilltop for Mathô's last stand. Polybius does not say — did not know? — the identity of the last rebel to be killed on the field, though what he does say strongly indicates that it was not Mathô. These epic details have been Flaubert's inventions; he did not rely on any oral French tradition. Being a great storyteller, he described Mathô's fall (defeat in this case, not death) in the most natural way, the way our culture mandates for the telling of such stories. Flaubert is universally considered a master storyteller; but what of those countless mute and inglorious Flauberts who created much the same plot for their own narratives? They too, like Herodotus, and Turoldus, and Frederick Whittaker (Custer's first biographer) knew how to tell a tale of overcome heroism in the best, most effective way; "das Volk" lack the inclination to invent the finely wrought line, the incandescent metaphor, the school-learned philosophy that may elevate a narrative out of its created world to a more encompassing universe. What they, we, know quite well, are the larger structural elements of narrative, the knowledge that comes from listening and most of all from living.

We see also in the Custer analogues just how closely allied the genres of history and folklore can be. Herodotus and Polybius took many of their sources from oral tradition. The story of the annihilation of Charlemagne's rear guard (and the death of one of its leaders, a Hrulandus) had been in oral circulation for over two centuries before "Turoldus," whoever he was, wrote his heroic epic of defeat. *La Salammbô* is unarguably literature; but to what extent are Froissart's chronicles history? Or those of Herodotus? Conversely, then, is oral history really literature in disguise, or closet folklore, or the makings of authentic history? Hayden White once remarked (to a National Institute for the Humanities seminar of which I was a member) that historians had drummed him out of the profession — for his heretical writings about the influence of literary style and structures on the writing of history. The results of the research presented above argue his case, though from a different perspective. Historians may be attempting to reconstruct the past, and to give it a theoretical structure, while artists may be merely fancifully re-creating it; yet they, like the "folk" whose often inartistic accounts only folklorists study, are united by limits of human epistemology. But that matter, to beg off the question, is not within the scope of this book.

Custer's Last Stand is not a traditional narrative of today, yet the hero's-last-stand scenario is still being recreated: a hero, or a small group of men, are defeated by a hated enemy. When I spoke on this topic at the Hebrew University of Jerusalem in 1972, neither faculty nor graduate students had any resistance to placing Saul or the Jewish zealots at Masada within this paradigm. And they even suggested contemporary parallels, the "Negev Thirty-five," overrun by Egyptian troops in that desert in a recent war. (Though there are now no longer any sabers, the hilltop becomes a dune, and other adjustments are made to adapt this narrative cluster to its enviornment.) And Vietnam veterans who were my students have told me about similar accounts of heroic last stands of units overrun by the enemy. One can predict, reasonably safely, that as long as one's compatriots (or allies) are defeated by a hated enemy, stories of the last stand will reemerge.

A final example of traditional narratives that have been re-created for their expressive content today comes from an entirely different area of human activity, religious conversion. Yet just as the Custer story seems almost inevitable given certain conditions — the defeat of prestigious friendlies by a hated or despised alien force — so a number of conversion narratives seem to derive from lived experiences. One of my informants (for *The Art of the American Folk Preacher*) interviewed in 1968, the Reverend Rubin Lacy of Bakersfield, California, had been a blues singer during the late 1920s and the 1930s, supplementing his sporadic earnings by working as a laborer for a railroad. He remembered that period of his life, during which he had too often indulged his appetites for things of the flesh, with some embarrassment.

Then one day, while he was working with a track gang doing some repair work, he was involved in an accident which hospitalized him for several weeks. Lacy was vague about the extent of his injuries, but whatever the actual case, his recollection was that he was near death. Then one night the Lord appeared to him and asked why he had never followed the straight path. The singer then "struck a bargain" with God: in return for healing, Lacy promised to give up his former sinful ways and enter His ministry. The healing happened; and the ministry gained a new, fervent apostle.

The morpohology of this conversion narrative was one that I was to hear repeatedly in subsequent years. Lacy was black, but the conversion stories of white preachers in eastern Kentucky as well as those of other blacks in North Carolina and Virginia were much the same. In every case the would-be convert had a deep sense of wrongdoing (a "troubled soul"). He soon experienced a period of intense inner turmoil, during which the Lord or one of His angels visited the penitent, shortly after which he resolved his spiritual turbulence and thenceforth led an exemplary life.

The structure of this related experience is like that of the most famous convert of the Middle Ages, the fourth-century Bishop of Hippo, St. Augustine. In the *Confessions* he wrote of the struggles within himself between "two wills, the one old, the other new, the first carnal, the second spiritual," laying "waste my soul" (1960 p. 189). At that crucial moment in his spiritual life, Ponticianus visited him and told him of his own conversion, overwhelming Augustine with horror and shame (1960, pp. 195 ff.). Left alone, he wondered how long he would have to endure his soul's torture:

> And lo, I heard from a nearby house, a voice like that of a boy or girl, I know not which, chanting and repeating over and over, "take up and read, take up and read". . . . I checked the flow of my tears and got up for I interpreted this solely as a command given to me by God to open the book and read the first chapter I should come upon. . . . I snatched it up, opened it, and read in silence the chapter on which my eyes first fell: "not in rioting and drunkenness, not in chambering and impurities, not in strife and envying; but put you on the Lord Jesus Christ, and make not provision for the flesh in its concupiscences." No further wished I to read, nor was there need to do so. Instantly, in truth, at the end of this sentence, as if before a peaceful light streaming into my heart, all of those dark shadows of doubt fled away.

Within a year he had accepted baptism and a few years beyond that he was ordained in Hippo.

We should note the profuse emotional expression in Augustine's writing, characteristic of the man and of his age. Everything is seen in extremis: the sins of his early life are many and great, his soul is tormented by a profound confusion, and after his sudden glimpse of Grace, a peaceful light streamed into his heart. First, all was purple; then the deepest black; finally, it is all clarity and (white) light. Such was the medieval tendency to view life in striking, absolute terms.

The passion that was typical of the fourth-century personal-conversion narrative had not diminished a thousand years later when the great Majorcan alchemist and mystic Ramon Lull converted to the faith of his inheritance. He too led a life of dissipation until his thirty-first year; like Augustine, and many other medieval saints, Lull's conversion dates seem carefully chosen. One night, while penning an amorous song to his most recent mistress, a divine presence came to him in his lonely chamber; his biographer, E. Allison Peers (1946), describes it thus:

> As he gazed abstractly into space, he saw that Something was gazing at him. There, a little to his right, against the wall was "Our Lord Jesus Christ hanging upon the cross." It was no delusion of the imagination. . . . He [Lull] trembled with fear. His pen fell from his grasp. He could neither think nor reason. (p. 11)

On the following night he again sat down to write his song of love, and again the apparition appeared to him:

> This time hardly had he begun when, looking up, he saw the crucified again. At this second appearance "he had a much greater affright than at the first," and, pushing away the paper, flung himself upon the bed again, burying his face in his hands to shut out the terrible and persistent visitation. . . . Three times more . . . Ramon took up his pen again to complete his song, and three times more there appeared that Figure "in great agony and sorrow," gazing at him. . . . Our Lord Jesus Christ desired none other thing than that he should wholly abandon the world and devote himself to His service. (Peers 1946, p. 246)

Lull's conversion became an active reality. Giving up all of the things of the world, he went to Palma to learn Arabic so that he might teach the gospel to the infidels. And in this service, a decade after his conversion, Lull found the martyr's death he had sought.

His narrative unfolds artfully. How often do we find that the (male) saints of the Middle Ages have led an early life in the bonds of turpitude, only to refine those base lusts suddenly to a pure love for God. St. John of the Cross wrote poems about his encounters with God as though they were love poems describing erotic liaisons: we may recall the popular theory of de Rougemont that the love lyrics of the troubadours were meant secretly and really for the Virgin; and we know what the medieval Church made of the ostensibly sensuous Song of Solomon. Lull was not persuaded the first few times his Lord appeared to him, but only after the conflict within him had built to an intolerable climax. And then the absolute response: to "wholly abandon the world."

In Lull's account as in Augustine's so much of the surface of the narrative and so much of its underlying morphology—awareness of sin, distress, divine visitation, and harmonious resolution—are alike that one may suspect a little pious borrowing, or imitation of the hallowed Father. We remember how the later scholastics debated the correctness of the early Fathers, how they revered them, how in so many ways they sought to imitate their virtues. To emulate their virtues was virtue in itself.

Or perhaps both are indebted to the New Testament's most famous convert, Paul. His sins were not the same ones of the flesh, yet as Luke testifies, God came to Paul as violently as to any unregenerated lecher:

> And as he journeyed, he came near Damascus: and suddenly there shined round him a light from heaven:
> And he fell to earth, and heard a voice saying unto him, Saul, Saul why persecutest thou me?

And he said, Who art thou, Lord? And the Lord said, I am Jesus whom thou persecutest: it is hard for thee to kick against the pricks.

And he trembling and astonished, said, Lord, what wilt thou have me to do? And the Lord said unto him, Arise, and go into the city, and it shall be told thee what thou must do. (Acts 9:3–6)

Paul, now blind, was led to Damascus where he fasted for three (!) days until God's emissary, Ananias, came to him and filled Paul with the Holy Spirit, "and immediately there fell from his eyes as it had been scales: and he received sight forthwith, and arose and was baptised" (Acts 9:18). Blindness, symbolizing the error of the old law, and the regaining of sight in the light of the new, was to become one of the most popular religious literary "events" of the next 1,500 years.

The Reverend Lacy had surely never heard of Ramon Lull and probably not of Augustine. I know that he had never read the *Confessions* — he hardly read at all. They did not inspire his conversion narrative, though possibly Paul did. That lawyer-turned-apostle may have also inspired itinerant evangelist Jed Smock who, stopping off at Indiana University after an autumn pilgrimage through Kentucky and Tennessee, related to those of us who would listen his depraved adventures as a hippie, when he found that "carnal gratification became the driving force of my life." In Africa, Smock was following his shadowy pursuits with several birds of the same feather when "on Christmas day God sent a messenger when an Arab walked into the midst of our hippie band, planted a cross, and preached Jesus. Although most of the children of disobedience mocked him, through the blood of the cross I received a word of peace." Like the conversion of Justin Martyr, whose conversation with "a certain old man" in a field near the sea led to his commitment to the faith, evangelist Smock found God in the words of a stranger. "And like the Prodigal Son, I came to myself, departed from certain lusts which were warring against my soul, and made the decision to arise and seek the home of my Father."

St. Paul may have been the model for all of these holy men, but William James (1958) thought the answer lay elsewhere — in a psychological polygenesis. He characterized human psychic life as a succession of constantly readjusting and changing goals, each usually succeeding the other gradually and in relative harmony. One's life is marked by a constant change in the center of interests and in one's system of ideas, from more central parts of consciousness to the more peripheral — and the reverse. As emotional commitments alter, we learn that what is important one month may mean little the next. Our emotional experiences may oscillate greatly, causing "the divided self." However, when the focus of emotional excitement over a particular goal becomes permanent, and if that concern or goal is religious, we experience what James termed a religious conversion. "To say that a man is 'converted' means, in these terms, that religious ideas, previously peripheral in his consciousness, now take a central place, and that religious aims form the habitual centre of his energy" (1958, p. 162).

Strong emotional events may generate mental rearrangements; the emotions thus produced by such "shocks" often achieve permanence.

James perceived two conversion-experience genres, one a gradual development or moral and spiritual habits which he termed "volitional," and the other a sudden and instantaneous self-surrender. The latter interests us here. During such conversions, James noted, the penitent sees himself or herself as something of a passive spectator to a process imposed from without. At such moments the convert is said to be visited by the spirit of God, and an entirely new nature is breathed in, allowing him or her to partake of the very substance of the deity. In James's scheme, the impulse that will eventually seize the convert already exists in the subject's unconscious, or beyond the "field of consciousness." The most important consequence of having such an unconscious life is that the ordinary fields of consciousness are liable to incursions from it, and because we cannot guess their source, they appear to be unaccountable impulses to act (or to refuse to act), and they give rise to obsessive ideas. "Automatism" is the name given to the sphere of effects due to uprushes into consciousness of energies originating in the unconscious.

The convert is likely to have a "pronounced sensibility; second, a tendency to automatism; and third, suggestability of the passive type" (1958, p. 194). Yet while we may dissect and analyze this process exhaustively in psychological terms, the change that occurs in the human convert is spiritually profound. Nothing of what James says really explains conversion, but only attempts to describe it, in such metaphors as "fields" and "spheres." James himself admits that conversion may well be a divinely inspired act, though he thought that God may be acting through the convert's unconscious.

But what of the form of the narrative of conversion? Scholars and theologians may debate causes, but how does it happen that the personal accounts of conversions, spanning 1,500 years and three times that many miles, are yet so similar? To approach that question we should ask first what options are open to those who wish to communicate this central experience. How else might one's rebirth be told? The convert must state — presumably as a result of feeling — that his or her former life has been depraved. Of what dramatic significance is it to us if we are told that a rather ordinary, bland person, not much more sinning than most, has suddenly repented of his or her ways? Such a conversion story pales beside the penitential change of the colossal reprobate, and is in itself hardly interesting. More important, such a conversion would hardly be instructive to others. The convert is really likely to feel that his or her former life was in some way wrong, or vile, or base to give point and meaning to the very act of conversion. Augustine (like Francis after him), had to claim to have given himself over to lechery and debauchery completely so that his subsequent piety would become all the more striking. God's ways are not so mysterious here: Lull seems the least likely sinner to want to give his life for his Lord. That Lull was chosen shows us that even the most seemingly unregenerate blasphemer may be saved in the most glorious fashion.

Augustine wrote of the two spirits warring within him. Such a narrative provides tension, drama, conflict. Lacy lay "on a bed of affliction," tortured with pain, reluctant to eschew his riotous ways until the end. He was a man whose conversion narrative he would want to recall, framed in such a way that we would want to retell.

We should assume sincerity in these converts, and we must allow them to feel that the change from one way of life to another has meaning. The convert does not think of having given up one good life merely for another equally meaningful. Such psychic events may happen, but we do not call them conversions, nor are they compelling stories when we hear about them. They are simply not the kind of stories that will confirm us in our faith or in the power of the Almighty or which will perhaps some day convert the heathen.

As in all well-conceived narratives, even personal narratives, there must be contrast. In conversion stories the old life is contrasted with the new: "therefore if any man be in Christ he is a new creature: old things are passed; behold, all things are become new" (2 Corinthians 5:17). The old should seem to have been wicked, willful, and depraved, even more evil that it may actually have been; the new must be supremely holy, obedient to God's will, and chaste. Before, a life of wretchedness and shame; after, righteousness and peace. If the conversion is to be dramatic, it should occur suddenly, swiftly. To many it no doubt seemed so. And the impelling agent should come directly from God. Anything less diminishes the impact of the confrontation between sinner and Judge. In the struggle, God's glory is the greater if His triumph is over a truly degenerate soul; what is the magnitude of a victory over a modestly licencious penitent?

These truths have transcended time and place. Conversion—at least in the West — is a universal. So is God's role; and the psychology of the convert appears also to be a constant. The penitent's means of expressing this universal experience is, perhaps not so surprisingly, consistent, because so much of the tradition and situation in which personal narrative would arise is constant throughout the West. On the road to Damascus, in Hippo and Palma, in contemporary America, people find God in similar ways and talk about it in similar ways.

The human factors that inspired the creation of these and other legends re-created anew though in the mold of traditional belief-narratives, are much harder to determine than to identify. However, at least two elements seem to be involved: the desire to have events occur in a certain way, to shape reality for our own ends; and the forming of that reality from the everyday observation of the lifeworld. We so strongly want life to have a particular, individual structure that we rearrange our perceptions to make that "happen"; and we shape our wish-fantasies according to materials that we find in our lives and that our culture has given to us.

We recall that Truman Capote was at one time receiving sixty to seventy letters a week inquiring about the survival of John F. Kennedy. And though he thought it was a vicious and nasty hoax, many of his correspondents expressed the great hope that Kennedy was in fact alive, no matter what his condition, because it was vitally important to them. A need is felt; there are many reasons for citizens to want Kennedy to remain alive. They deeply admired him and the work he was doing, so of course his death brought in its wake a great deal of uncertainty; the unsettling situation in Washington was mirrored in millions of unsettled psyches; they abhorred violence and the waste of a young and talented life, and wished to undo all of those evils by returning him to life.

The narratives of conversion also express an urgent need — on the part of the convert — though in these stories that need is contemplated retrospectively. The feeling that one's present life is somehow wrong can be a major component in one's psychological being, a feeling crying out desperately for rectification. Given that need, the rest of the conversion narrative falls into place. If one converts, the past must be seen to have been excessively sinful, or at least empty. The conversion itself will be an emotionally upsetting experience, very likely climaxed by a visitation from the deity to whom the convert is about to vow allegiance and obedience. And to give the conversion point, the convert's present life must be serene and meaningful.

The Custer legend-cluster shows us even more cogently the influence of one's cultural heritage of narrative elements. The tradition precedes the individual. For instance, the hero must be defeated by an overwhelming horde of the enemy; what kind of hero would he be, what would we think of the martial valor of his men, if he were defeated by an inferior force of the hated enemy? Such narratives exist, and may well correspond to specific realities, but the leader of the defeated army could hardly be considered a hero. Whether the battle actually goes well at first or not, we want to think that it did; we will assume that the hero will be among the last to be killed, if not the very last (what kind of hero would he be if he were not?); we will want to think that only through treachery and/or the cowardice of one of more of his men he is defeated at all; and we assume that his great pride in himself and the skill of his men will delay his call for help — until it is too late. Not all of these elements need be present, certainly. But, given the basic need to explain why a favored hero would be defeated by a despised enemy, many or all of the above narrative elements will be present. If they are altered, and so appear in conflictingly variant form, the purpose of the narrative will not have been to glorify and to justify the hero.

The narrative of Custer/Roland/Leonidas/the "Negev thirty-five", etc. is one of praise. The ritual murder stories are hateful, and they are meant to inspire hatred. Both narratives strongly affect the listener; both are meant to incite action. The Custer-paradigm tales rouse the hero's fellow citizens to vengeance, whether against the Indians, the Japanese ("Remember Pearl Harbor"), the Spanish ("Remember the Maine"), or the Mexicans ("Remember the Alamo"). Ritual murder stories incite hatred against the alleged killers of the young child: in Chaucer's *Prioress's Tale* the guilty Jews are arrested and punished (or, as in other variants, they are killed wholesale); and the recent function of the tale in Los Angeles was to arouse hatred, fear, and contempt of the supposedly responsible Chicanos, as it was against the blacks near Washington, D.C. The story is, shamefully, an embodiment, a manifestation, a creation of some dark need, brought to life, leading to the punishment of some hated group.

Given the hatred, many stores — not simply this one — could come into being. This narrative is at hand, but the elements in it are the inheritance of our culture. The victim is always young, and thus innocent as well as helpless. He/she is mutilated brutally as well as murdered, heightening the heinousness of the crime. And the villains are said to require this sacrifice as part of their religious rituals, thus condemning them as intrinsically debased creatures, whose very religious (or ethnic) fundamentals require the murder of innocents. A destructive need establishes the conditions for the narrative, whose details are supplied by our culture. The "Ritual Murder" probably projects the desire to mutilate and destroy the detested minority; always a young boy is said to be the victim, and his mutilation is a symbolic castration. Though 'they" do it to "one of us" in this tale, the reverse is at the bottom of the tale teller's (sub-rosa) desires. Genetic monogensis is not necessary to explain this spontaneous development, nor is any notion of a collective unconscious, however modified. The individual psyche and the inheritance of one's culture supply most of the narrative components of those traditional narratives current today, as they did for Chaucer, St. Augustine, Herotodus, and the early Arthurian romanciers.

CHAPTER 15

Urban Legends:
The Modern Folktales

ELIZABETH JANE HOWARD'S SHORT STORY "Mr. Wrong" (1979) shares several narrative episodes with two (possibly three) popular contemporary oral narratives—urban legends—and its emotional core is similar enough to them to invite comparison. Direct borrowing is a possibility; and while I will discuss, among other aspects of narrative, the recent, ongoing relationship between literature and oral narratives, this chapter will not be merely a source study. Far from it; I intend to use this similarity as a point of departure for a discussion both of the behavior of these new folktales in circulation and of the flexibility a writer of known sophistication can employ in their presentation.

Because Mrs. Howard's story is not widely known in the United States, it needs to be summarized:

> Meg Crosbie, a twenty-seven-year-old who has always lived four hours' drive from London with her parents, has gone to the capital to start a life on her own. She is quiet, shy, lonely, socially inept, bored (and probably boring), and timid. She works as an assistant in a china and knickknack shop. She is lucky in being able to buy a (used) car in her first few weeks in London, enabling her to drive home on weekends. During her first such trip, on a rainy and foggy freeway (the M 1), she hears "heavy, laboured, stertorous, even painful breathing" coming from the back of the car. She is frightened, but no other harm befalls her. On the next week's trip home, this time in fog and sleet, she sees a hitchhiker—a girl, bareheaded, who "looked wet through, cold and exhausted," an "air of extreme desolation about her" (p. 17). When Meg offers her a lift, the "astonishingly pale" girl whose face was "actually livid" got into the back seat while a man, appearing suddenly out of the rainy night, got into the front beside her. Meg finds him thoroughly detestable; so when he asks that she pull over onto a roadside turn-off so that he may satisfy "a need of nature" (p. 19), she turns to the pale girl in the back to chide her for not talking at all during the ride. But the girl has disappeared. The next portion of the journey erupts into an argument when the stranger refuses to acknowledge that he knew or knew of a girl like the

one Meg described as having been in the back seat. Stopping at a service station several miles further along, Meg asks her hitchhiker to leave; when she asks the attendant if he had seen the man in the front of her car, he replies that he "didn't see anyone. Anyone at all" (p. 25). The rest of the journey is completed uneventfully. On the next weekend Meg tries to sell her car, which she now feels is haunted, and is unable to return home, having to remain in London in order to answer telephone inquiries about the vehicle. During the week she discovers, in an old newspaper photograph being used to wrap china, that the girl hitchhiker had been a murder victim eighteen months before, and that her body had been found near an abandoned MG. On the fourth weekend trip home during a "fine misty rain" (p. 44), she pulls into a service area to take off her sweater when the stranger's hand reaches out in front of her. Helplessly, she remains in the car, feeling "the knife jab smoothly through the skin of her neck" as "speechless terror overwhelmed her. . . . " (p. 45)

The reader is not told whether the rider is, as Meg thinks, a ghost, or the actual killer of the pale girl a year ago, the police having arrested "Mr. Wrong." The behavior and ghostly disappearance of the pale girl is never explained at all. The story is, as Todorov has described the genre, fantastic (1975). It has purely supernatural elements: Meg's MG is probably the same car used by the murderer eighteen months before, and it may be haunted by the ghost of the murdered girl whose mysterious disappearance from the back seat seems to have really occurred.

The story is strikingly similar in several particulars to the well-known legends, "The Killer in the Back Seat" and "The Vanishing Hitchhiker." The latter tale has been frequently commented on and analyzed, owing to its great popularity, and will be reserved for later. I shall begin with a version of the "The Killer in the Back Seat," collected in fall 1981 in Providence, Rhode Island, from a nineteen-year-old student at Brown University. Tim Barton heard this version "a few years ago" from a "storyteller" who would "swear [that his] story actually happened":

> A woman drives into a gas station. The gas station attendant starts to fill up the gas tank, then goes into his office. He returns shortly and gives her a piece of paper. As he gives her this, he says "That will be [X] number of dollars." The note says, "Don't turn around. There is a man in the back seat. Just calmly get out of the car and follow me." She does, and soon after, a police car arrives, and arrests a man with a pistol who had been hiding in the back seat.

Howard's story differs from Barton's legend (which I will call "TB 1") and others like it in at least one important respect. In the "Killer in the Back Seat" tales the victim is always rescued, probably because a

survivor is necessary to tell the tale. This is a story of terror survived; as
Linda Dégh has observed of another legend ("The Roommate's Death"),
the focus is on the fear of the survivor (1969). A narrow escape is essential to the aesthetic of "The Killer in the Back Seat." In other stories
the victim may have a friend murdered—as in "The Boyfriend's Death"
and "The Roommate's Death" stories—but those deaths serve only to
heighten the terror of the victim, who survives. Dead women tell no
tales. Ms. Howard presents a negative image of the legend. In the folk
legend ("The Killer in the Back Seat") the service area or parking lot
is a place of safety, a secure well-lighted place in the midst of the surrounding darkness; in the short story, when Meg pulls off the road into
such an area, her assailant decides to strike. No gas station attendant
will help her; two weeks before, in fact, the attendant had been oblivious to her need: rather than seeing the assailant in the back seat, he
had not seen "anyone at all" (p. 25).

Even though the situation in the two narratives is similar—a young
woman alone at night and an unknown assailant in her back seat—the
difference in the ending of the two stories does not argue for a direct
relationship. But when "Mr. Wrong" is set beside "The Vanishing Hitchhiker," the similarity is clearer. The following version was reprinted in
Brunvand's *The Vanishing Hitchhiker* (1981, p. 25):

> A traveling man who lived in Spartenburg was on his way home one night
> when he saw a woman walking along the side of the road. He stopped his
> car and asked the woman if he could take her where she was going. She
> stated that she was on her way to visit her brother who lived about three
> miles further on the same road. He asked her to get in the car and sit by
> him, but she said she would sit in the back of the car. Conversation took
> place for a while as they rode along, but soon the woman grew quiet. The
> man drove on until he reached the home of the woman's brother, whom he
> knew; then stopped the car to let the woman alight. When he looked behind
> him, there was no one in the car. He thought that rather strange. . . .

Most saliently, the sex of the driver is reversed, but then the point
of most "Vanishing Hitchhiker" tales is not so much the fear of the
driver but the eeriness of the event. In Ms. Howard's narrative we are
fearful for the driver. Some of the descriptive and situational details
of the horror legend are in the short story as well. Meg assumes that
the pale girl will get in beside her, but, like the girl in the legend, she
chooses the rear seat. The disgusting man gets in front. (For the next
trip the legends are shifted, and the killer is appropriately in the back
seat.) When the girl disappears—Meg has just chided her for not con-

tributing to the conversation—some physical sign of her presence is sought: moisture on the back seat. This detail also appears in some of the legends (Brunvand 1981, p. 27; Beardsley and Hankey 1942, p. 314).

Brunvand lists nine elements that characterize the "Vanishing Hitchhiker" legend (1981, p. 20); not all are stable, active episodes—four are the more labile descriptive features—but the ensemble further demonstrates the proximity of "Mr. Wrong" to this popular legend: driver; authentication; setting; hitchhiker; her address; choice of seat; disappearance; concern; identification (see Bennett 1984). In the British short story the privileged character is, primarily, a driver who offers a lift to a hitchhiker who, in turn, chooses to get into the rear seat. After a while the hitchhiker disappears, the driver is concerned, and, a few weeks later, while glancing at an old newspaper, identifies her. "Authentication" in literature is seldom the same as in legends, as in Brunvand's example when the tale teller "identifies" the driver as a "traveling man" from Spartenburg. The legend is usually believed, the short story almost never. Yet there is the willing suspension of disbelief—and we know quite a few particularizing details about Meg Crosbie, details imparting verisimilitude: her purchase of the MG, her job in the London china shop, and her weekend drives home. The setting is there, of course: fog and cold rain. The girl hitchhiker's address is not given, though her disgusting companion wants to be dropped off between Northampton and Leicester. But not all legends have all of these nine elements, just as Propp showed that not all folktales have all his functions. "Mr. Wrong" has more than enough to demonstrate its similarity with folk legends, even if the labile elements are not thought to be present. The stories are close, especially the account of Meg's final trip compared to the tale of the "The Killer in the Back Seat."

Nevertheless, my point here is not to argue for a genetic relationship between these three stories. Instead, their similarity provides a point of departure for observations about the fluidity of narratives in oral tradition and the changes that can occur when an imaginative writer tells (relates in written prose) the "same" story.

For the purpose of this demonstration, we can identify two traditions of "The Killer in the Back Seat" tales. In the first (I), exemplified by TB 1, the victim-driver, unaware of any danger, routinely pulls into a gas station where the attendant "rescues" her, using a fabrication to get her into the safety of the station office, and (usually) calling the police. Barton's second version (TB 2) is also of this type, but with the clever ruse on the part of the attendant of telling the woman that the money she has given him is counterfeit and that she will have to come with him into the office. No mention is made of police. In one of the versions supplied by the Indiana University Folklore Archives, the woman driver is on a highway "one night" when a truck tries to get her to pull off the highway, but she refuses. However, when she shortly sees that her gas is low, she drives into "this awful looking filling station." She gives her credit card to "the rough looking attendant," who subsequently tells her that she will have to come into the station for a minute. There he tells her that "there was a man laying [*sic*] in the back of her car." The truck is an extraneous element in this tale, but it has a very definite place in those versions of the second tradition. (For another taxonomy, see Cord 1969, pp. 48 ff.).

In these stories the woman driver (in one collected instance a boy is out driving with his girl friend) is on the road alone when another vehicle, usually a truck, signals her to pull over, by either blinking its high beams or blowing the horn. The driver is frightened, but is finally stopped, sometimes halting voluntarily. The other driver approaches the victim and tells her (them) that an assailant is hiding in the back seat. The place where the revelation is made can be a wide spot in the road, a narrow dirt road (where the driver thinks the truck incapable of following), or a place not specified. Sometimes the police come to the rescue; sometimes it is the truck driver; in one instance (Indiana University Folklore Archives legend 5; hereafter the form "IU 5" will be used) the woman drives back to her house (Brunvand notes one version in which the husband then restores order [1981, pp. 52–53]). The second traditional (II) differs in that help comes from another driver whose signals are at first misinterpreted; in those tales the victim-driver is frightened early in the tale, but for the wrong reason; later she will learn why she should have been frightened—for the right reason.

Another legend (IU 3) presents a conflation of details: a woman is driving home at night when she notices that she is being followed by another car with its high beams on. She drives into a gas station

> that was open since this was rather late at night, got out of her car quickly and went up to the attendant to tell him she was being followed and to call the police. The other car also followed her into the filling station keeping its bright lights on. The driver got out of the car and explained that he had seen a Negro man crouched down in the back seat of the car.

Does this tale belong to Tradition I or II? For my purposes it does not matter; IU 3 is cited merely to demonstrate how labile, ancillary elements in a narrative change, even though the essential tale—composed of several constantly recurring narrative elements—remains: victim, threat, and rescuer. Not all of these elements are active: "rescuer" is defined by his action, and the victim is defined by her movement — driving alone (usually at night), presumably unable to cope with an assailant in her back seat, quickly frightened by the headlights of another car or truck. "Threat" implies bodily harm that would have been perpetrated by the person in the back seat — and, while in none of the legends examined does he actualize this threat, he is nevertheless designated in the legend's title as "killer." In various versions he carries, or brandishes, a knife, a gun, or an axe. An early writer on this folktale suggested "Assailant in the Back Seat," but no assault is ever made (Cord 1969, p. 47).

The migration, deletion, and alteration of narrative elements are understood by folklorists; such changes are so common that some scholars define folklore mainly in terms of change. Not only do tales of the same type (or "tradition" as I have designated them here) constantly shift episodes and descriptive details, but elements from other tales entirely interchange, much as the Finns had observed in their study of the traditional folktale (Thompson 1977, p. 436). Tale IU 2 begins with the distinctive situation of a couple parked in a local lovers' lane:

> There was this couple parking, and when it came time to leave they took the side road home. Well a car passed them, and all of a sudden it turned around and started blinking its lights and honking its horn at them. Well this really worried the couple, so that at first he tried to get away from the car. But finally it upset the girl so much that they stopped the car to find out what was wrong with them. Just as soon as he stopped, the car pulled beside him, and the man said, "I just wanted to warn you that there was a man on top of your car with an axe in his hand waiting for you to get out."

As with so many of these tales, just the slightest examination will reveal the unlikely character of the story. A man with an axe is on top of the car but the couple inside do not hear anything unusual. When the presumed assailant is seen in the back seat, he is unwaveringly identified as having evil intent by another driver on the road; if it was thought that the car simply had a passenger in the back seat — the reaction that we would all have — there would be no story. And, in the case of IU 2 above, when the "rescuer" pulls alongside the innocent couple, what does the axe-wielding man on the roof do — nothing? — while the brief conversation about his discovery is allowed to proceed.

But such considerations are beside the immediate point, which is a demonstration of how episodes from other tales — other types of tales — get attached to foreign material. Most commonly "The Killer in the Back Seat" begins with the victim, a woman, alone on the road, usually at night. The couple, parking, presumably in a lovers' lane, is an import from one of two other tales, either "The Boyfriend's Death" or "The Hook." Brunvand's example of the former begins, "This happened just a few years ago out on the road that turns off 59 highway by the Holiday Inn. This couple were parked under a tree out on this road. Well, it got to be time for the girl to be back at the dorm, so she told her boyfriend that they should start back. But the car wouldn't start . . . (1981, p. 6).

Here the tales part company and go their different ways: the victims of "The Killer in the Back Seat" version of IU 2 start right up but are soon stopped by the other car. The boyfriend in "The Boyfriend's Death" gets out of the car to go for assistance, and his body is found the next morning hanging from a tree above the car by people coming along the road. A similar beginning is to be found in "The Hook," as Duncan Emrich's reprint (1972) shows:

> I heard this story at a fraternity party. I heard this guy had this date with this really cool girl, and all he could think about all night was taking her out and parking and having a really good time, so he takes her out in the country, stops the car, turns the lights off, puts the radio on, nice music; he's really getting her in the mood, and all of a sudden there's this news flash comes on over the radio and says to the effect that a sex maniac has just escaped from the state insane asylum and the one distinguishing feature of this man is that he has a hook arm, and in the first place this girl is really, really upset, 'cause she's just sure this guy is going to come and try and get in their car. . . . (1972, p. 333)

To placate her fears, though he is angry at his missed opportunity, the boyfriend starts the engine and "goes torquing out of there" for her house. When they get there, he gets out to open the door for her and finds caught in the handle a hook (1972, p. 334).

"The Boyfriend's Death" has no hero, only a terrorized young woman. We are not told whether the killer is ever caught, or even whether he is ever seen again. He functions merely as an agent to kill the boyfriend, whose corpse functions only to terrorize the girl, which terror is the emotional core of this story. "The Hook" does not differ much in this respect. Though the boyfriend escapes, he is hardly heroic. The girl is frightened as soon as she hears the radio announcement, but the real terror of her situation is not known until she and her boyfriend return home and find the attached (detached?) hook. Both stories end on notes of terror, though soon alleviated because in both cases the terrorized victim has escaped, on the one hand when "others" arrive and enable her to get out of her imprisoning car, on the other when she is safely in front of her house. The hookman can't hurt her then. In the former the boyfriend is killed, often grotesquely, but the real victim of the story, the girl, is frightened but not physically harmed.

"The Killer in the Back Seat" has victim, hero, and villain. The hero is usually not revealed until the climax of this narrative (Barnes 1984); he has, from the first, been threatening, or hostile, or at best indifferent. In a few instances the victim is rescued by her husband; she has driven, not to the gas station or along a narrow road for aid, but to her own driveway. The husband has not been a participant before he storms out of his house to his wife's rescue. Unlike the other rescuers in "The Killer in the Back Seat" legends, he is (obviously) not a threat. The other heroic actants' sole intention has been to warn the victim, or else he has devised some clever ruse to get the victim to safety—in his gas station office, for instance—and out of the dangerous car. The villain never appears as a particularized individual. He is simply a man with an axe, a gun, or a knife. He may be black (50 percent are in Cord's sample, 1969, p. 50), or simply a man, but it is always understood that he means to do the victim violent bodily harm. What she fears, what she is alerted to, is a nameless, impalpable danger, fear itself. Almost always the victim is a woman alone, temporarily isolated from her society which, in this narrative context, is protective. One cannot imagine the victim as a professional wrestler or even a college football player. The emotional core of this narrative (and many related ones) depends upon the victim's helplessness—in our society on being an undefended woman, as she is still commonly perceived. Many women are quite capable of taking care of themselves physically, but the effect of the story is not enhanced if the driver-victim is expert in judo.

In only one instance that I know of is the "victim" male. I collected this version from Brown University student Paul Medeiros in November 1983; he had heard it in Oklahoma City about eighteen months earlier. Paul's informant reported that, on a cross-country bus at a stop for refueling and servicing, all the passengers were asked to disembark. One of them noticed, however, a man with a gun "hiding behind one of the rear seats." In order to get the driver off the bus inconspicuously, the informant shouted in through the front door, "Hey, could you open the luggage compartment so that I could get some stuff out of my bag?" When the driver complied he was told about the backseat gunman, and the police were informed. I have not encountered this version anywhere else, indicating its lack of interest for the popular imagination. It is the one version of the backseat "killer" type with a male victim-driver, and significantly, in this story, the driver is not terrorized. He is, once he learns about the situation, completely in charge. No terror here; not a very good story, either.

The nighttime setting of most of these terror tales further reinforces the feeling of fearful vulnerability. Nighttime isolates, removing one from contact — however much dependent only on sight — with others, and with safety. Night creates shadows which mislead, hiding friend and foe alike. The fear of the dark is very old in our culture, surprisingly old in our literature. It is no mistake that the backseat "killer" stories are set at night.

Although Brunvand and others classify "The Killer in the Back Seat" differently from "The Vanishing Hitchhiker" (Bennett would classify it as a ghost story: 1984), the tales are related — to each other and to yet others — by their emotional cores, by the similarity of setting (an automobile, and the terror inflicted upon its occupant[s]), and by the ease with which they exchange episodes; certain motifs can be added to provide bridges between related narratives. Fig. 15.1 is not an attempt at establishing provenance, merely a graphic illustration of the episodic relationship between several urban legends. The legend types are shown linked by those motifs which have been found to join them in actual performances (see Barnes 1984). A brief description of the emotional core of each is listed in the right column.

"The Hairy Hand," a legend collected in Devonshire (but also reported to me by a native of Lawrence, Massachusetts) may have been familiar to Ms. Howard; the tale has no consistently related ending, but the emotional core is constant; a hairy hand appears from (?) the rear of a moving car to threaten the driver in the front. The innocent stop for gas, here shown linking "The Killer in the Back Seat" with "The Vanishing Hitchhiker," has not been collected as a folk legend but is the idea of Ms. Howard, as is the (possible) conflation of "The Hairy Hand" and the backseat "Killer."

Elizabeth Jane Howard makes the chilling weather during the nighttime drives an important part of her setting. Meg is vulnerable, lonely, timid, still not entirely on her own in the large world of London. Her father has always warned her not to give lifts to strangers, yet she feels, presumably, that the girl with the livid face must be harmless enough. She becomes frightened, just as the women drivers in their cars are alarmed by the blinking lights of trucks trying to hail them, when she

Fig. 15.1. Episodic Relationship between Urban Legends

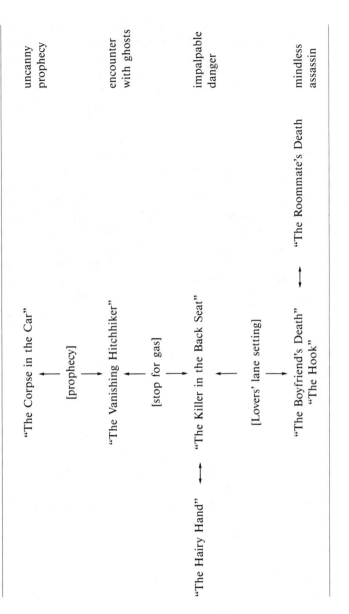

sees the girl's picture in an old newspaper and learns that the girl has been killed near the highway. The folk legends may have two reversals: the "other" driver is the hero; and the villian's presence is only suddenly made known. Howard removes those twists of plot; the gas station attendant is no hero, he has not the slightest interest in the fears of the victim, and the villain is known almost from the first. His lethal intent is not anticipated right away, though Meg does find him repulsive, with his "horrible" breath of stale smoke and peppermints (p. 18), and "underneath that was a smell like rotting mushrooms" (p. 19). Only before her third trip home does she suspect the murderous notions of her hitchhiker, but then it is too late.

Again, the debt of Howard's short story to one or more folk legends is not my central concern. This is an exploration of the several ways in which these relatively simple folk narratives interchange, drop, and add narrative elements. Their performance, in this respect, despite most tellers believing in them, is much like the traditional folktale. Linda Dégh (1969, p. 68) has noted stylistic similarities. Nearly everything that has been learned about the transmission process of folktales during the last century is applicable to the life history of the legend. However, judging from the ways these legends are being classified, one important lesson seems not to have taken hold; today they are still being grouped by "subject." The Indiana University Folklore Archives catalogues them under "Legends, V, Modern Horror Legends, The Man in the Back Seat." Significantly, Brunvand includes "The Killer in the Back Seat" in his section, "'The Hook' and Other Teenage Horrors," not with the "Classic Automobile Legends" in which he has listed "The Vanishing Hitchhiker."

Some legends, whose narrative thrust is very slight indeed, make this genre extremely hard to define and classify. One would think that the salient feature of "The Vanishing Hitchhiker" stories would be a hitchhiker who vanishes. Yet this legend antedates the automobile, and early versions have the mystery take place in a horse-drawn carriage instead of in a car (Bennett 1984). Other early versions (one of them in Brunvand 1981, p. 34) have neither vehicle nor hitchhiker, but do include that other important narrative element, the revelation that the pivotal character (or some other apparition) is in reality only the seemingly corporeal form of a revenant. In the Brunvand version a priest comes to a house unbidden by the young man who answers the door and lets him in; the clergyman shortly recognizes in a protrait on the wall the woman who had earlier invited him to visit. The young man announces that it is a picture of his dead mother.

Can these tales be classified in some way other than by subject?

Propp's morphology does not seem applicable — Nicolaisen (1987) uses Labov's six-part scheme — since so many of the legends have such sparse narrative elements. There is often no "Villainy," often no "Hero," no "Donor," no "Helper." Often there is a victim, but this function is not the same as Propp's victim-hero. Many of the tales are no more complex than single motifs, though Christiansen's *Migratory Legends* was completed before many urban legends had been analyzed. The Indiana Universty Archives classified "The Killer in the Back Seat" by emotional effect while Brunvand includes it with "Teenage Horror Stories," privileging the presumed age of the creators and transmitters. There is, as noted, disagreement on the subtypes of the tale.

"The Killer in the Back Seat," though simple, can be classified in at least three other functional ways. The stopping place — where the would-be victim goes for aid, or comes to rest unawares, or is coerced — can be a parking lot, a gas station, a wide place on the road, or her own home's driveway. The rescuer is often a truck driver but as often as not is just the "other driver"; it can be the gas station attendant, the driver's husband, and/or the police. Another variant of "The Killer in the Back Seat" legend concerns the thrust of the narrative, involving the victim's awareness and perception of the villain. In one variety of this legend, the victim is unaware of the assailant's existence until he is pointed out by the rescuer — often the gas station man. In the second type, the victim(s) fear the driver of the other car, usually — but by no means always — a truck, and her (their) flight is from it.

What has been here designated as the "Tim Barton" versions combine the functional role of the "other driver" with that of the gas station attendant. Only when the car stops by the roadside, or in the owner's driveway, can the trucker be the rescuer. The "other driver" as rescuer is the more potentially dramatic of the two traditions having, as it does, two reversals of expectations instead of one. It also has the feature of dramatic tension from nearly the beginning of the tale when the "other driver" ominously blinks his lights into the victim's eyes. In tradition II there is not a threatening "other driver," hence no implied (and imagined) danger to the victim. There is no tension throughout (except that which may be implied, paranarratively, by the teller) and only an after-the-fact consideration that there was any danger at all.

The legends we have examined proceed from tranquillity through threat to tranquillity restored (equilibrium-disequilibrium-equilibrium), but this is far too broad to make meaningful distinctions possible. And the scheme is too much like the traditional, "classic," folktale — or like much of narrative fiction, for that matter — to distinguish the legend from those genres on such a basis. Of course, this structural similarity to fictions demonstrates the artistic nature of folk legends, certainly as revealed by their telling. True or not — and occasionally a legend may relate an actual event or a fact — they have become indistinguishable in several ways from consciously wrought fictions. If there is a "natural" way of telling stories, if there is a "natural narrative," it is manifest in the style and the structure of the telling. That "nature" is, as has been argued elsewhere in this book, culturally transmitted.

One affective element common to all of the legends considered here is revelation (see Barnes 1984, p. 77). To the woman driver it is the presence of the man in the back seat. To the accommodating driver it is the discovery that his hitchhiker is a revenant. To the lovers who rush away from their secluded spot it is the discovery of the proximity of the hookman. To the girl left in the stalled car, it is the delayed knowledge that the scraping she has heard throughout the night is from the feet (or the fingernails) of her boyfriend's corpse. To the girl left alone in her room it is the discovery that the scraping she heard during the night was that of her dying roommate. That revelation forces the victim to consider the danger just narrowly escaped and gives the tale's audience, empathetically, that chill which is one of these legend's most consistently maintained messages. "Revelation" hardly seems a viable basis for classifying, however, though it does work with those that have been examined here.

Morphology may be brought to the aid of yet another genre (see Barnes 1984), though not — as already noted — the way Propp formulated it for the heroic folktale. The pivotal character in our legends is not a hero, but the victim. This in itself says something about the tenor of life in contemporary urban America. When there is a hero, he is not the focus of the narrative. The villain may be real — he usually, though not always, is — and nearly always his motivations are nebulous: to commit a crime, of course, but for what purpose? Robbery is rarely implied — he is the "killer" in the back seat. But why kill? In many stories the killer is demented, reinforcing Joseph Conrad's insight that terror is essentially irrational: we are terrorized by that which cannot be reasoned with, that which strikes out without cause or provocation.

So there is victim, villain (threatener, real or implied), and rescuer. Only the victim is embued with dimensionality. The villain is mute (in the narratives I have seen), and often may not be actualized — be brought to "life" by the narrator — at all. And the rescuer customarily has little to say indeed: one line is usually all he gets, and that is not memorable in itself but only effective (and affective) for the relief it brings the victim. The narrative relies on the revelation of the unexpected for its effect. Roles and/or situations are commonly reversed, and we the audience do not learn the true nature of the characters, who are defined by their intentions, until the end of the story. That revelation, in fact, determines the end.

The above structural outline is intended to be generative; it does not describe all urban legends, or even one of them. These automobile/horror stories are too varied in makeup to accomplish that. The outline does provide the elements of deep structure from which legends are generated, including those elements of reversal and affect in the narrative that characterize the genre's members.

A large variety of other legends surprise the listener, at the same time and in the same way that the sympathetic character in them is also surprised. A great many stories in the United States turn upon the suddenly exposed nudity of victims. In some legends, such as that of the passenger in the back of the camper, returning from vacation, whose vehicle's sudden lurching thrusts the passenger onto a public thoroughfare, nude (or often nearly so); our sympathy is with the victim, but since the circumstance of the tale makes it funny, we are not greatly embarrassed (see Nicholisen 1987, pp. 73 ff.). In others, where one person (or a couple) are found nude by surprise — surprise birthday parties are the favored situations here — their moral transgressions invoke our negative judgments. Such tales often have morals attached, such as the common story about the engaged couple caught frolicking about in a house where they have been hired to baby-sit; we may not condemn public nudity, but most of us do feel that in such situations the couple's nudity is a transgression against their roles; they are being paid to babysit, and nude cavorting around the house is not acceptable. We condemn them even while we may at the same time sympathize with their playfulness and their being "caught." The nude in the back of the camper is wholly blameless; we sympathize with him (her?), though not embarrassment but humor is evoked.

All of these legends evoke high-intensity emotions; the narratives seem designed to evoke shame, fear, anxiety (alligators in the sewers, poisonous snakes in the carpet, parts of rodents in Coke bottles, etc.), anger and outrage (at the arrogant and pretentious management of hotel restaurants, for instance, who will not give away the proper recipes for some of their foods), and embarrassment (the solid cement Cadillac/Porsche, as well as the nude in the RV). These high-intensity emotions seem to make urban legends "tellable," and formed as they are around reversals and surprises they are well-nigh irresistable.

234 Folklore and Literature: Rival Siblings

To return once more to literature: did Elizabeth Jane Howard know any of the "revelation" legends, and did she use them as a basis for "Mr. Wrong"? Urban legends have been heavily collected in Great Britain, but that is no evidence for her awareness of them. I do not want to make this chapter stand or fall based on the presumed relationship between her fiction and modern folklore. Yet my personal prejudice is in favor of such a genetic connection. If Ms. Howard thought of the plot of "Mr. Wrong" on her own, it would be a striking coincidence. If there is no polygenesis in this case — as I think — then we have another instance of the lasting relationship between literature and folklore, more specifically between "ordinary" people as tellers of stories and skilled artisans of tales. They have much in common, probably more than separates them.

For instance, in nearly all of the oral versions of "The Vanishing Hitchhiker" the weather is unpleasant. It is raining or sleeting or very foggy, and it is cold and damp. Beardsley and Hankey thought that such "background" details provided the rationale for picking up the hitchhiker (1942, p. 308). Elizabeth Jane Howard's victim, Meg Crosbie, feels sorry for the pale girl she sees standing in the sleet and violates her own rule never to give a lift to strangers, because the weather is so bad and the poorly dressed girl appears to be painfully chilled. But if the bad weather is a distributional element, embodying a causative action, a functional role, it is also descriptive, integrational (according to the system of Barthes 1982, pp. 263–64). The bad weather induces Meg, as well as the kind drivers of countless folk legends, to offer the hitchhiker a lift, thus establishing the chronological and logical causal chain. But it also establishes the mood of the encounter and further suggests the ominous nature of it. In fact, while bad weather may heighten one's inclination to offer lifts to strangers, there is also a resistance to doing so because the hiker will get one's car wet and dirty. In a narrative setting, however, bad weather or whatever kind is the right one for the story, distributionally and integrationally. Folktale tellers and Ms. Howard have understood this.

"Mr. Wrong" conflates at least two legends, it would seem, legends that are related by mood, situation, affect. Ms. Howard has made this conflation effortlessly and effectively. But the most impressive manifestation of her skill as a narrator is the period of reflection she places between the second trip (incorporating "The Vanishing Hitchhiker" legend) and the third (which incorporates "The Killer in the Back Seat"). During this period, which occupies about one-quarter of the narrative, Meg decides to sell her car, having become convinced that it is haunted;

but she cannot. She sets to work on an especially tedious job at the shop, wrapping a great many china pieces, and then discovers in an old newspaper photograph the hitchhiker's picture. But mainly during that two-week period, she worries. She considers what has happened to her during her trips home to her parents, and she worries. Folk narratives rarely afford such psychological glimpses. During this interval, the reader's tension builds with hers. This seeming pause roughly corresponds to what Labov has termed "evaluation"; Howard's ten pages devoted to this interval are not all evaluative, but much of this kind of material appears here, as Labov predicted, at the juncture between complication and resolution. Having such similar plots in both writing and oral circulation better enables us not only to see what the author is doing right but to appreciate the aesthetic sense of oral tellers.

CHAPTER 16

What Is Natural Narrative?

WILLIAM LABOV'S WORK CONTAINS "the only body of data-based research dealing with aesthetically structured discourse which is not, by anybody's definition, literature" (1967, p. 39). His research and his analysis have been the stimulus for further scrutiny in other, though related, fields, particularly speech-act theory, language acquisition, cognitive psychology, elementary education, the new study of "narratology," and folklore. In folkore, Labov's work has helped nurture the waxing interest in the personal-experience story; his "Narrative Analysis: Oral Versions of Personal Experience," coauthored with Joshua Waletzky, and a revised version which appeared as a chapter in *Language in the Inner City* entitled "The Transformation of Experience in Narrative Syntax," have been influential.

Originally, Labov sought to determine whether the reading problems of black children from the inner cities were related to dialectical differences. Labov's conclusion was that they were not but stemmed from "political and cultural conflicts in the classroom" (1972). The 1967 essay described the purpose of his research: "the ultimate aims of our work will require close correlations of the narrator's social characteristics with the structure of narratives, since we are concerned with problems of effective communication and class and ethnic differences in verbal behavior" (p. 13). Thus his excursus into personal-experience narratives intended to reveal how narrative techniques — and their speaker's resultant performance — varied among speakers of differing classes and ethnic groups.

Labov's work has assumed such importance among narratologists that his analysis of narratives deserves close scrutiny, particularly some of the fundamentals of his rationale in his study of memorates: that the analysis of simple narratives is basic to an understanding of more complex narratives, and that unschooled narrators are "natural." One of his working hypotheses was that the "Danger of Death" stories were "original productions", a moot point. I also want to examine his tentative finding, one that has been utilized by speech-act theorists, that first-person experience stories tend both to be lucid and coherent and to contain predictably situated evaluative clauses, while those narratives that relate vicarious experiences, such as the repetition in a television drama, are typically confused and incoherent.

In all, about six hundred interviews were recorded during the fieldwork for four of Labov's sociolinguistic projects, including black and white informants from rural and urban areas, ranging in age from ten to seventy-two. None had graduated from high school. Labov found it most useful to work with the clause as his basic unit of speech, though it was occasionally necessary to refer to cases in which both phrases and individual words were grouped. Labov felt that it was important to analyze narrative on levels lower than that of the sentence because previous analyses had proved unproductive by dealing with "substantial" blocks of narrative material defined at various levels of abstraction according to the activity described (as has been the case with Propp's morphology). As Labov said, "most attempts to analyze narrative have taken as their subject matter the more complex products of long-standing literary or oral traditions. Myths, folk tales, legends, histories, epics, toasts and sagas seem to be the results of the combination and evolution of simpler elements. . . . in many cases, the evolution of a particular narrative has removed it so far from its originating function that it is difficult to say what its present function is" (1967, p. 12).

This assumption interests folklorists and narratologists in several ways. First, that Labov and his associates collected relatively simple narratives does not mean that all memorates are uncomplicated. A narrative, after all, can be "complicated" in any of several ways. Students of mine at Brown University, for instance, recorded several first-person experience stories of considerable length—their recitations took nearly half an hour—and of considerable complexity. Mini-narratives were embedded within the framework of the encompassing structure. Katherine Young—and many others, we can be sure—has collected (in Devonshire) a self-referencing narrative that has, within forty lines or so, when transcribed, embedded narratives and subtle shifting of tenses. Such a story, though an oral, folk narrative, is not a simple story according to the definition of Gerald Prince (1973, pp. 39–40), and it is certainly not a kernel story. Even Labov's collected narratives have several kinds of complications in them; the following account, Labov's #4 (1967, p. 6), was in response to a question whether the informant had ever seen any shooting:

Oh yes, I can remember real well. I was just a girl. 'Fact, stayed with me quite a while.

Well, there's a fellow, his name was Martin Cassidy 'n' Bill Hatfield. Mr. Cassidy's mother give him some money an' tell him to get a bushel of peaches. An' he went down to Martin's house. An' Martin had some moonshine there.

Back down there, they make their own liquor, you know. So — we call it moonshine. Today they call it white lightnin'; but at that time we call it moonshine.

While it is probably true that, during its evolution, a narrative will be altered in style and possibly even structure, and will evolve away from its originating function, that really only tells us that a different (and more sophisticated?) social context for storytelling may well alter the function the story once filled in its simpler setting. An evolved form — say, the *Chanson de Roland* — will almost certainly have a function different from that of its originating, or seed, story, but that difference is self-evident: the shorter heroic lays from which the *Chanson* seems to have emerged, to follow through on this illustration, were sung/recited for purposes quite different from those of the epic we now celebrate in our classrooms. Moreover, the function of complicated, evolved stories is often known (as in the case of most myths, histories, epics, toasts, and others), and while it may not bear a close relationship to its simpler parent, knowing all about the one may not be of any help in knowing about the other. And, further, some relatively simple forms have derived from those more complex (not the other way around), such as ballads from romances. Knowing about the function of one does not necessarily help with the other. The idea for the plot of "Rip Van Winkle" is said to come from Irving's knowledge of Germanic legend and mythology; but as this plot structure is transformed in American fiction it is hardly a myth anymore, and while it has reverberations of the originating legend, the short story no longer carries the same meaning.

Labov's extenders assume these hypotheses in their applications of his findings to literature. Mary Louise Pratt, in *Toward a Speech-Act Theory of Literary Discourse*, applies Labov's six narrative functions to several lengthy narratives — Henry Miller's *Plexus*, George Eliot's *Silas Marner*, Jane Austen's *Jane Eyre*, Albert Camus's *The Fall*, F. Scott Fitzgerald's *The Great Gatsby*, and Herman Melville's "Bartleby the Scrivener," among others — and finds that functional components — abstract, orientation, complication, evaluation, resolution, and coda — can be effectively applied to these literary works (and by implication to any other), complex and "evolved" as they are. While it is true, as

Labov points out, that some simple narratives are strung together, and complex stories may have embedded constituent stories to produce longer narratives, it is questionable whether the study of function, in this sense, is a substantial aid to understanding longer tales.

Labov's assumption seems to be that the complex narratives have their historical and structural bases in simple ones, and that simple memorates have psychological priority. But there is no guarantee that studying simple forms will reveal essential matter about complex ones, which may be radically different in numerous ways. Do we know very much more about *King Lear* if we know that Shakespeare's source, Geoffrey of Monmouth, probably took the story from the oral folktale "Love Like Salt"? And why should we study a memorate (necessarily) as a key to understanding, say, an Icelandic family saga, any lengthy history, or *The Education of Henry Adams*? The constituent short stories, "cannibalized" as Raymond Chandler put it, of *The Big Sleep* and *Farewell, My Lovely*, tell us a lot about the compositional genesis of those novels, but little about their meaning or even the author's principles of organization.

The study of many folktales of the Aarne-Thompson type 301 have not been greatly helpful or universally convincing in analyzing the stylistics of *Beowulf*; but of course the "John the Bear" stories are not epic fragments, they are fairy tales, and Labov's research was on personal-experience stories. We don't want to compare artichokes and aardvarks for their similarities. But that seems to be the implication of Labov's statement that, in order to understand folktales, myths, epics, toasts, and sagas, we would profit by studying the personal-experience story.

Labov and his associates used two kinds of taping procedures: in one the speaker was alone with the interviewer; in the other the recording was made in the presence of the informant's peer group. The type of story elicited, however, is of continuing interest in what follows. Assuming that the "fundamental structures" he was seeking were to be found in oral versions of personal experiences, Labov sought the "original productions of a representative sample of the population" (1967, p. 12), being careful to avoid "the products of expert story-tellers that have been re-told many times." (Expert storytellers are usually more histrionic, pace the actor in an oral performance; their style of narration is more engaging, but the structure—in Labov's sense—is not necessarily different).

At "a certain point in the conversation" the interviewer asked the informant, "were you ever in a situation where you were in serious danger of being killed, where you said to yourself—'this is it'?" (1972,

p. 365). Sometimes other questions were asked, such as "were you ever in a fight with a guy bigger than you?" But the "Danger of Death" stories were the more frequently used and have been the object of nearly all references to this project: we think mainly, almost exclusively, of the "Danger of Death" tales in relation to this research on first-person experience narratives.

Labov's descriptive phrase "original production" is quite important, showing that he was seeking "not the products of expert story-tellers that have been re-told many times, but the original productions of a representative sample of the population." Futhermore, "original production" is ambiguous: it could mean an "initial production" or one that is merely "inventive." But the context, "re-told many times," suggests that the former meaning was intended. So one is not pedantically or arbitrarily quibbling to point out that hardly any—probably none—of these informants would have been recorded telling such a tale for the first time. An oral narrative in which the teller claims to have been in serious danger of getting killed will have been rehearsed and retold many times, and very likely borrows stylistic traits and histrionic techniques from similar tales which the informant has heard. The memorat may be original to the speaker—describing in a personal style an event in which he/she participated—but is not likely to be only rarely told.

We all have an individually varying stock of stories that are important to us, but which usually fit some socially structured category: what we were doing at the time of Pearl Habor (or the Kennedy assassination), stories of our Ph.D. comprehensives or orals, the birth of our child, our finest day of fieldwork. Art Buchwald begins an essay with the thought that "everyone has his own favorite airline story from years gone by"; and Robert Graves once listed those episodes that he thought any successful potboiler should include:

> murders . . . ghosts, of course . . . and kings. . . . a little foreign travel is usually needed. . . . school episodes, love affairs (regular and irregular), wounds, weddings, religious doubts, methods of bringing up children, severe illnesses, suicides. But the best bet of all is battles. . . .

Roger Abrahams presented a paper at the 1977 American Folklore Society meeting on "The Most Embarrassing Thing That Ever Happened" (subsequently published in *Folklore Forum*, 1977).

As Labov himself observed of his informants,

> The narrators of most of these stories were under social pressure to show that the events involved were truly dangerous and unusual, or that someone else really broke the normal rules in an outrageous and reportable way.

Evaluative devices say to us: this was terrifying, dangerous, weird, wild, crazy; or amusing, hilarious and wonderful; more generally, that it was strange, uncommon, or unusual—that is, worth reporting. (1972, p. 371)

Not all of us may have stories for each category or telling situation, but most of us can relate personal experiences about many of them. And we have told these memorats several—probably many—times, have worked and reworked the diction, the timing, the histrionics, each time benefitting from the feedback we have gotten during each telling. The product, after a time, may no longer closely resemble the original, and this is also to the point. A story relating an event in which we were in danger of death will have been often told, more often reformulated mentally, and may well be one of the most polished and derivative stories in our repertoire, and so is hardly the right subject to evoke a tale which will be an "original production," an example of how a teller will "naturally" recapitulate experience.

Also deserving attention are Labov's conclusions on the form of narratives of vicarious experiences. "Many such narratives of vicarious experience" were collected, though only one is printed in *Language in the Inner City*. As Labov notes, this retelling of a television episode from "The Man From U.N.C.L.E." begins in the middle of the action without the orientation section that first-person narrative always contain. No note is made of the time interval between the original viewing and Labov's interview. This may have been important, for in this "Man From U.N.C.L.E." retelling, an "original production" may well be involved—if the retelling is close enough in time for the subject not to have told it previously, and if the subject matter was not important enough for the informant to have thought about the story very much at all—which was probably the case.

One characteristic of vicarious-experience recapitulations is a confused and ambiguous proniminal reference, though for Labov the important fact of this performance is that none of the events are evaluated:

This kid—Napolean got shot
And he had to go on a mission.
And so this kid, he went with Solo.
So they went
And this guy—they went though this window,
and they caught him.
And then he beat up them other people.
And they went
And then he said

that this old lady was his mother
and then he— and at the end he say
that he was the guy's friend. (1972, p. 367)

The absence of evaluative sentences is important to Labov's analytic scheme because such passages are used by the narrator "to indicate the point of the narrative, its raison d'être: why it was told, and what the narrator was getting at" (1972, p. 366). By not evaluating his own narrative, the speaker indicates that he has no purpose in telling the story, in turn causing the story's grammatical as well as functional disintegration.

Significantly, Pratt picks up on this demonstration to show how *The Sound and the Fury* and *The Stranger* use similar grammatical features intentionally to depict estrangement and a radical disorientation from society and the world, what Sartre termed in Camus's work "discrepancy, divorce, and disorientation," ideal for fiction of the absurd. Pratt cites the following passage from the point of view of Faulkner's character Benjy for her demonstration:

> Through the fence, between the curling flower spaces, I could see them hitting. They were coming toward where the flag was and I went along the fence. Luster was hunting in the grass by the flower tree. Then they put the flag back and they went to the table, and he hit and the other hit. Then they went on, and I went along the fence. Luster came away from the flower tree and we went along the fence and they stopped and we stopped and I looked through the fence while Luster was hunting in the grass. (Cited in Pratt 1977, pp. 182–83)

Experience with the writing of real psychotics would point up, once more, the difference between reality and verisimilitude. Benjy expresses himself far too coherently and conventionally to be taken seriously for an actual mentally deprived person. This passage is, no doubt, a very effective—and conventionally arranged—communication of what we have come to expect of the writing of mentally deficient people. But it is not what they actually express in their writing; and any stylistic generalizations about the styles of the handicapped or of children relating vicarious experiences must account for the real thing, not the fictional simulation of it.

Pratt's observations of literary style may be helpful to our understanding of these two (and other, similar) novels; but Labov's conclusions should not lead so unquestioningly to such interpolations. For one thing, such narratives as an episode from "The Man From U.N.C.L.E." series are not likely to be high-intensity events, and so the narrator is not likely to remember them clearly, nor is he/she likely to relate them often, if at all (unless asked to do so by a sociolinguist); if Labov had not asked the question, we do not know whether his informant would have ever related this television episode to friends. The discrepancy between clarity in first-hand accounts and disorientation in vicarious ones does not always hold, Labov's findings and Pratt's confirmation to the contrary.

For the following example I am indebted to Elizabeth Tucker, who collected hundreds of children's narratives; the following specimen is by a "Patricia," in the fifth grade, whom Tucker profiles as "an avid reader" whose "two stories from books showed her ability to recapitulate remembered details without difficulty" (Pratt 1977, p. 72). The following is Patricia's retelling of a story she had seen pictorialized recently in a TV cartoon:

> There's this—there's this fly out of all the flies in the United States, and it's real strong. The flypaper, uh, flyswatter can't kill him. . . . insecticide can't kill him, and no flypaper can hold him. And well, his girl . . . his girlfriend lives in this little sugarbowl that cracked, and uh, Fearless Fly stays in this matchbox, and he goes in there and he's known as Herman and when there's trouble he gets into his Fearless Fly costume. And his glasses—his glasses is antennas, they get real weak, he can't do anything. And uh there's these old uh, Chinese men that are trying to kill 'im, and the old fat one's acting like that he's dying, he goes, "Go-go get Fearless Fly, I wanta pay him my respects and tell him that I'm sorry," so the skinny ones goes and gets Fearless Fly, says, "Fearless Fly, um, he's dyin', and he wants to pay you his respect." So he um, he looked at his watch, and he found out that it was just a trick, and, um, but he went there anyway, and when he landed on his arm, he landed on the old man's arms, he goes, "I'm here," and he goes, he goes, "I'd like to say I'm sorry," and, um, he said, "here's a token of my grandfather's watch," and so it had a bomb in it. And so he took it and he goes, "I can't take this," and he gave it back and, um, all of a sudden it blew up. And they never have been able to catch 'im. (1977, pp. 220–21)

Patricia had recently seen the TV cartoon and obviously enjoyed it enough to remember the story, at least in outline. Notice there are coherence, evaluative remarks, and a reasonably clear plot structure, a climax, and a concluding narrow escape.

We do not know what transpired between interviewer and informant in the "Man From U.N.C.L.E." demonstration, but Tucker (certainly) and I have collected enough contrary evidence to rule out the possibility that vicariousness is the determining factor in incoherent narratives. Lack of incentive seems to be more important; if the narrator is requested to relate a story he or she has little interest in, so little that it has not entered his/her repertoire of his/her own volition, that story is not likely to be coherently well told. But if the story has been warmly received initially, if the hearer spontaneously decides that it is a good enough story to remember and an exciting experience to re-create, then the telling is much more likely to be clear, pronoun references will be understood, the story will in general be purposefully structured. "Danger of Death" stories will usually fall into this category.

Can we speak of "natural narrative"? No and yes. Clifford Geertz has persuasively argued that, just as the human mind, or the human personality, does not become "human" outside of society, so the style, the functional structure of relating personal experiences, even the inclination to tell such stories, does not occur apart from culture. Did Labov's informants tell "natural narratives," did they recount experience in a manner that is innate, or unschooled, in humans? Or did they tell their tales the way they did because it was the way all of their acquaintances told stories, the way narratives are related in print and to a great extent in film? Is "natural narrative" natural because it has become second nature, the way such performances have always — in our culture — been done? Before we tell stories we hear them. We know how they are told; we are exposed to different styles, and we constantly discern critically among them as we develop our own styles. As Pratt has put it:

> We are all perfectly aware of the "unspoken agenda" by which we assess an experience's tellability. We know that anecdotes, like novels, are expected to have endings. We know that for an anecdote to be successful, we must introduce it into the conversation in an appropriate way, provide our audience with the necessary background information, keep the point of the story in view at all times, and so on. And as with any speech situation, literary or otherwise, we form firm judgments all the time about how "good" an anecdote was and how well it was brought off by its teller; in fact, we are expected to express this judgment as soon as the anecdote ends. We recognize narrative expertise when we hear it, and when narrative speech acts fail, we can almost always say why: the experience was trivial, the teller longwinded, or we "missed the point." (1977, pp. 50–51)

We tell and retell our own personal-experience narratives frequently, even continually, and the human inclination is to improve on previous versions. If we are to understand and analyze narrative, as was Labov's attempt, we will have to do more than ask informants if they ever had an experience in which they thought they were in danger of death. We will want to know how each individual has first formulated each specific narrative (a nearly impossible project, of course), how it develops through subsequent serial retellings, and how the subject has been influenced by the style of others — acquaintances, professional writers, and all the others who put such notions "in the air." This will probably never be achieved, I grant, but it is the direction that researchers interested in such matters must continue to head. Narrative, like narration, is not "natural" if we mean by that a phenomenon antecedent to or outside of culture; to understand narrative more thoroughly — how it functions and in what ways it exceeds the lexicon and syntax through which it is conveyed — we will want to scrutinize it more thoroughly in its social context as a creation of the individual psyche, which is, in turn, a symbiotic part of that context.

Still, Labov's research has shown us a great deal about narrative and narrators. It is one of the most commonplace clichés of literary criticism that narrative (as with all literature) creates its own world. The orientation and coda of Labov's analysis show that all of his informants at least implicity recognize this transforming quality of storytelling. The orientation section implicitly acknowledges that the storyteller is taking listeners into "another world," one where they will need to be filled in on what has already happened so that they will understand what is going to happen in the story; they need, in short, to be oriented. In response to a question about a street fight the informant may have been in, he responded,

> Well, I had quite a lot. Well, one, I think, was with a girl [laughter]. Like, I was a kid, you know.
> And she was the baddest girl — *the baddest girl in the neighborhood.* If you didn't bring her candy — to school, she'd punch you in the mouth. And you had to kiss her when she['d] tell you. This girl was only about twelve years old, man, but she was a killer. She didn't take no junk. She whupped all her brothers. (1967, p. 17)

And it is only after the speaker has provided all of the above background information, has filled in his listeners with what he feels is essential to understand the story he is about to tell, that he begins. His audience has now been transported to the other world, that of the told story. After his tale is done and his point has been made, he can return the audience to the present, immediate world from which he first began his departure several minutes before. Another teller finished an account of "the last cartoon you saw on television" with the coda, "And that was that." And there we are, back at the originating point.

Complication and resolution subsume distributional elements, those episodes that tell the story, that establish a conflict in the plot, and then resolve it. In all of the published personal experience stories the narrative begins with an equilibrium, then proceeds to a disruption of that static state — disequilibrium — and concludes, is resolved, with a second equilibrium, which Todorov has already pointed out is not identical with the initial state (1977, p. 111): A peace returns to the neighborhood of Labov's teller of tale #7, after he was whupped by the baddest girl in town, but it is not the peace of the initial situation. The baddest girl now knows that at least one of the neighborhood boys will fight back, and in the end her dominance has been checked. Stability returns, but now it is the truce created by a confrontation of equals. Peace through strength.

Evaluations are the speaker's (the writer's) means of ensuring that the audience fully understands the significance of what has been said. These metanarrative comments on the story make explicit — about the "moral" of the tale or the feelings of the teller (which may not be at variance) — what unembellished narration may not get across. Evaluative remarks are the speaker's instant supplementation, and immediate criticism and explication, ensuring that the point of the story is not clouded by errant interpretations. Complication and resolution are the meat and bones of the story, providing its interest; evaluations convey the implicit message, foreground the correct meanings, and explicate intentions.

Can there be a natural narrative? Todorov thought not, that there is no primitive narrative, that no narrative was natural: "a choice and a construction will always preside over its appearance" (1977, p. 55). By "natural" he seems to mean narrative that would come from creatures who have almost no experience with society, the stories of those people who were raised by wolves, those creatures sociologists used to talk about. We mean something else by "natural narrative," not the concept of Labovian speech-act theorists. "Natural" describes the way narratives must develop, the distributional elements they are likely to incorporate, as well as the integrational.

Custer and the Epic of Defeat demonstrated how the story of the defeated (military) hero recurs throughout history with a surprising repetition of detail, even though the narratives bear no genetic relation to each other. The kernel beliefs seem to be only that a respected soldier is defeated (usually killed) in combat with a detested enemy; given that sparse core, a great many supplementary episodes have occurred polygenetically to different relaters of this narrative (Rosenberg 1974a). Since the defeated warrior is cherished and honored by his countrymen—though occasionally his admirers consist of a relatively small coterie—his defeat must be at the hands of a much larger force of the enemy, and his own unit is proportionately reduced in size: the multitude overcome the few. The addition of a traitor would not seem necessary to further apologize for the defeat, but such a character occurs commonly enough—in the *Chanson de Roland*, in the deaths of Gawain and Arthur, at Thermopylae—and is created by Custer's admirers at the Little Bighorn. At first the hero's men should be successful so that their qualitative superiority is established; later, the enemy's quantitative edge will give them victory. The hero may summon help—as do Roland and Custer, allegedly—but it is too late. Custer/Leonidas/Saul/Gawain/Byrhtnoth have a chance to escape (Rosenberg 1974a), but choose to remain with their men and to share their fate. This episode is only apparently insignificant; it is an important integrational element, establishing the hero's choice in his death, which makes of it a martyrdom and not merely a casual sacrifice. One person survives, again on the surface a trivial detail in the larger drama, but the recurrence of such an actant suggests the universality of his/her employment.

All of these distributional and integrative elements occur repeatedly because of the way our culture has decided, collectively, over several millennia, that certain stores must be told. If a warrior is to be heroic and held in esteem by his followers/countrymen, he cannot have led a larger force to its defeat at the hands of a small but skillfully superior enemy. And so on; all the elements in this narrative type reflect the way our culture believes that heroes are defeated and the way their defeat must be related—if they are to be considered heroes. Compare the Custer of the early poems and biographies with the Arthur Penn movie *Little Big Man*.

There is no question of literary borrowing here. The story of the first known defeated hero, Saul, was in oral currency for several centuries before commitment to the writing of the Old Testament. Herodotus, whose account of the Spartan stand at Thermopylae was taken largely from peasants living in the area, did not read Scripture for assistance in putting his story together. The *Chanson de Roland* is based quite sketchily on an actual defeat during one of Charlemagne's retreats, developed into an epic with overtones of the New Testament—especially the death of Christ—and not of Saul's death on Mt. Gilboa. And the American public—the American folk—who collectively created a "chanson de Custer" did not consciously create a hero's death for the Boy General along known, or knowing, lines. The death they created for him developed from their belief. It was a narrative, like nearly all of the others, that was "natural" in its genesis. The stories of Saul, Leonidas, Byrhtnoth, Lazar, Bjarki, Constantine Paleologus, James IV at Flodden, the Jews as Massada, Janos Hunyadi, and of Custer were told in the natural way that our culture learns to create, re-create, and transmit such stories. Nobody has to tell us how to do it.

In 1975 Frederick Forsyth published *The Dogs of War*, a novel about an attempt by a British industrialist to bring about a coup in a small African nation where, surreptitiously, platinum has been discovered. The discovery of the mineral and the industrialist's attempt to suppress news of it, for his own profit, comprise what Propp would term "preliminary action," though occupying well over one hundred pages. The more privileged episodes concern James Manson's employment of a private army to subvert the platinum-owning nation; and the physical bulk of the novel describes the preparations of the mercenary army, and then their attack on "Zangaro."

(I suppose that it is merely pedanty to try to identify the real model of the fictional "Zangaro." One of Manson's conspirators researches the geography of the tiny country and reports: "It's shaped like a matchbox, the short edge along the seacoast, the longer sides stretching inland. . . . Behind the plain lies the river Zangaro, then the foothills of the Crystal mountains, the mountains themselves, and beyond that, miles and miles of jungle up to the eastern border" [p. 62]. It sounds much like the actual equitorial Guinea. The notion of distant mountains containing great hidden wealth recurs frequently in the folklore of the West, even the American West. Some time around 1726 Sieur de la Verendrye heard from some nearby Indians about the "Montagnes de pierres brillantes," the Rockies, which were soon to be called "the Shining Mountains" [Lavender 1963, p. 32]. Today there are Crystal mountains in Italy as well as Washington State. There's gold in them thar hills; but that is yet another kind of story.)

But it is first necessary to "find" the precious metal in the Zangaran hills, so that James Manson will get the idea to take over the country and get possession of the mineral rights, and finally to enable Carlo Shannon, the mercenary leader, to turn the country over to the "right" people immediately following the success of the coup. Once the "preliminary matter" of the platinum's discovery is established, the rest of the narrative can proceed logically.

The ore is found by an old prospector, an old African hand, Jack Mulroony. While prospecting in the Crystal mountains of Zangaro, he finds what he believes is a large, surface deposit of tin. Sending a large sample back to corporate headquarters in London—"ManCon" of Sir James Manson—the corporation chemists soon discover that the Crystal mountains are one of the world's largest, and richest, platinum deposits. Inevitably, Sir James begins an elaborate series of subterfuges and cover-ups to keep the bonanza secret. Mulroony, who doesn't know what he has discovered, is brought back to the main office, patted on the back, and returned to duty, in remote Africa. The corporation's analytical chemist is bribed to remain silent. Manson then plans to establish a dummy corporation to possess Zangaran mineral rights once the coup he proceeds to plan for—and which comprises the bulk of the novel's plot—has taken control of the country away from its current rulers.

This sequence of episodes has an analogue, not surprisingly, in legends that arose in and around the great mineral discoveries at Virginia City during the 1850s, and following. Each of the episodes also has analogues in legends that have been generated in an impressive number of other bonanzas, but legends of the Comstock lode country will suffice here.

Forsyth's Jack Mulroony "was one of the last of the old prospectors"; his London headquarters usually "gave him the little jobs" which kept him in "the wild country that was miles from civilization," but it was the life he liked best. "He preferred to work alone; it was his way of life" (1974, p. 21). Now while a man of such solitary habits is important for the succeeding episodes in the novel (making it "easy" and plausible to reassign him even deeper in the bush), the persona of the lone prospector is a common one (Rosenberg 1981). In the American West, at Virginia City and elsewhere, he was a figure often noted because resented or suspected. Like Jack Mulroony, who "could tell an unsafe mineshaft by instinct, and the presence of an ore deposit by the smell" (Forsyth 1974, p. 20), the American prospectors are said to have had an uncanny sense about the presence of gold or silver, and to have worked their claims in places inaccessible to other men.

The key episode, again, is the discovery of a precious metal. Whether in fiction—*The Dogs of War* is just one example—or in life or legend, our assumption is that, if such a bonanza is found, it will be coveted by the greedy or the "ambitious." Rapacity may be assumed in such situations, and following logically is the assumption that various attempts will be made to keep the bonanza secret and controlled by a few hands.

Some details in this narrative—an early failure to recognize the nature of the precious metal—do not seem to be integrative (but rather, decorative), even though they occur regularly. Mulroony collected bags of earth samples, believing them to be alluvial tin buried in the Crystal mountains: "Everything he saw about him said 'tin' " (1974, p. 24). Many anecdotes have been told about the failure of the early prospectors at the Comstock lode to recognize silver ore, even when it was in their pans. They were looking for the sparkle of gold, and heavy blue clay, what reporter Dan de Quille called the "blasted blue stuff" (1976, rpt. 1947, p. 19), obscured their search for gold. It was to be the richest silver deposit they would ever hear of, let alone find. At ManCon, when all the samples had been tested, Sir James Manson was stunned: "Jesus Christ. A ten-billion-dollar mountain" (1974, p. 32).

Someone involved with the bonanza will try to keep the wealth for himself. The solitary habits of the prospector facilitate secrecy; usually, though, the secret does get out. At Virginia City, prospecting had been going on for a number of years before a lot of gold and silver was found. As soon as O'Reilly and McLaughlin struck it rich, "Pappy" Comstock (for whom the lode was subsequently named) swindled his way into their claim by arguing that the claim was originally his and that O'Reilly and McLaughlin were poaching on his preserve (Beebe and Clegg 1950, p. 10). Sutter and his foreman Jim Marshal tired hard to keep the latter's discovery of gold secret, but within days everyone in California knew that gold had been discoverd at the mill's raceway, and within weeks everyone in the United States knew it. Back in San Francisco, several years later, the Bonanza Kings arranged to have the very rich ore from the Consolidated Virginia mine brought up at night through the contiguous shafts of the Gould and Curry while they bought up stock in their own mine, then cheap (Beebe and Clegg 1950, p. 43). When they leaked the news of their bonanza to the market, they multiplied their profits. Fair and Mackay supervised the mine in Nevada; Flood and O'Brien manipulated the stock market in San Francisco.

Since Forsyth's Mulrooney doesn't know what he has discovered, there can be no attempt to deceive; that task falls to his London employer, who first bribes the chemist in his corporation to maintain secrecy. Then he tells his two most trusted personal assistants about the discovery and promises to split the profit with them if they agree to work with him in private. A dummy corporation is established to mine, refine, and market the platinum rather than sharing the profit with ManCon's stockholders. And then, to ensure that he will gain mineral rights, Sir James plans a coup, privately financed by himself, to bring his puppet into power. In outline, then, on the analytic level of what folklorists call episodic motifs, *The Dogs of War* is similar to legends that developed about the Virginia City bonanzas in the middle of the last century, and which have recurred frequently in Western history whenever significant amounts of precious minerals have been discovered.

Given the one episode of the discovery of wealth, the rest of the episodes follow "naturally." Their succession is not rigidly inevitable, and any account may delete one or more; as legends were told, on the scene, the narrative was usually brief, consisting of the discovery and one or two further integrational elements. But full accounts, such as Forsyth's book or Dan de Quile's *The Big Bonanza* are likely to include all of those just mentioned, and more. "The Discovery of Mineral Wealth" is the abstract of a narrative whose episodes follow naturally, based upon what we know about such discoveries in life. The attempt of one or a small group of people to keep the discovery, and of course the wealth involved, to themselves is a natural complication of this abstract implying a very limited set of resolution possibilities—success or failure. The Comstock lode story is one of success for Fair, Flood, Mackay, and O'Brien, though there is some disaster in their later lives—but that is another narrative. Forsyth's Manson is finally defeated, though his attempts to keep the platinum bonanza secret are successful; by the time the coup succeeds—although Manson's mercenary, Shannon, turns the country over to an honest politician-in-exile—we are well beyond the "Discovery of Mineral Wealth" narrative limits.

CHAPTER 17

Folklore in Recent Literary Theory

UNTIL VERY RECENTLY THE folktale's interest to students and scholars of literature had greatly faded; but the current fashion of narrative
theory — narratology — has revived the importance of the folktale to
serious literary research and theory (as opposed to the allegedly more
"trivial" study of folklore for its own sake). Whether narratives are
analyzed on a linguistic model (in which the relatively simple structure
of the folktale readily lends itself for use as an illustrative example),
as "basic" story or "mininal" or "kernel" tale, or as examples (pro and
con) of the linear narrative par excellence, the folktale is the exemplary
narrative of choice. This chapter will scan some of the ways in which
the folktale has made its academic reappearance.

Several narrative theorists have argued that nearly any story can be
analyzed using a (somewhat modified) linguistic model: Pierre Guirard
is quoted (in Dorfmann 1969, p. vii) as saying that

> it is now recognized that we owe to linguists, and more particularly to phon-
> ologists, definitions and methods of structural analysis which have furnished
> new *models* and a new epistemological framework for the historian, the
> sociologist, and the anthropologist. Thus we must not be surprised if today
> literary criticism approaches this problem in the light of linguistics.

Better known than Dorfmann's work is the published material of
Todorov, Barthes, Greimas, and Prince — among many others. Frequently
their systems of analysis assume or seek to prove that narratives are
analogous with the sentence: the action is a verb, descriptions are ad-
jectives, characters are nouns (Todorov 1977, p. 119). For Greimas there
are dynamic predicates or functions (approximating acts); and static
predicates or qualifications (approximating descriptions).

But, as Barbara Herrnstein Smith has devastatingly argued, the putative analogy is by no means exact, and in fact the organization of

fiction is so different from the structure of the sentence that comparisons are bound to be distorting:

> A language, however, is a very different sort and order of thing from *plot structures*, and there is no good reason to assume a priori that the specific criteria for a *grammar* of one would be at all relevant to a *theory* of the other. (1978, p. 180)

In response to the assertion that literature is a "system of signs," Smith replies that while it (literature) may be studied as a system constituted by a set of conventions which shape our expectations and responses, it does not follow either that this system is "directly analogous to the one that constitutes a natural language" – or that literature is a communicative system. Whereas languages are stable and economical, literature is continually innovative, uneconomical, and ambiguous (1978, pp. 193–94).

To supplement these generalizations, I would like to specify one instance. Gerald Prince's *A Grammar of Stories* (1973) has achieved a certain notoriety among narratologists. Closely following Chomsky's *Syntactic Structures* (1966), Prince analyzes narrative by seeking to reveal what he calls the minimal story and (after Chomsky) the kernal story. For Chomsky the kernel sentence was the matrix from which all utterances derived:

> Thus every sentence of the language will either belong to the kernel or will be derived from the strings underlying one or more kernel sentences by a sequence of one or more transformations. (1966, p. 45)

For transformational grammarians the kernel provides keys to the sentence's origins, meaning, and constructional ambiguity:

> . . . in order to understand a sentence it is necessary to know the kernel sentences from which it originates . . . as well as the transformational history of development of the given sentence from these kernel sentences. (1966, p. 92)

Understanding the sentence is thus reduced to explaining how kernel sentences are themselves understood, these being the basic "content elements" of sentences (1966, p. 92).

Isolate the kernel sentence, and you have decomposed the subject sentence and defined its meaning. Decompose a narrative into its kernel story, and it will be laid bare to the most perfunctory inspection. Additionally, Prince attempts to set out the methodology and the principles by which all narratives may be so usefully decomposed. Prince seeks the kernel story of which the surface manifestation is an elaboration; Propp had claimed that his own morphology would enable the researcher to analyze the folktale, and then, by retrogressing the analytic process, identify the primordial tale.

Prince illustrates his method on a version of "Little Red Riding Hood," and so comes under the purview of this book. But, relatively simple as that folktale is, there are still problems. Though propositions are stored in memory when we input data (Clark and Clark 1977, pp. 143–44), these propositions are not necessarily the same as kernel sentences in minimal stories. Chomsky's kernels have grammatical limitations (1966, p. 800), whereas the proposition as the basis of memory storage datum does not (Clark and Clark 1977), pp. 145 ff.). Furthermore, propositions are stored by logical principles, and are not lexical-specific.

A Grammar of Stories states that "a minimal story is equivalent to the smallest series of events composed by the minimum number of conjunctive features and constituting a story" (1973, pp. 18–19). But, while Prince's methodology attempts to establish objective criteria for the definition of narrative, the final arbiter is the reader's intuition—another Chomskian idea. "John was rich and he was miserable" and "John was rich, then he was poor" are, according to Prince, "clearly" not stories (p. 20). But another reader's intuition might differ. Prince's *Grammar* posits as a minimal story the stipulation that it must contain three conjoined events, of which the second is active and the third must be the inverse of the first (1973, p. 19). But isn't this unduly complicated? Prince's inductive method does not use actual narratives in its elements of proof; in "The Three Ravens" (Child 26), stanza nine embodies what many thousands of listeners have accepted as a valid story:

> She buried him before the prime,
> She was dead herselfe ere euen—song time.

These ballad lines describe only two conjoined events—she buried him, and then she died; are they insufficient to constitute a story? Reflecting on basic narratives, novelist Ursula Le Guin proposed the line carved in stone, *Tolfink carved these runes in this stone* (1981, p. 194) as the simplest narrative of all, yet in one reader's perception—and a very perceptive reader at that—this is still a narrative. And Le Guin's definition was formed from her experience with actual narratives, those she had read and those she had herself written. Barbara Herrnstein Smith formulated the matter this way: "it may be that the innermost kernel of narrative structure is the sense of what it means for *something* to have *happened*" (1978, p. 185). This lacks the sense of precision which the influence of science had led us to hope for; yet it may be the best description of narrative yet proposed. Todorov, after Aristotle (though arrived at independently), suggests that the minimal complete plot consits in the passage from on equilibrium to another (1977, p. 111). Clearly he and Prince are of the same mind (as are many of the French structuralists); yet perceptive as this definition appears to be, it demands elements superfluous to what has actually been accepted as a good story by, no doubt, millions of listeners over centuries.

Todorov asserts that there is no such thing as a natural or primitive narrative (1977, pp. 53–55) if we recall that stories do not conform to nature but are selected, chosen, crafted by narrative conventions. Yet some stories are less crafted than others, or so narratologists have implied when they have chosen folktales for their examples. To demonstrate how his own calculus of narrativity works when applied to an extant story, rather than to one of his own creations constructed specifically to illustrate one of his theorems, Prince uses a version of "Little Red Riding Hood." Todorov once cited the *Odyssey* as an allegedly primitive narrative that should have been simple, plain, and pure — if the theorists were right, but he finally observed that few contemporary works "reveal such an accumulation of 'perversities' " (1977, p. 55). "Little Red Riding Hood" has no such perversities. Yet, though the version Prince uses has only fifty-seven lines — approximately six hundred and eighty-five words — Prince's calculus, as manifest in his descriptive charts, occupies more than four pages (1973, pp. 84–86).

Yet if linguists occasionally play fast and loose with folklore, the favor has been on occasion outragously returned. In discussing "The Hero Pattern and the Life of Jesus," folklorist Alan Dundes (1980, pp. 223–61) demolishes linguistics and philology as disciplines in the name of folklore. Arguing for a connection between "mother" and "sea" (pp. 242–43), he says that "it is tempting to argue from linguistic data" that being thrown onto or into a body of water does not so much symbolize birth as it does being thrown onto the mother. For proof we are told that Latin *mare* "could conceivably be related to" *mater*. A parenthetic comment reminds us that French *mer* and *mere* are homophonic. Dundes admits that he is not interested in the sea-mother relationship in all languages, but if he can make the connection in just one, it "is surely of interest." Moving right along, "one wonders" whether "Mary" isn't derived from either "sea" or "mother." *Mary* "may be related" to the Hebrew *Miriam* "which could be construed" as containing Hebrew *yam,* "sea." The stodgier OED is more positive about the Mary/Miriam connection but mentions nothing about a body of water. Dundes found it "curious" that Latin *lacus* (lake) and *lac* (milk) are "related." Citing the orthographic similarity between French *boîte* and *poitrine,* he guesses that "the floating 'chest' might be literally just that, a floating female bosom." Thus this argument has developed from "could conceivably" to "may be" to "could be construed as," pausing along the way to cite as demonstrations homophones (assumed to be genetically related) and orthographic similarities. This argument is to be found in one paragraph; and if the reader is not convinced, there is the final disclaimer: "Please note that the association exists *regardless* of the validity of the above admittedly highly speculative philological musings." Dundes's argument is true, he tells us, regardless of whether we accept his demonstration of proof—which argument would render that demonstration irrelevant.

But the present book is not about the treatment of philology by folklorists, and the above paragraph is not central to the present argument. More germane is the linguist's concept of deep structure and its inextricable relationship to what has been termed the "basic story" by Seymour Chatman (1978, pp. 117–18). The Finnish method seems to imply such an idea, but only apparently so. The tale-type is not a "basic story" or even a version of it; and the archetype is almost inevitably an approximation, reconstructed in broad outline (by a methodology already described below). In any event, a folklorist engaged in a full-scale historic-geographic study might find the archetype of no more interest than an oicotype or a subtype whose popularity gave it great weight in his or her calculations. In such an instance, by no means rare, the idea of a "basic story" would be even harder to identify. And further, more than five decades ago, Propp had complained about the slipperiness of tale-types. They blend and bleed, fade and shift shapes unpredictably; stability has to be the norm of the life of the folktale in transmission, or else the Finnish method would be useless. But changes do perversely occur, sometimes radical changes.

So, when Seymour Chatman writes (1978, p. 117) that "one of the most important observations to come out of narratology is that narrative itself is a deep structure quite independent of its medium," he would not be supported by folklore research over the past century. A reader/viewer, according to Chatman, would be expected to recognize the similarities between two of the "texts" analyzed in Chatman's essay—Maupassant's "Une Partie de Campagne" and Jean Renoir's film of it, with the same title — but in a number of instances genetically related stories might not be easily identifiable, perhaps not at all.

Barbara Herrnstein Smith is quite correct when she points out that in the Cinderella folktale (A-T 510) — an example used by Chatman — there is no such phenomenon as the "basic story" and that the idea itself, a kind of Platonic ideal, is not even theoretically useful. In most, but by no means all, of the versions of Cinderella collected by Cox in the last century and published in 1893:

> we find an initially ill-treated or otherwise unfortunate heroine, though sometimes her name is not Cinderella but Cencienta or Aschenputtel, Eschenfettle, Fette-Mette or Tan Chan; and sometimes she isn't the youngest stepchild but the oldest daughter; and sometimes she is not a heroine but a hero; and usually the fairy godmother is a cat, a cow, or a tree; and the glass slipper is often a gold ring. Moreover, the turns of plot in many of these tales are likely to be disturbing or intriguing to someone who knows only one set of versions of the Grimm brothers' version.

Smith then cites an Icelandic version, collected in 1866, in which the heroine (named Mjadveig) marries a ship's captain, and later invites her stepmother on board for a dinner at which they serve her the salted flesh of the heroine's stepsisters, whom Mjadveig and her husband have previously murdered (1981, p. 212).

Smith's argument would have been further strengthened if she had been aware of the assumed genetic relationships between tales belonging to the same type, which, if true, make the "basic story" even more problematic to identify. Those who have studied folk narrative realize that a tale will vary in each performance, written or oral, and the variations include, in addition to transmitted narrative constituents: the relation between performer and audience (an interaction in the case of oral performance), situation, and context. So we must agree with Barbara Herrnstein Smith when she writes that the story is "some set of particular tellings . . . in accord with some particular, but arbitrary, set of relational criteria" (1981, p. 215). Later in the same essay (p. 222) she outlines those influences that may cause variation in the reenactment of each of the performed versions of a narrative:

> individual narratives would be described . . . as the verbal acts of particular narrators performed in response to — and thus shaped and constrained by — sets of multiple interacting conditions. For any narrative, these conditions would consist of (1) such circumstantial variables as the particular context and material setting (cultural and social, as well as strictly "physical") in

which the tale is told, the particular listeners or readers addressed, and the nature of the narrator's relationship to them, and (2) such psychological variables as the narrator's motives for telling the tale and all the particular interests, desires, expectations, memories, knowledge, and prior experiences ... that elicited his telling it on that occasion, to the audience, and that shaped the particular way he told it.

With this declaration of principles or narratology, Smith reconciles literary study with folklore, invoking speech-act theory as the conjoining rationale. Robert Georges had more than a decade before (1969) urged the same philosophy upon his fellow folklorists.

Closely related to the question of the "basic story" is an example given by Smith, albeit anecdotally (1981, p. 216): a colleague had once argued that all of the novels of Charles Dickens were versions of the Cinderella story. Smith's response was to point out that in such interpretations a great deal depends upon who is establishing such an "analogy." *Great Expectations* is a Cinderella story in the sense that Pip does "move" from rags to riches; it is not a Cinderella version in any sense that would be meaningful to a traditional folklorist conducting historic-geographic research, or to anyone familiar with that methodology. But the question also involves not only the researcher but the level of abstraction at which the comparison is made. At the level of cardinal distributional units found in the commonest versions of the folktale (or motif clusters as outlined in *Types of the Folktale*) one would be hard put to connect Dickens's novels and the Cinderella framework:

I. The persecuted heroine
II. Magic help
III. Meeting the prince
IV. Proof of identity
V. Marriage with the prince
VI. The value of salt

This is, of course, quite broad in outline; a motif analysis, being more specific about narrative and descriptive details, would further show that Dickens's novels have little in common with this folktale. But, if the level of analytical abstraction is simply "rags to riches," the connection can certainly be made — but to what purpose? So many different (and disparate) narratives would have to be included (Horatio Alger stories, a biography of Bing Crosby, the romance of *Sir Launfal*, etc.) that the comparison would not be helpful in illuminating the literary text — or the folktale.

The folktale is also often cited by narratologists for its simple linearity. Now linearity in narrative operates on at least two levels: language and episode (narrative unit). The first concerns the fact that words are arranged on a page sequentially and that Latin alphabet readers read them (arguably) as Suzanne Langer once suggested (1942, p. 76), "one after another like beads on a rosary." And we hear language spoken in the same "linear, discrete, successive order." The other sense of linearity addresses itself to the chronological relationship of a narrative's episodes.

I was once seduced enough by this philosophy to publish an article whose thesis was that oral narrators in a traditional society had an innate advantage over authors in that the sense of simultaneity which narratives, especially written narratives, can only imperfectly recreate is best established when the audience knows the story in advance and can therefore make three dimensions out of what is necessarily a two-dimensional tale. Reality, William James's "blooming, buzzing confusion," is multidimensional, simultaneous. Edmund is planning further evils while Lear is being rebuffed by Regan and then Goneril; and all the while Kent, Gloucester, Edgar, and Cordelia are preparing, reacting, acting. But we cannot see them all acting at the same time; Shakespeare's stage did not have a split screen.

Similarly, we follow the intricate machinations of the Jackal as he systematically plans the assination of de Gaulle; all the while the detective who eventually kills him is tracking him, but our attention may shift, alternately, from criminal to detective back to criminal (and so forth) even though they would, in reality, be acting simultaneously — and we must comprehend the action of Forsyth's *Day of the Jackal* as though these characters were acting simultaneously. Even more so with that far more complicated, and considerably better novel, Don DeLillo's *Libra*; at the same time that a faked attempt is being plotted on President Kennedy's life, others are scheming to actually do the deed — not to miss — while the chief actor in their scenario, Oswald, has a life and a history and an ambition of his own, sometimes corresponding with theirs, sometimes not. By constantly shifting the time spans in which episodes are realized, DeLillo attempts a sense of simultaneity.

On reading a story for the first time the reader is — when compared to someone listening to a known tale — at somewhat of a disadvantage. When the written (or cinematic) narrative assumes a one-time audience, the spatial fullness and complexity of the fictive scene may be lost; the one-performance narrative, typified by the paperback novel, substitutes information for imaged richness. In Kenneth Burke's aphor-

ism, "the hypertrophy of the psychology of information is accompanied by the corresponding atrophy of the psychology of form" (1968,
p. 33). Plots depending for their impact on the revelation of information can be experienced only once with interest. If knowing who done
it is all a story has to offer, we will probably not read it again. Thus
the thoughtful writer, one who wants to be reread, educates his/her audience to participate more creatively in their mutual aesthetic experience; when such an author is read again, when an oral narrator is heard
again, the audience will have increased its competence by just enough
to accomodate that work/recitation.

But the "beads on a rosary" metaphor does not accurately describe
the reading process; for though we do usually read the words of a text
sequentially, Barbara Herrnstein Smith once again corrects us (1978,
p. 174):

> (1) we normally scan as we read, taking in (and anticipating) more than one
> word at a time; (2) our expectations and recollections are organized not only
> linearily but heirarchically, comprehending and subsuming simultaneously
> a number of structural patterns of various unit sizes, for example, from
> phoneme to canto, from morpheme to total semantic field. . . .

The level of narrative episode has been of greater interest to contemporary narratologists. But in this regard Professor Smith somewhat dis-
appoints us. The usual claim for the folktale (seldom made by folklorists, as it happens) is on behalf of its direct linear simplicity. Smith replies
that "it can be demonstrated not only that absolute order is as *rare* in
folkloric narratives as it in any literary tradition but that it is virtually
impossible for any narrator to sustain it in an utterance of more than
minimal length" (1981, p. 223). Leaving aside the vagueness of the
phrase, "minimal length," the question can, again, only be resolved by
a determination of what level is being analyzed. At the level of narrative episode, the traditional wisdom seems to be correct—based on
the several score folktales which I examined for just this purpose. I
worked with English and American tales, since translations are always
somewhat suspect. None of the folktales in the Briggs anthology or
those American tales collected by Leonard Roberts exhibited any of the
"perversities" that Todorov complained about in the *Odyssey*.

Within the tales, however, are many brief analepses or disgressions
in which a teller will explain sufficient background so that his/her listener will understand why something happened, why someone reacted
as he/she did. The hero's brothers respond in such-and-such a way
because of the king's notorious strictness, and they are fearful. I char-

acterize these analepses as brief because they are subsumed in subor-
dinate clauses, or in obvious apostrophes. They do not involve distribu-
tive units; they would not appear in a motif breakdown of the tale. Propp
has called them motivational aspects, not part of the action proper.
Smith disappointed us in this analysis, but perhaps not entirely; it is
a matter of the level of discourse being decomposed, and she is not very
wide of the mark.

In his now-famous study of the personal experience story, William
Labov defined narrative as "any sequence of clauses which contains at
least one temporal juncture" (1967, p. 28). He did not find it necessary
to theorize about three conjoined events or passages from one equilibrium to another. Of course Labov's narratives were simpler structures
than the novel and epics which he hoped one day to comment on. His
intention was first to understand te simple narrative structures, then
work from those to the more complex ones. The personal-experience
narratives were simple enough, in fact, for him to define his memorate
as "one verbal technique for recapitulating experience, in particular, a
technique of constructing narrative units which match the temporal sequence of that experience." Barbara Herrnstein Smith (in a different
context) has argued that, while fictions, including folk narratives, are
almost necessarily riddled with analepses, few narratives evolve in a
chronologically straight line: she cites chronicles, news reports, gospels,
and personal anecdotes as having antecedent-event sequences upon which
the narratives are based (1981, p. 224). This observation is supported
by the narratives Labov has printed—in "Narrative Analysis" and in
Language in the Inner City—though Smith does not include Labov in
her bibliography or notes.

Nevertheless, these conclusions are not for all time. Folklorists have
begun studying the personal-experience narrative, not expecting to find
traditional (or repeated) material in them but nevertheless considering them folkloric, presumably because they were orally transmitted.
These folklorists have found that, the more a narrative—even a personal-
experience narrative—is told and retold, the more fictionalized it
becomes. Memorates drift irreversibly to the condition of fabulates
(fictions). We, as tellers, incorporate those techniques in our personal-
experience "true" stories which will make them more interesting, and
that is a "natural" enough development. The teller's ego inevitably
becomes involved—in telling an interesting story or a memorable tale,
in being known among the circles of his/her listeners as a raconteur
of talent. In short, we fictionalize our realities. So, while personal-
experience stories are likely—during the initial retellings of their life

histories—to be linear, they are very likely to acquire "perversities" and complications as they mature with repetition.

The discipline of folklore has no quarrel with semiotics, which as almost always practiced, is comparative, diachronically and synchronically, cross-generically and cross-culturally. The Finnish method invites these comparisons, the marshaling of all relevant "texts" to bear on the problem. In the classic historic-geographic studies there may be no "basic" text, no target item that all other texts are meant to illuminate, so all texts have at least a potential relevance, and so must be examined. The folklorist may view any cultural artifact as a signifier, one whose meaning has been determined by its users, but which nevertheless needs interpretation. Because of the nature of their work, folklorists never abandon culturally and historically based criticism for some social-science version of the New Criticism.

Thus folklore—particularly the folktale—has reappeared among the concerns of literary critics. The putative simplicity, directness, and naïveté of folkloric productions have attracted narratologists who have thought that, by analyzing this uncomplicated narrative form, they will find something of value in their concern for more "serious" narrative. Looking for simplicity and directness, some critics have found simplicity in the folktale; expecting to find complications even in this narrative material, other critics insist that folktales are as "twisted" chronologically and as intricate as most literary works. Critics have, in short, found in folklore what they had hoped to find and are able to use folkloric illustrations to demonstrate whatever they have wanted to. Thus as a willing and malleable tool has the folktale returned to academic departments of literature.

And some members of literature departments have taken an interest not only in the folktale but in the oral performance of different kinds of narratives. They see in such events a parallel with the presentation of narratives of their own experience and interest (particularly epics), and—following somewhat in the wake of the Parry-Lord findings—have suggested that the compositional principles of literature may be helpful in understanding those of oral narrative. The key that unlocks this cerebral gate is Plato's.

In their very useful and often insightful analysis *The Nature of Narrative* (1966), Robert Kellogg and Robert Scholes were among the first scholars to suggest that oral performers always had an ideal performance in mind before each recital. Folkloric performances vary, according to their analysis of the experience, because no reciter is ever able to perform up to a self-conceived and self-imposed standard of perfection. Each performance is witness to the compromise of perfection on behalf of the expedience of the actual performance; each performative act is necessarily an imperfect rendering of the ideal.

Though he knows quite a lot about folklore, Kellogg is not a folklorist, but rather a literary scholar whose primary interest is in the early English Renaissance, an era heavily influenced by Platonic thought. I do not mention this to disqualify his opinion; his analysis of the oral performer's cognitive process is neither a silly guess nor an indefensible notion: Platonic thought has been monumentally influential in our culture, after all, and as a descriptive principle it would seem to do as well in representing oral performances as it does in describing literary ones. On one occasion, Kellogg was addressing an audience of literary historians and critics of early Renaissance literature, academics interested in and accustomed to dealing with, fixed texts. In explaining oral narrative to such an audience, the advantages of comparing the unfamiliar (oral tradition and performance) with what would be known to them are obvious. Kellogg wrote:

> If we grant that a work of written literature really exists only when, through the agency of the inked shapes on the page, a connection is made between the mind of an author and the mind of a reader, and that the work is the reader's experience during those minutes or hours of "intersubjectivity," there is still a constant authorial state of mind behind each such reading "performance." In oral literature such is not the case. As a constant behind each performance is not the mind of an author but an ideal performance, an aspect of the tradition that is shared by performer and audience alike. For this reason the performer in an oral tradition is analogous not to an author but to a skillful reader of written literature. As written work remains in a kind of limbo until a reader picks it up and "performs" it, so an oral work exists as an abstract body of rules and ideas until a performer embodies some of them in a performance. (1973, p. 58)

What could this ideal performance be? Countless studies of individual tale-types (carried on under the aegis of the now much maligned Finnish historic-geographic method) have shown that the archetype can only be identified as a statistical composite. If there is some ideal narrative, it is unknowable, and hence all known versions are not variants of a hypothetical original (unless they are variants of a performance that may never have existed), but in some way all are variants of each other. Each performance of an oral narrative is inseparably tied to the time, place, and performative circumstances of recitation. What ideal performance, or idea of an ideal performance, can be in the mind of the auditor who has never heard two versions of any oral epic narrative which have been performed alike? Could it be his/her own ideal striven towards, an ideal abstraction which never quite duplicates that ideal in the actual event, which has never succeeded in that exact duplication?

The written text may remain in "a kind of limbo until a reader picks it up," but that is not at all the situation wth oral performance, which may be an abstract set of rules and ideas. But these abstractions govern the mode and style of performance, and not the story, the plot. Performer and auditor do not have precise notions of story (as opposed to discourse, or which their notions are, with several exceptions, even less precise, however much the performer (the guslar, for instance) insists that he/she has gotten the story down by heart.

The comparison between unread text and unrecited "ideal performance" is also imprecise. It is, in fact, misleading. The written text is fixed, unvarying. If I do not read it today, it will not change; if I pick up the book that contains it a week from now — or next month, next year — it will not have changed. I, the reader, will have changed, but how much like the oral performer is the literate reader of narrative? The oral performer's renditions are constantly changing, constantly in flux, constantly responding to the exigencies of the performative moment.

Barbara Herrnstein Smith (1981, pp. 209–232) has made an analogous argument in her assault on those narratologists who have postulated the ontology of a "basic" story which is separable from its various realized multiforms. After establishing her own definition of narrative as the (collective) "verbal acts of particular narrators performed in response to — and thus shaped and constrained by — sets of multiple interacting conditions," she further argues that

> since all the formal properties of an individual narrative would be regarded as functions of all these multiple interacting conditions rather than as representations of specific, discrete objects, events, or ideas, the expectation of a conformity or formal correspondence between any of the properties of a narrative and anything else in particular simply would not arise. (1981, p. 222)

It is this persistent notion of what is ultimately a Platonic ideal that I want to assess for its validity as a cognitive map of oral performances.

Recently, a similar idea has been proposed by Gerald L. Davis (in *I Got the Word in Me, And I Can Sing It, You Know* [1985]); Davis believes — following Kellogg's and Plato's suggestion — that the oral sermon's variability is caused by the failure of the preacher to realize his own ideal; but in this scholar's thought Platonism is modified and adjusted until it more adequately describes the oral performative situation. Davis begins with the comment that "African-American narrative performance is guided by concepts of *ideal* forms and *ideal* standards. The notion of an ideal form is as compelling for the African-American performer as it is for his or her audience."

Davis avoids falling entirely into a Platonist fallacy, though, because he sees the black American folk sermon as one in which "performer" and "audience" are actively locked into a dynamic exchange. The analysis of African-American narrative performance begins with a Platonic statement and ends with something else. Davis's argument opens with the assertion that such performances are "guided by concepts of ideal forms and ideal standards." But then Davis seems to shift the grounds of his argument: during performance, when both preacher and congregation ("performer" and "audience") are in an dynamic, interpersonal exchange, "the audience compels the performer to acknowledge the most appropriate characteristics of the genre system" (Davis 1985, p. 26); this sounds much like the argument of a speech-act theorist, more so when Davis goes on to talk of "the 'ideal' in terms of "that particular performance environment." That performative moment occurs before the performer is given congregational permission to "individuate" into his or her own "genius and style." This is a conditional ideal, its perfection reset by the conditions of each performance.

Speech-act theory can thus provide a useful approach by accounting for the exigencies of individual performances. But Davis does not seem to want to let go of Plato; and where I think he has somewhat strayed is in his citation of (the same) Robert Kellogg for the Platonic support of speech-act theory. (Davis's Kelloggiana was gleaned from a paper delivered at an MLA meeting.) The citation begins with a stylistic analysis in which the scholar remarks that the performer

> makes every attempt to conform his performance, in style, in form, and in content to a tradition that already exists in his mind and in the mind of his audience. His performance, in other words, is an attempt to reexperience a thing that already exists in some ideal way in tradition. (Kellogg cited in Davis 1985, p. 26)

Davis says that Kellogg's "postulation of ideal forms in folk narrative performance" is not intended to approximate literary archetypes but is rather like a "dynamic usage of folk ideational structures in performance" (Davis 1985, p. 26). Happily, just like his own idea.

In any event, whether Davis misreads Kellogg (so as to make him (correctly) describe Davis's own concept of the situation) or not, he then constructs a diagram of an "African-American validation model." This graphic representation begins with an "Ideal form" within a squared balloon, and then proceeds toward a "Realized form." (On Platonism see Smith 1981, pp. 208ff.) On the way Davis notes that the "Ideal form" is initially interpreted (by the performer) who infuses it with the "most appropriate characteristics" of an ideal form. Then, the audience "accepts, rejects, and/or modifies" the performance's interpretation. If he/she is rejected, Davis observes, the interpretation is adjusted until the audience accepts the new interpretation. The final phase occurs when the performer "imprints [his or her] own style on [the] performance" (1985, p. 28).

Though Davis's prose suggests that he understands the intricate interrelationsip among the tradition, the performer's individual talent, and the audience's response, what he calls a "validation model" (p. 28) is not helpful. That graphic cognitive map suggests to the reader, because it uses the terms "Ideal form" and "Realized form," that it is Platonic in conception and operation.

This "validation chart" is more confusing than clarifying. It should be, but is not, a flowchart; in fact it doesn't conform to any known chart or graph type (see Stewart 1976 passim). The line from "Ideal form" could lead to "Realized form" in any direction—it doesn't have to be circular any more than it has to be clockwise—though making it loop clockwise seems to argue for the closeness of Ideal form and Realized form, which the author wants to point out.

The "Idealized form" should be like a seed—a starting point that grows as it assumes its own life; it does not spiral arbitrarily, however much under control, toward a "Realized form." The goal of the aesthetic performance is like a germinated seed, not a blueprint; the artist does not aim for some abstraction such as an "Ideal form" which he or she necessarily falls short of; the artist does not move from point A to point N, as if closely following a fixed plan; rather, he or she exploits and develops major ideas, themes, exempla, etc. along the way— many of these being serendipitous opportunities that occur to the performer during the performance. Preaching on the Twenty-third Psalm, it suddenly occurs to the Reverend Rubin Lacy to invoke the Four Horsemen; the next time he preaches this sermon, he will not do the same thing (Rosenberg 1970, pp. 70–72). Performance is composition.

The arrows on Davis's chart do not indicate other influences exerting pressure on the preacher's performance: surroundings, circumstances, the performer's mood, the congregation's personality, the heat in the church building, etc. Davis's arrows indicate a mechanical progression from "Ideal form" towards "Realized form," and that is nearly all.

The performer's ideal form is never that of the audience, and in the hundred or so sermons that I witnesses and recorded (discussed in *The Art of the American Folk Preacher* [1970] and *Can These Bones Live?* [1988], the congregation, even the most active ones, did not impose major modifications on their minister in quite the way that Davis suggests. If the congregation were bored or tired or otherwise unresponsive, the preacher might invoke any of several paralinguistic or histrionic ploys to enliven them. But such alterations of original operational notion per se were not governed by the congregation. The listeners did not indicate what alternative was more desirable, only that the performance of the moment was inadequate. The performer decided what to do about it. And I collected no evidence that the preacher's subsequent performances were altered to placate a congregation's past boredom.

Davis's idea of the sermon's core motif, which the preacher announces early in the performance and is then "released" by the audience in order to establish the *realized* form of the event, is not the same as the Platonist's "basic story." Davis's idea acknowledges the preacher's/performer's great freedom (which he or she actually has) in the fulfillment of the sermon; Plato's original conception would not. Davis's idea does not restrict the sermon to being a variation on a traditional theme; Davis falls just shy of arguing that each realized performance is an imperfect rendering of that great sermon in the sky. His is the precise way to view this performative phenomenon; Plato is dead, and regarding the spontaneous African-American folk sermon — and the oral composition of nearly every narrative — it is time to put him to rest.

Folklore and Literature:
Some Conclusions

THE NATURAL WORLD ITSELF IS HOLISTIC and seamless; in our attempts to study it, we have rigidly compartmentalized our knowledge. Time also is seamless; yet we partition it into seconds, minutes, hours, days, weeks, months, years, etc. Segmented time enables the modern world to function efficiently. When we taxonomize our methods of understanding the world, when we try to define its ontological parameters, as is commonly done in university departments today, we inadvertently fragment our understanding of the observed world; no longer unified and seamless, it is subdivided into supposedly manageable fragments; we have, as a result, chemistry, botany, literature, astronomy, physics, folklore, and the rest. Look at any college catalog.

Yet the formation of new combinatory disciplines out of older existing ones — the "new" psycholinguistics out of the intersection of the extant psychology and linguistics, to use just one common example — demonstrates the necessity to delineate new fields of study, so that we can explore those interstices that suddenly appear between the older, entrenched academic territories. As our knowledge expands, we discover that even the regions within the parameters of our disciplines, in which we seek to extend that knowledge, have only been sparsely examined, and that borders of these disciplines are inadequate.

Physics and chemistry are contiguous at several points, one of which we now call physical chemistry; and we have devised such discrete transgeneric disciplines as astrophysics, sociobiology, biochemistry, agroecology, psychobiology, biogeography, pathobiology, biochemistry, photochemistry, psychacoustics, psychobiology, social psychology, etc. The nature of the matter that biologists and physicists experiment with has forced a number of interrelated disciplines to be created, each with the intent to fill in the interstices of knowledge between already mapped regions. The materials examined in this book, the products and processes of literature and folklore, both "soft" disciplines, are obviously closely enough related to each other to justify my belief that they should be studied as contiguous and symbiotic subjects. They are hermit crabs operating out of the same shell; they are sibling rivals.

But the personal inclinations of many researchers hermetically seal off their deliberations and evaluations, quarantining them from closely related subjects and disciplines. The literary scholar may have a deeply felt disdain for folklore, the product of ignorant and uncouth people, not the sort one wants to know — or study. That judgment has not been decided by the nature of the subject matter but by socially determined considerations. Stratification and status have become the primary criteria by which the worthiness of disciplines is judged. I have been at a tenure-decision meeting in which the candidate was condemned (by one committee member) because her specialty was in the popular ballad; it was granted that she excelled in this area, but the decision of this colleague implied that it was better to be a mediocre Shakespearean than a first-rate ballad scholar. (After the meeting he admitted as much to me.)

One of the arguments of this book has been that folklore should be understood not only in its own right but as a valuable body of knowledge, and a methodology, related to literary study. We learn about history so that we may place literature within a meaningful context. Literary biography is also closely kin, studied in order to learn more about the literary product. Specialized studies — of Chaucer and the medieval sciences, of Freudianism and the stream-of-consciousness technique, of Shakespeare's education, of Coleridge's (or Washington Irving's) knowledge of German philosophy and mythology, and of D. H. Lawrence's anthropology — are all legitimate literary studies. V. A. Kolve's recent (1984) outstanding book examines medieval narrative art as it relates to, and illuminates, Chaucer's *Canterbury Tales*. But folklore study has few advocates, though all of us are carriers and many are transmitters of folklore.

Despite our literacy, we are all still heavily oral: much of what we learn in this technologically dense culture derives from the orality that swirls around us at every social moment. We are all of us full-time receptors and transmitters of lore. How do we behave at the dinner table? How do we respond to people we meet on the street, in an elevator, at the check-out counter? How do we raise our children, respect our parents? What do we really feel about fast foods? How should we conduct our lives? According to the coded messages of television narratives? Or according to the way our parents implicitly modeled our attitudes, tastes, and convictions? A relatively recent branch of linguistics, pragmatics, studies the unspoken rules of behavior by which we all live and conduct our lives; hardly an area of contemporary life is thus left out. None of these behaviors is transmitted to us in writing. Some writers, of course, focus on the lore of their characters: Singer, Malamud, Turgenev, Simms, Faulkner, Dickens. But nearly every writer, just in the act of describing people and their cutoms and beliefs, necessarily touches upon some aspect of folklore.

This book also argues for an expansion of our epistemological awareness. To understand literature, it is often necessary to learn about folklore; to enhance our appreciation of the folkloric performance, it may be important to consider narrative as text. Folklore and literature are contiguous disciplines. The literary scholar commonly invokes the aid of skills not purely literary (are there any purely literary approaches? —perhaps the purest were the New Critics, perhaps deconstructionists); but more usually the literary critic is a biographer, a sociologist, a (literary) historian, a (clinical) psychologist, a linguist, a philosopher — and sometimes he or she needs to be a folklorist, as Milman Parry and Albert Lord discovered. Literature was not created in a "clean room"; it should not be studied as though it were, as if we were technicians trying to preserve its sterile purity.

In such an interdisciplinary study as the present book, inevitably one of the disciplines will seem in some way or other favored. Such favoritism as exists here has not been generic or disciplinary; it has not been concerned with the processes or the products of the material; rather, it has been for the education of literary scholars and critics about the methods and procedures of folklore. This has been a consciousness-raising exercise. The folklorists I know are better acquainted with literary history and theory than are the English-department people about folklore, ethnology, or cultural anthropology. English is part of every liberal arts curriculum; folklore is taught in only a few schools in America.

The ultimate aims of both folklore — particularly verbal lore — and literature are to appreciate and to judge aesthetic performance. Each discipline has its own kind of material; the most important differences between them have been discussed in this book. Yet the similarities by far outnumber and outweigh the differences. Differences will always seem to be highlighted and will seem irreconcilable when the aesthetic subjects of one discipline are evaluated by the criteria established for the judgment of the other. A Child traditional ballad suffers when judged by the standards formulated to appraise grand-opera arias or even art lieder, yet the ballad is not inherently inferior because of that.

As the "art" in "art literature" suggests, schooling and formalized expression are given precedence over simplicity and basic psychological expression. James Joyce and Shakespeare used folk ballads in their works and obviously found beauty in them; the Elizabethan playwright was popular in his time and shortly after, and is now strictly a "classic." Coleridge and Auden (among hundreds) have imitated ballad forms in their poetry, finding something of value in the form. *Beowulf* was probably popular at the time of its various compositions and performances, was somewhat denigrated during the early years of the twentieth century, and is now considered by the academy to be indisputably high art. Homer composed a guidebook of cultural behavior and laws—if Eric Havelok's *Preface to Plato* is to be taken seriously—and is now the most classic of all.

Folklore theory has already make a significant, though often unsung, contribution to literary studies: in structuralist theory, in oral-formulaic analyses, in comparative folktale studies, and in performance analyses. So much has been made of those facts here because they are frequently forgotten; conversely, it is seldom overlooked that, in evaluating narrative folklore, the evaluator uses techniques and theories and criteria learned in literature classrooms. Parry and Lord realized that new criteria had to be developed, but their innovations have been slow to catch on.

I have tried to tell my students that monodisciplinary knowledge is incomplete, almost necessarily so, often dangerously inadequate. When you are on the trail of something, be prepared to follow it however far and in whatever direction it may lead. When possible, develop the skills (as well as the knowledge) to be able to keep on the track. Disciplinary knowledge, that which is conducted within the boundaries of a single field, may not lead to any satisfying understanding; the real world does not have arbitrary, restraining boundaries. Unidisciplinary approaches impose an artificial and unnecessary limitation on the scope of exploration, and thus on the results of that exploration. The researcher must have the inclination and the skills to track down his/her quarry whatever turns it may take, over whatever fences and walls it may seek to hide itself, in whatever directions it may flee.

Bibliography

Aarne, Antti, and Stith Thompson. 1964. *The Types of the Folktale*. Helsinki: Academia Scientiarum Fennica.

Abrahams, Roger D. 1972. "Folklore and Literature as Performance." *Journal of the Folklore Institute* 9:75–94.

————. 1977. "The Most Embarrassing Thing That Ever Happened to Me." Paper given at American Folklore Society meeting.

St. Augustine. 1949. *The Confessions of St. Augustine*. Trans. Edward Pusey. 1960 rpt. New York: Modern Library.

Barakat, Robert A. 1965. "The Bear's Son Tale in Northern Mexico." *Journal of American Folklore* 78:331–34.

Barnes, Daniel R. 1966. "Some Functional Horror Stories on the Kansas University Campus." *Southern Folklore Quarterly* 30:309–12.

————. 1970. "Folktale Morphology and the Structure of *Beowulf*." *Speculum* 45:422–34.

————. 1984. "Interpreting Urban Legends" *Scandinavian Yearbook of Folklore*. 40:67–78.

Barthes, Roland. 1982. *A Barthes Reader*. Ed. Susan Sontag. New York: Hill and Wang.

Bartlett, Frederick C. 1932. *Remembering*. Cambridge: Cambridge University Press.

Basile, Giovanni Batiste. 1943 rpt. Il *Pentamerone*. Trans. Sir Richard Burton. New York: Liveright Publ. Corp.

Baugh, Albert C. 1959. "Improvisation in the Middle English Romance." *Publications of the American Philological Society* 103:418–54.

————. 1967. "The Middle English Romances: Some Questions of Creation, Presentation, and Preservation." *Speculum* 24:1–31.

Beardsley, Richard K. 1943. "A History of the Vanishing Hitchhiker." *California Folklore Quarterly* 2:13–25.

Beardsley, Richard K., and Rosalie Hankey. 1942. "The Vanishing Hitchhiker." *California Folklore Quarterly* 1:303–35.

Beebe, Lucius, and Charles Clegg. 1950. *Legends of the Comstock Lode*. Oakland: Grahame H. Hardy.

Bennett, Gillian. 1984. "The Phantom Hitchhiker: Neither Modern, Urban, nor Legend?" *Centre for English Cultural Traditions and Literature Conference Papers*, ser. 4. 45–78.

Benson, Larry. 1966. "The Literary Character of Anglo-Saxon Formulaic Poetry. *PMLA* 81:334–41.

Benson, Larry, and Theodore M. Anderson, eds. 1971. *The Literary Context of Chaucer's Fabliaux*. Indianapolis: Bobbs-Merrill.

Berger, Thomas. 1964. *Little Big Man*. New York: Dial Press.

Boccaccio, Giovanni. 1930. *The Decameron*. Trans. Frances Winwar. New York: Modern Library.

Bolte, Johannes, and Georg Polivka. 1913–32. *Anmerkung zu den Kinder- und Hausmärchen der Bruder Grimm*. 5 vols. Leipsig: Dieterich'sche Verlagsbuch handlung.

Booth, Wayne. 1967. *The Rhetoric of Fiction*. Chicago: University of Chicago Press.

Bowden, Betsy. 1987. *Chaucer Aloud*. Philadelphia: University of Pennsylvania Press.

Bransford, J. D., J. R. Barclay, and J. J. Franks. 1972. "Sentence Memory: A Constructive Versus Interpretive Approach." *Cognitive Psychology* 3:193–209.

Brémond, Claude. 1970. "Morphology of the French Folktale." *Semiotica* 2:247–76.

———. 1973. *Logique de récit*. Paris: du Seuil.

Briggs, Katherine M. 1970. *A Dictionary of British Folktales*. Part A. *Folk Narrative*. Bloomington: Indiana University Press.

Brown, Mary Ellen Lewis. 1976. "Beyond Content in the Analysis of Folklore in Literature: Achebe's *Arrow of God*." *Research in African Literature* 7:44–52.

Brunvand, Jan Harold. 1981. *The Vanishing Hitchhiker*. New York: W. W. Norton.

Bryan, W. F., and Germaine Dempster. 1941. *Sources and Analogues of Chaucer's Canterbury Tales*. Chicago: University of Chicago Press.

Burke, Kenneth. 1968 rpt. "Pschology and Form." In *Counter-Statement*. Berkeley: University of California Press.

Carey, George. 1971. *Maryland Folk Legends and Folk Songs*. Cambridge, MD: Tidewater Publ.

Cate, W. A. 1932. "The Problem of the Origin of the Griselda Story." *Studies in Philology* 29:389–405.

Cather, Willa. 1954 rpt. *My Antonia*. Boston: Houghton, Mifflin Co.

Chambers, R. W. 1921. *Beowulf: An Introduction to the Study of the Poem*. Cambridge: Cambridge University Press.

Chatman, Seymour. 1978. *Story and Discourse: Narrative Structure in Fiction and Film*. Ithaca: Cornell University Press.

Chaucer, Geoffrey. 1977. *Complete Poetry and Prose*. Ed. John Hurt Fisher. New York: Holt, Rinehart and Winston.

Chomsky, Noam. 1966. *Syntactic Structures*. The Hague: Mouton.

Chrétien de Troyes. 1975. *Yvain, or the Knight with the Lion*. Trans. Ruth Harwood Cline. Athens: University of Georgia Press.

Clark, Herbert H., and Eve V. Clark. 1977. *Psychology and Language: An Introduction to Psycholinguistics*. New York: Harcourt Brace Jovanovich.

Clements, Robert J., and Joseph Gibaldi. 1977. *Anatomy of the Novella*. New York: New York University Press.

Colby, Benjamin N. 1973. "A Partial Grammar of Eskimo Folktales." *American Antropologist* 75:645–62.

Comfort, W. Wistar, introd. and trans. 1914. *Arthurian Romances by Chrétien de Troyes*. Rpt. 1975. London: J. M. Dent and Sons.

Conrad, Joseph. 1963 rpt. *Under Western Eyes*. New York: Anchor Books.

Cooke, Thomas D. 1978. *The Old French and Chaucerian Fabliaux*. Columbia: University of Missouri Press.

Cord, Xenia E. 1969. Further Notes on "The Assailant in the Back Seat." *Indiana Folklore* 2:47–54.

Cormier, Raymond. 1972. "Tradition and Sources: The Jackson-Loomis Controversy Re-examined." *Folklore* 83:101–21.

Crosby, Ruth. 1938. "Chaucer and the Custom of Oral Delivery." *Speculum* 13:413–32.

Culler, Jonathan. 1977. *Structural Poetics*. Ithaca, NY: Cornell University Press.

Davis, Gerald L. 1985. *I Got the Word in Me and I Can Sing It, You Know*. Philadelphia: University of Pennsylvania Press.

Deese, James. 1970. *Psycholinguistics*. Boston: Allyn and Bacon.

Dégh, Linda. 1969. "The Roommate's Death and Related Dormitory Stories in Formation." *Indiana Folklore* 2:54–74.

Deighton, Len. 1972. *Close-up*. New York: New American Library.

De Quille, Dan (William Wright). 1947 rpt. *The Big Bonanza*. New York: Alfred A. Knopf.

Dickson, Arthur. 1929. *Valentine and Orson*. New York: Columbia University Press.

Dobson, Richard Barrie, ed. 1970. *The Peasant's Revolt of 1381*. New York: St. Martin's Press.

Dorfman, Eugene. 1969. *The Narreme in the Medieval Romance Epic*. Toronto: University of Toronto Press.

Dorson, Richard M. 1957. "The Identification of Folklore in American Literature." *Journal of American Folklore* 70:1–8.

Drake, Carlos. 1968. "The Killer in the Back Seat." *Indiana Folklore* 1:107–9.

Dundes, Alan. 1964. *The Morphology of North American Indian Folktales*. *Folklore Fellows Communications* 195.

———. ed. 1965. *The Study of Folklore*. Englewood Cliffs, NJ: Prentice-Hall.

———. 1980. *Interpreting Folkore*. Bloomington: Indiana University Press.

Durrell, Lawrence. 1961. *Justine*. New York: Pocket Books.

Eberhard, Wolfram, and Pertev N. Boratav. 1953. *Typen turkische Volksmarchen*. Wiesbaden: F. Steiner.

Eisenstein, Elizabeth L. 1979. *The Printing Press as an Agent of Change*. 2 vols. Cambridge: Cambridge University Press.

Emrich, Duncan. 1972. *Folklore on the American Land.* Boston: Little, Brown, Inc.

Faulkner, William. 1931. *The Sound and the Fury.* New York: J. Cape and H. Smith.

Finnegan, Ruth. 1970. *Oral Literature in Africa.* Oxford: Oxford University Press.

————. 1977. *Oral Poetry: Its Nature, Significance, and Social Context.* Cambridge: Cambridge University Press.

Foley, John Miles. 1984. *Oral-Formulaic Research and Scholarship.* New York: Garland Publishing.

Forsyth, Frederick. 1972. *Day of the Jackal.* New York: Bantam Books.

————. 1975. *The Dogs of War.* New York: Bantam Books.

Fowler, David C. 1968. *A Literary History of the Popular Ballad.* Durham, NC: Duke University Press.

Frappier, Jean. 1959. "Chretien de Troyes." In *Arthurian Literature in the Middle Ages,* ed. Loomis. 157-91.

French, Walter Hoyt, and Charles Brockway Hale. 1964. *Middle English Metrical Romances.* 2 vols. New York: Russell and Russell and Co.

Froissart, Jean. 1968. *Chronicles.* Trans. and ed. Geoffrey Brereton. Baltimore: Penguin Books.

Fry, Donald K. 1968. "Old English Formulaic Themes and Type-Scenes." *Neuphilologus* 52:48-53.

Geertz, Clifford. 1973. *The Interpretation of Cultures.* New York: Basic Books.

Gennette, Gerard. 1980. *Narrative Discourse.* Trans. Jane Lewin. Ithaca, NY: Cornell University Press.

Georges, Robert A. 1969. "Toward an Understanding of Story-Telling Events." *Journal of American Folklore* 82:313-29.

Gibbs, A. C. 1966. *Middle English Romances.* Evanston, IL: Northwestern University Press.

Gill, Chris. 1981. "Profs Say Writing Skills Need Work." *The Dartmouth,* November 11, 1981.

Golding, William. 1955. *Lord of the Flies.* New York: Coward-McCann.

Goody, Jack, ed. 1968. *Literary in Traditional Societies.* Cambridge: Cambridge University Press.

Greimas, A. J. 1971. "Narrative Grammar: Units and Levels." *Modern Language Notes* 86:793-806.

Griffith, Dudley. 1931. *The Origin of the Griselda Story.* Seattle: University of Washington.

Haymes, Edward R., ed. 1973. *The Haymes Bibliography of Oral Theory. Publications of the Milman Parry Collection.* Cambridge, MA: Harvard University Press.

Hibbard, Laura. 1960. *The Medieval Romance in England.* New York: Burt Franklin.

Hill, Roy L., ed. 1964. *Rhetoric of Racial Revolt.* Denver: Golden Bell Press.

Hoffman, Daniel. 1961. *Form and Fable in American Fiction.* New York: Oxford University Press.

Howard, Elizabeth Jane. 1979. *Mr. Wrong.* New York: Penquin Books.

Hunt, Margaret, trans. 1972. *The Complete Grimms' Fairy Tales.* Ed., James Stern. New York: Pantheon Books.

Jacobs, Melville. 1971. *The Content and Style of an Oral Literature.* Chicago: University of Chicago Press.

James, Henry. 1897. *The Spoils of Poynton.* London: W. Heinemann.

James, William. 1958 rpt. *The Varieties of Religious Experience.* New York: New American Library.

Jason, Hedda. 1977. "Precursors of Propp: Formalist Theories of Narrative in Early Russian Ehtnologists." *Poetics and Theory in Literature* 3:471–516.

———. 1982. "The Fairy Tale of the Active Heroine: An Outline for Discussion." In *Journées d'Etudes en Littérature Orale* 79–97.

Jason, Hedda, and Dimitri Segal. 1977. Eds. *Patterns in Oral Literature.* The Hague: Mouton.

Jones, Charles W. 1963. *The Saint Nicholas Liturgy and Its Literary Relationships.* Berkeley, CA: University of California Press.

Jones, Gwyn. 1972. *Kings, Beasts, and Heroes.* London: Oxford University Press.

Jones, Gwyn, and Thomas Jones, introd. and trans. 1949. *The Mabinogion.* London: J. M. Dent.

Joos, Martin. 1967. *The Five Clocks.* New York: Harcourt, Brace and World.

Kahn, Edward. 1973. "Finite-State Models of Plot Complexity." *Poetica* 9:5–21.

Kail, Johanes. 1889. "Uber die Parallelstellen in der Angelsachsischen Poesie." *Anglia* 12:21–40.

Kellogg, Robert. 1973. "Oral Literature." *New Literary History* 5:58.

———.1976 "What Is an Oral Epic?" Paper given at annual MLA meeting, New York City.

Kellogg, Robert, and Robert Scholes. 1966. *The Nature of Narrative.* New York: Oxford University Press.

Kendall, Calvin B. 1983. "The Metrical Grammar of *Beowulf*: Displacement." *Speculum* 58:1–30.

Kennedy, Charles W., trans. 1940. *Beowulf: The Oldest English Epic.* New York: Oxford University Press.

Kittredge, George Lyman. 1886. "Sir Orfeo." *American Journal of Philology* 7:176–202.

Klaeber, Fr., ed. 1936. *Beowulf.* 3d ed. Boston: Heath and Co.

Krohn, Kaarle. 1971. *Folklore Methodology.* Trans. Roger L. Welsch. Austin: University of Texas Press.

Labov, William. 1972. *Language in the Inner City.* Philadelphia: University of Pennsylvania Press.

Labov, William, and Joshua Waletzky. 1967. "Narrative Analysis: Oral Versions of Personal Experience." In *Proceedings of the 1966 Annual Spring Meeting of the American Ethnological Society,* ed. June Helm. Seattle: University of Washington Press.

Langer, Suzanne. 1942. *Philosophy in a New Key.* New York: New American Library.

Lavender, David. 1963. *Westward Vision*. New York: McGraw-Hill Book Co.

Lehmann, W. P., and Tokemitsu Tabusa. 1958. *The Alliteration of the Beowulf*. Austin: University of Texas Press.

Levi-Straus, Claude. 1955. "The Structural Study of Myth." In *Myth: A Symposium*, ed. Thomas Sebeok. Bloomington: Indiana University Press.

———. 1966. *The Savage Mind*. Chicago: University of Chicago Press.

Lewis, C. S. 1964. *The Discarded Image*. Cambridge: Cambridge University Press.

Lindahl, Carl. 1987. *Earnest Games*. Bloomington: Indiana University Press.

Loomis, Laura Hibbard. 1942. "The Auchinleck Manuscript and a Possible London Bookshop of 1330–1340." *PMLA* 57:595–627.

Loomis, Roger Sherman. 1958a. "Arthurian Tradition and Folklore." *Folklore* 69:1–25.

———. 1958b. "Objections to the Celtic Origin of the 'Matiere de Bretagne.'" *Romania* 79:47–77.

Loomis, Roger Sherman, ed. 1959. *Arthurian Literature in the Middle Ages*. Oxford: Oxford University Press.

Lord, Albert. 1965. *The Singer of Tales*. New York: Atheneum.

Lowes, John Livingston. 1927. *The Road to Xanadu*. Boston: Houghton Mifflin.

Lüthi, Max. 1976. "Parallel Themes in Folk Narrative and in Art Literature." *Journal of the Folklore Institute* 4:3–16.

Magoun, Francis P., Jr. 1955. "Oral-Formulaic Character of Anglo-Saxon Narrative Poetry." *Speculum* 28:446–67.

Malamud, Bernard. 1966. *The Fixer*. 1986 rpt. New York: Pocket Books.

Marchalonis, Shirley. 1976. "Three Medieval Tales and Their Modern American Analogues." *Journal of the Folklore Institute* 3:173–84.

Mehl, Dieter. 1967. *Middle English Romances of the Thirteenth and Fourteenth Centuries*. London: Routledge and Kegan Paul.

Miller, George. 1967. *The Psychology of Communication*. Baltimore: Penguin Books.

Moore, John Robert. 1916. "The Influence of Transmission on the English Ballads." *Modern Language Review* 11:387–95.

Morize, Andre. 1922. *Problems and Methods of Literary History: A Guide for Graduate Students*. Boston: Ginn and Co.

Nabokov, Vladimir, trans. 1960. *The Song of Igor's Campaign*. New York: McGraw-Hill.

Nicolaisen, W. F. H. 1987. "The Linguistic Structure of Legends." *Perspectives on Contemporary Legend* 2:61–76.

Olson, Paul A. 1961. "Chaucer's Merchant and January's Heaven in Erthe Heere." *English Literary History* 28:203–14.

Ong, Fr. Walter J. 1981. *The Presence of the Word*. Minneapolis: University of Minnesota Press.

———. 1982. *Orality and Literacy*. New York: Methuen.

Opie, Peter, and Iona Opie. 1975. *The Classic Fairy Tales*. Oxford: Oxford University Press.

Panzer, Friedrich Wilhelm. 1910. *Studien zur germanische Sagengeswchichte.* I. *Beowulf.* Munich: C. H. Beck.

Parry, Milman. 1930. "Studies in the Epic Technique of Oral Versemaking. I. Homer and Homeric Style." *Harvard Studies in Classical Philology* 41–80.

Peers, E. Allison. 1946. *Fool of Love: The Life of Ramon Lull.* London: SCM Press.

Pike, Kenneth. 1964. *Phonemics.* Ann Arbor: University of Michigan Press.

Pratt, Mary Louise. 1977. *Toward a Speech-Art Theory of Literary Discourse.* Bloomington: Indiana University Press.

Prince, Gerald. 1973. *A Grammar of Stories.* The Hague: Mouton.

Propp, Vladimir. 1968. *Morphology of the Folktale.* Trans. Lawrence Scott. Second English ed. Bloomington: Indiana University Press.

Radin, Paul. 1957 rpt. *Primitive Religion.* New York: Dover.

Ramsey, Lee C. 1983. *Chivalric Romances.* Bloomington: Indiana University Press.

Ranke, Kurt, ed. 1966. *Folktales of Germany.* Lotte Bauman, trans. Chicago: University of Chicago Press.

Richmond, W. Edson. 1954. "The Textual Transmission of Folklore." *Norveg* 4:173–96.

———. 1963. "Den Utrue Egteman: A Norwegian Ballad and Formulaic Composition." *Norveg* 10:59–88.

Ridley, Florence. 1965. "A Tale Told Too Often." *Western Folklore* 153–56.

Rimman-Kenan, Schlomith. 1983. *Narrative Fiction.* New York: Methuen.

Roberts, Leonard. 1969. *Old Greasybeard: Tales from the Cumberland Gap.* Detroit: Folklore Associates.

Robinson, Fred N., ed. 1957. *Poetical Works of Chaucer.* Boston: Houghton, Mifflin Co.

Rogers. W. L. 1966. "The Crypto-Psychological Character of the Oral Formula." *English Studies* 67:89-102.

Rosenberg, Bruce A. 1967. "Lord of the Fire-Flies." *Centennial Review of the Arts and Sciences* 11:128-39.

———. 1969. "The Oral Quality of Rev. Shegog's Sermon in William Faulkner's *The Sound and the Fury.*" *Literatur in Wissenschaft und Unterricht* 2:73-88.

———. 1970. *The Art of the American Folk Preacher.* New York: Oxford University Press.

———. 1974. *Custer and the Epic of Defeat.* University Park: Penn State Press.

———. 1975a. "Folktale Morphology and the Structure of *Beowulf:* A Counter-Proposal." *Journal of the Folklore Institute* 11:199-210.

———. 1975b. "The Three Tales of Sir Degaré." *Neuphilologische Mitteilungen* 75:39-51.

———. 1976. "Kennedy in Camelot: The Arthurian Legend in America." *Western Folklore* 35:52-59.

———. 1978. "Olrik's Laws: A Judicial Review." *Folklore Forum* 11:152-62.

———. 1979. "Simultaneity and Linearity in Narrative." *Southern Folklore Quarterly* 43:121–31.

———. 1980. "How Natural is Natural Narrative?" In *Folklore on Two Continents*, eds. Nicholai Burlakoff and Carl Lindahl. Bloomington, IN: Trickster Press.

———. 1981. "The Folklore of the Gold Rush." *Huntington Library Quarterly* 44:293–308.

———. 1986. "Reconstructed Folktales as Literary Sources." In *Historical Studies and Literary Criticism*, ed. Jerome McGann. Madison: University of Wisconsin Press.

———. 1987. "The Complexity of Oral Tradition." *Oral Tradition* 2:73–90.

———. 1988. *Can These Bones Live?* Urbana: University of Illinois Press.

Rosenberg, Bruce A., and Jerome Mandel, eds. 1970. *Medieval Literature and Folklore Studies*. New Brunswick: Rutgers University Press.

Rosenberg, Bruce A., and John Smith. 1974. "The Computer and the Finnish Historic-Geographic Method." *Journal of American Folklore* 84:149–54.

Rosenberg, Bruce A., and D. K. Wilgus. 1970. "A Modern Medieval Story: 'The Soldier's Deck of Cards.'" In *Medieval Literature and Folklore Studies*, ed. Bruce A. Rosenberg and Jerome Mandel.

Rosier, James L. 1962. "Design for Treachery: The Unferth Intrigue." *PMLA* 77:1–7.

Rumelhart, David E. 1975. "Notes on a Schema for Stories." In *Representation and Understanding: Studies in Cognitive Science*. Eds. D. G. Bobrow and A. M. Collins. New York: Academic Press.

———. 1977. "Understanding and Summarizing Brief Stories." In *Basic Processes in Reading: Perception and Comprehension*. Eds. D. Laberge and S. J. Samuels. Hillsdale, NJ: Laurence Erlbaum Associates.

Russo, Joseph A. 1976. "Is 'Oral' or 'Aural' Composition the Cause of Homer's Formulaic Style?" In *Oral Literature and the Formula*. Eds. Benjamin A. Stolz and Richard S. Shannon. Ann Arbor, MI: Center for Coordination of Ancient and Modern Studies.

Sachs, J. S. 1967. "Recognition Memory for Syntactic and Semantic Aspects of Connected Discourse." *Perception and Psychology* 2:437–42.

Samarin, William J. 1967. *Field Linguistics*. New York: Holt, Rinehart and Winston.

Sargent, Helen Child, and George Lyman Kittredge. 1932. *English and Scottish Popular Ballads*. Boston: Houghton, Mifflin and Co.

Sanders, Chauncey 1952. *An Introduction to Research in English Literary History*. New York: Macmillan Co.

Sands, Donald, ed. 1966. *Middle English Verse Romances*. New York: Holt, Rinehart & Winston.

Schlauch, Margaret M. 1927. *Chaucer's Constance and Accused Queens*. New York: New York University Press.

Severs, J. Burke, ed. 1967. *A Manual of the Writings in Middle English: 1050–1500*. New Haven: Connecticut Academy of Arts and Sciences.

Shakespeare, William. 1964. *Cymbeline*. Ed. Robert B. Heilman. Baltimore: Penguin Books.

Shiffrin, Deborah. 1981. Rev. of Wallace Chafe, ed., *The Pear Stories*. *Language* 57: 959–63.

Smith, Barbara Herrnstein. 1978. *On the Margins of Discourse*. Chicago: University of Chicago Press.

———. 1981. "Narrative Version, Narrative Theories. In W. J. T. Mitchell, ed., *On Narrative*. Chicago: University of Chicago Press.

Stewart, Ann Harleman. 1976. *Graphic Representation of Models in Linguistic Theory*. Bloomington: Indiana University Press.

———. 1983. "Double Entendre in the Old English Riddles." *Lore and Language* 3:39–52.

Sulin, R. A., and D. J. Dooling. 1974. "Intrusion of a Thematic Idea in Retention of Prose." *Journal of Experimental Psychology* 103:255–62.

Sydow, Carl Wilhelm von. 1922. "Beowulf och Bjarke. Skrifter utgivna av Svenska Litteratursallskapet." *Studien i Nordisk Filologi* 14:1–45.

Tannen, Deborah. 1982a. "Oral and Literate Strategies in Spoken and Written Narrative." *Language* 58:1–21.

———. 1982b. *Spoken and Written Language: Exploring Orality and Literacy*. Norwood, NJ: Ablex Publ. Corp.

Tedlock, Dennis. 1971. "On the Translation of Style in Oral Narrative." *Journal of American Folklore* 84:114–33.

Thompson, Stith. 1955–58. *Motif-Index of Folk Literature*. 6 vols. Bloomington: Indiana University Press.

———. 1965. "The Star-Husband Tale." In Dundes, ed., *The Study of Folklore*. Englewood Cliffs, NJ: Prentice-Hall.

———. 1977. *The Folktale*. Berkeley: University of California Press.

Titon, Jeff Todd. 1989. *Give Me This Mountain*. Urbana: University of Illinois Press.

Todorov, Tzvetan. 1969. *Grammaire du Décaméron*. The Hague: Mouton.

———. 1975. *The Fantastic*. Trans. Richard Howard. Ithaca, NY: Cornell University Press.

———. 1977. *The Poetics of Prose*. Trans. Richard Howard. Ithaca: Cornell University Press.

Tupper, Frederick, Jr. 1910. *The Riddle of the Exeter Book*. New York.

Utley, Francis Lee. 1961. "Folk Literature: An Operational Definition." *Journal of American Folklore* 74:193–206.

———. 1964. "Arthurian Romance and International Folktale Method." *Romance Philology* 19:596–606.

———. 1965. "Some Implications of Chaucer's Folktales." *Laographia* 22:588–99

———. 1969." Oral Genres as Bridges to Written Literature." *Genre* 2:91–103.

———. 1972. "Five Genres in the Clerk's Tale." *The Chaucer Review* 6:198–228.

Utley, Francis Lee, and William Edwin Bettridge. 1971. "New Light on the Origin of the Griselda Story." *Texas Studies in Literature and Language* 13:153–208.

Vinaver, Eugene. 1971. *The Rise of Romance*. New York: Oxford University Press.
White, Hayden. 1978. *The Tropics of Discourse*. Baltimore: Johns Hopkins University Press.
Whorf, Benjamin Lee. 1969. *Language, Thought, Reality*. Ed. John B. Carroll. Cambridge: MIT Press.
Wittig, Susan. 1978. *Stylistic and Narrative Structures in the Middle English Romances*. Austin: University of Texas Press.

Index